Nudging Public Policy

ECONOMY, POLITY, AND SOCIETY

The foundations of political economy—from Adam Smith to the Austrian school of economics, to contemporary research in public choice and institutional analysis—are sturdy and well established, but far from calcified. On the contrary, the boundaries of the research built on this foundation are ever expanding. One approach to political economy that has gained considerable traction in recent years combines the insights and methods of three distinct but related subfields within economics and political science: the Austrian, Virginia, and Bloomington schools of political economy. The vision of this book series is to capitalize on the intellectual gains from the interactions between these approaches in order to both feed the growing interest in this approach and advance social scientists' understanding of economy, polity, and society. This series seeks to publish works that combine the Austrian school's insights on knowledge, the Virginia school's insights into incentives in nonmarket contexts, and the Bloomington school's multiple methods, real-world approach to institutional design as a powerful tool for understanding social behavior in a diversity of contexts.

Series Editors

Virgil Henry Storr, associate professor of economics, George Mason University; Don C. Lavoie Senior Fellow, F. A. Hayek Program for Advanced Study in Philosophy, Politics, and Economics, Mercatus Center at George Mason University

Jayme S. Lemke, senior research fellow, Mercatus Center at George Mason University

Titles in the Series

Nudging Public Policy

Examining the Benefits and Limitations of Paternalistic Public Policies

Edited by
Rosemarie Fike, Stefanie Haeffele,
and Arielle John

ROWMAN & LITTLEFIELD
Lanham • Boulder • New York • London

Published by Rowman & Littlefield
An imprint of The Rowman & Littlefield Publishing Group, Inc.
4501 Forbes Boulevard, Suite 200, Lanham, Maryland 20706
www.rowman.com

86-90 Paul Street, London EC2A 4NE

British Library Cataloguing in Publication Information Available

Library of Congress Cataloging-in-Publication Data

Names: Fike, Rosemarie, editor. | Haeffele, Stefanie, editor. | John, Arielle, editor.
Title: Nudging public policy : examining the benefits and limitations of paternalistic public policies / edited by Rosemarie Fike, Stefanie Haeffele, and Arielle John.
Description: Lanham, Maryland : Rowman & Littlefield Publishers, 2021. | Series: Economy, polity, and society | Includes bibliographical references and index.
Identifiers: LCCN 2021035459 (print) | LCCN 2021035460 (ebook) | ISBN 9781786614858 (cloth) | ISBN 9781786614865 (paper) | ISBN 9781786614872 (ebook)
Subjects: LCSH: Political planning—Citizen participation. | Economics—Psychological aspects.
Classification: LCC JF1525.P6 N84 2021 (print) | LCC JF1525.P6 (ebook) | DDC 320.6—dc23
LC record available at https://lccn.loc.gov/2021035459
LC ebook record available at https://lccn.loc.gov/2021035460

Contents

List of Figures and Tables

FIGURES

TABLES

Introduction

Rosemarie Fike, Stefanie Haeffele, and Arielle John

Behavioral economics has become an increasingly popular means to influence the decisions that individuals make, particularly through public policy in the United States and around the world. Behavioral economics, influenced by psychology and other cognitive sciences, identifies the various ways in which real-world people fail to meet what economics calls "rational expectations." People have biases and make mistakes, sometimes resulting in worse outcomes than if they behaved like the strictly rational agents in neoclassical economic models. Such ideal agents have access to all of the relevant knowledge and can quickly calculate trade-offs and probabilities in order to maximize their utility, or well-being. Real-world individuals, however, sometimes lack important information and over- or underestimate their abilities or the probability of particular outcomes. For example, someone may read a news article about a plane crash and become afraid to fly, even though air travel is significantly safer than driving (known as availability bias). In other words, people are fallible and human interactions are messy, especially compared to the tidy predictions of economic models built on the assumption of hyper-rational agents.

Identifying and acknowledging these biases and faults is the first step toward correcting them. For instance, once someone realizes that they eat the entire bag of cookies whenever they buy them, they may stop buying cookies or hide them in order to minimize their temptation. Likewise, many people find a "workout buddy" or hire a trainer to help them commit to getting up early and hitting the gym since they know they have a hard time getting out of their warm bed in the morning without external accountability. They may also rely on mental shortcuts or "hacks" for dealing with complex tasks and problems. Rather than try to memorize conversion tables for cooking, someone may download an app that can quickly calculate how many liquid ounces are in a cup or how to triple a baking recipe. People, while fallible, often find ways to overcome their biases on their own or with the help of their family, friends, and community. When they fail to do so, however, policymakers may be able to utilize the insights from behavioral economics to "nudge" them into making better, more informed decisions. This policy approach is often referred to as "nudging," or libertarian paternalism, as coined and advocated by Richard Thaler and Cass Sunstein (2008).

A principal justification for the use of nudges is to help individuals, all of whom suffer from cognitive limitations, make decisions that are objectively better for their long-term well-being. As Thaler and Sunstein (2008, 8) argue, "[b]y properly deploying both incentives and nudges, we can improve our ability to improve people's lives, and help solve many of society's major problems." The underlying assumption behind this ambitious goal is that policymakers are helping people make the decisions they would have made if they were somehow more rational and less susceptible to their cognitive biases. These nudges are not meant to eliminate choices or force particular outcomes, but instead to guard against outcomes that fall short of what a perfectly rational actor would choose by structuring the choice environment in a way that makes "better" choices more appealing to the decisionmaker. For example, policymakers may put a warning label on sugary foods to serve as another way to curb the temptation to eat an entire package of cookies. Or a policy may require employers to deploy an opt-out strategy for life insurance, in order to entice more people to stay signed up for the benefit and be better able to support their families.

Behavioral economics and the policies that are influenced by it point to an important element of real-world human interaction—people are flawed, and their choices do not always correspond to what economic models prescribe. However, this approach often still underappreciates other elements of the real world—particularly that people can learn and adapt and their ability to do so is shaped by the institutions within which they interact. This book attempts to fill this gap in the literature by exploring the institutional contexts within which nudges take place, and the ways in which people learn and adapt to overcome their own biases or to react to policies put in place to nudge their behavior (see also Abdukadirov 2016; Rizzo and Whitman 2019). Specifically, the chapters in this book explore the feasibility of using nudges as a public policy tool, both in theory and in practice, to achieve specific individual and social goals through the lens of market process economics.

The market process approach provides a useful critique of behavioral economics as it is often applied to public policy by examining the knowledge and incentive problems that plague policymakers in their role as choice architects. Despite well-intentioned goals, the institutional context in which policy decisions emerge presents severe challenges in their ability to achieve desired outcomes without suffering from negative unintended consequences. Understanding the institutional context in which decisions take place is central to the market process approach, because that institutional setting determines the knowledge available as well as the incentives that people face when interacting with one another. In markets, decisions are voluntary, and they take place within a system of private property rights, prices, and the feedback mechanisms of profit and loss. The market system itself helps flawed decisionmakers allocate resources effectively because the system provides meaningful feedback that guides their actions by altering their incentives. Prices and the pursuit of profits encourage people to shift resources toward uses that are highly valued by their customers and away from those that are not. Cognitively limited actors can thrive in market settings because they are able to make use of the dispersed information that exists within each and every individual (Hayek 1945). They do so not by collecting all the necessary data and quickly calculating their chances for success, but by adjusting their actions in response to market signals. For instance, a baker does not need to know that flour is in short supply because several wheat fields were destroyed by a hailstorm. They only need to see that the price of flour has increased, which will cause them to economize on flour or even shift to using a flour substitute for their baked goods. These signals carry valuable yet personally incomprehensible amounts of information that guide market actions. And since we know that humans are fallible and epistemically limited beings, these signals and heuristics are necessary for successful social interaction and exchange.

The political process, however, lacks a form of meaningful feedback that would guide cognitively limited policymakers to allocate resources effectively. When designing public policies, choice architects cannot access the information necessary to understand the preferences and constraints faced by all of the individuals whose choices they are trying to alter. When it is impossible to assess the needs and limitations of all of society, policymakers likely end up imposing their own preferences rather than helping others satisfy their own needs and desires and maximize their well-being (Rizzo and Whitman 2019).

Further, public policy decisions do not emerge in a vacuum. Politics is an exchange process and each attempt to implement a nudge policy will be subject to that political process. This creates opportunities for special interests and other rent-seekers to influence the way the policies are designed, further altering the ability of choice architects to maximize social welfare. For example, the U.S. Department of Agriculture aims to provide information on the best dietary practices in order to help Americans make better food choices and, therefore, have longer and healthier lives. However, the food pyramid and campaigns to encourage or discourage the consumption of particular foods are often based on biased studies or backed by agricultural interests (see Godoy 2016). These efforts may align with good health practices but may also represent rent-seeking efforts by particular industries and companies to persuade consumers to buy their products.

This approach also highlights the spontaneous and evolutionary nature of social institutions like culture and trust. Attempts from policymakers to generate these social institutions where they did not exist previously are unlikely to succeed unless they are aligned with the unique characteristics of the society in question (Boettke et al. 2008). This raises the question of whether seemingly successful policy interventions are even necessary, or if they align with revealed preferences rather than nudging people toward "better" outcomes.

As noted above, individuals respond to changes in their incentives in ways that are often unpredictable to policy designers. Additionally, policymakers themselves can fail to grasp their own biases. The market process approach highlights how policymakers themselves also suffer from cognitive biases that may result in the choice architects unconsciously designing flawed policies that have costly consequences. They may mistakenly think their preferences align with the "true" preferences of an otherwise biased populace or overestimate their ability to implement a policy that can shift behavior toward their desired outcome. For example, in an attempt to sway citizens to get health insurance, policymakers may neglect to understand the trade-offs faced by healthy young adults or those with tight budget constraints.

Many scholars in this tradition have warned their fellow academics as well as policymakers of their own biases and hubris. Adam Smith (1982 [1759], 233–234) famously dubbed "the man of system," arguing that he is

apt to be very wise in his own conceit; and is often so enamoured with the supposed beauty of his own ideal plan of government, that he cannot suffer the smallest deviation from any part of it. He goes on to establish it completely and in all its parts, without any regard either to the great interests, or to the strong prejudices which may oppose it. He seems to imagine that he can arrange the different members of a great society with as much ease as the hand arranges the different pieces upon a chess-board. He does not consider that the pieces upon the chess-board have no other principle of motion besides that which the hand impresses upon them; but that, in the great chess-board of human society, every single piece has a principle of motion of its own, altogether different from that which the legislature might chuse to impress upon it. If those two principles coincide and act in the same direction, the game of human society will go on easily and harmoniously, and is very likely to be happy and successful. If they are opposite or different, the game will go on miserably, and the society must be at all times in the highest degree of disorder.

Similarly, Frédéric Bastiat (2011 [1850], 2) observed that "a man absorbed in the effect which is seen has not yet learned to discern those which are not seen, he gives way to fatal habits, not only by inclination, but by calculation." This overconfidence to control fellow citizens, by both policymakers and social scientists that engage in policy research and debate, is what F. A. Hayek called the "fatal conceit." Instead, Hayek (1988, 76) contends that "[t]he curious task of economics is to demonstrate to men how little they really know about what they imagine they can design." Understanding that everyone has cognitive biases, even experts with the best of intentions, leads to a need to embrace humility over hubris (see Boettke 2012; Koppl 2018; Haeffele and Hobson 2019). It is from this approach that this book examines the role of nudges in public policy.

AN OVERVIEW OF THE BOOK

Several critical questions are relevant to those interested in the impact of behavioral economics on public policy: What exactly is a nudge? What are the ethical implications of and justifications for nudges? Are we able to have nudges without affecting one's freedom to choose? In what institutional context are nudges likely to work well and in what context are they likely to fail?

Each chapter in this book explores the ways in which individuals in society respond to attempts by policymakers to "nudge" them toward a specific outcome. Some chapters explore the theoretical arguments in favor of utilizing this approach to public policy, and others explore their feasibility and potential limitations. The chapters, authored by an interdisciplinary group of scholars, include discussions of Internet privacy laws, the sharing economy, education policy, environmental policy, as well as social issues such as trust and culture.

Chapter 1, by Mario J. Rizzo, provides an overview of the scientific foundations of nudges in public policy. Rizzo, whose research with Glen Whitman has provided a thorough critique of behavioral economics in public policy (see Rizzo and Whitman 2019), first outlines the development of the concept of rationality within economics, including the neoclassical conception of rationality, what it actually means, and the reasons why such a formal definition of rationality was incorporated into the framework of nudging. He then challenges behavioral economics' use of rationality as a prescriptive benchmark for human behavior. In demonstrating that people's behavior in the real world violates standard economic assumptions of rationality, behavioralists seek ways to "nudge" the choices of irrational economic actors closer to the normative ideal of what a rational economic actor would choose. Rizzo counters the behavioralists' position with several examples in which behavior that violates the standard rationality assumption is perfectly reasonable given the conditions under which the choice is being made. Finally, this chapter situates the discussion on nudges within the current policy landscape, demonstrating the limitations and weaknesses of the nudging approach and providing alternatives to our scientific understanding of human behavior.

In chapter 2, Jeffrey Bristol cautions against the uncritical acceptance of the premise that nudges *per se* are an improvement over other forms of public policy. Fundamentally, for Bristol, nudges are a form of social engineering and central planning. Therefore, nudges should be evaluated like all other legislative and policy tools, including criminal sanctions, which are often thought to be the opposite of nudges. By extending the insights from market process economics to nudges, Bristol disagrees with the notion that nudges dodge the pitfalls of sanctions just because nudges do not involve the use of force or penalties for noncompliance or because they are designed with the psychological makeup of the intended targets in mind. For social scientists and policymakers interested in maximizing the potential success of specific nudge policies, Bristol offers ways to categorize nudges that bring into focus the likely efficacy, restrictiveness, and cost of the various types of nudges.

Chapter 3, by Katarina Hall, calls for closer scrutiny of the relational context between policymakers and the citizens they attempt to nudge. Hall argues that nudges stand a better chance of benefiting their targeted demographic when they are designed and implemented in a governance space that is polycentric and decentralized. Polycentric governments have multiple, independent but related decision-making centers. Similarly, decentralized governments have units of authority that are closer to and more connected to citizens. Using insights from the Bloomington school of political economy, Hall contends that local government systems enjoy the advantages of both polycentrism and decentralization, as opposed to federal systems which tend to be more monocentric and centralized. Local-level policymakers designing nudges have better access to local knowledge and to the preferences of the public they serve than their federal-level counterparts. Furthermore, local governments tend to be less bureaucratic and therefore more responsive to internal and external feedback than federal governments. If policy success is constrained by policymakers' access to relevant knowledge and their incentives to discover and implement what works and to abandon what does not, we might, therefore, expect nudges to be more effective at the local level. Hall makes the case for the superiority of local-level nudges by contrasting the response of the Federal Emergency Management Agency compared to the responses of civil society groups—churches, community volunteer groups, and crisis centers—after Hurricane Katrina.

Oliver McPherson-Smith, in chapter 4, reassesses the practice of colonial migration through the lens of nudging and highlights the nuances and complications of this practice that is often lacking in the quantitative economic development literature. To do so, he examines and discusses the two historical instances of governments implementing nudges to encourage citizens to relocate and settle in new territories with preexisting indigenous populations: (1) the French state's efforts to facilitate migration to colonial Algeria and (2) the United States' efforts to encourage citizens to settle the western frontier through the Homestead Act. McPherson-Smith examines how these nudges altered the cost-benefit calculation of citizens who likely would have never left their place of origin in the absence of such policies. He also discusses the ethical implications of government nudges, arguing that the government is morally responsible for the disturbing impact these nudges had on indigenous populations as well as for incentivizing its citizens to be (often unknowingly) complicit in human rights violations. This chapter illustrates how the decision to settle in these locations implicitly reflects the policies of the state and, consequently, statistical metrics like high settler mortality rates did little to actually deter colonial settlement. While such economic development literature may point to broad patterns, they nonetheless miss important implications of colonialism on indigenous populations as well as citizens nudged to settle in new territories.

Chapter 5, by Erin Dunne, explores the social consequences of nudges and how they can impact social norms, culture, and identity. Dunne first provides a theoretical foundation to understand how nudges act on individual and group behavior, then applies this framework to the process of nation-building and identity formation. Using elements of Singapore's entrepreneurial nation-building efforts as case studies, this chapter analyzes the intentions and outcomes of various Singaporean government initiatives to nudge the country's diverse, initially fragmented population toward a distinct national identity. Using historical analysis, she argues that the success or failure of nudges is largely determined by the degree of buy-in from the nudged population as well as preexisting cultural norms and inclinations to accept or reject the nudge being offered. In short, creating a shift in culture, or a more narrowly defined social change, is not merely the project of elites acting as choice architects but a contested process of coproduction among stakeholders. Optimistically, the need for buy-in by the nudged population places limits on the extent to which this type of social engineering can succeed.

In chapter 6, James M. Strickland discusses the potential for nudge-like policies to improve the transparency of lobbying efforts. Registration can be a relatively simple task for lobbyists, as it requires visiting an office or filling out an online form, and submitting one's name, personal information, and the names of clients. Despite the simplicity of registering, however, there is a growing concern and evidence that not all lobbyists register and report on their activities. This is problematic given that voters have no information about the identities of unregistered, or "shadow," lobbyists who still engage in advocacy. Such unregistered advocacy can be particularly troublesome if the advocates are engaging in unethical activities or undermining the public interest in favor of private rents. Unregistered lobbyists and their clients deserve scrutiny, and nudges may be able to incentivize them to do so (even when the interests of the public and lobbyist may be dramatically at odds). Given this state of affairs, Strickland attempts to identify the conditions under which lobbyists are most likely to register with state authorities and comply with related reporting requirements.

Shannon Lee, in chapter 7, explores the nudges that influence, or discourage, involvement in voluntary postsecondary educational or training activities using signaling theory and human capital theory. Explicit in human capital theory is the belief that investments made into the stock of human capital have benefits for not only those that undertake those investments but society as well. Society has an interest in influencing its members to invest in their human capital to boost productivity and, therefore, governments may play a role in allocating resources toward promoting higher education each year. Increasingly, individuals within society place heavy emphasis on science, technology, engineering, and mathematics (STEM) education, and prioritize traditional four-year college education as the best path to a good job and a decent wage. This mindset, Lee argues, perpetuates a narrow view of education that is reinforced through government programs that provide incentives that encourage students to attend four-year universities instead of engaging in skilled trade apprenticeships, many of which are necessary to maintain and improve the nation's infrastructure. Lee concludes by proposing an alternative nudge: the provision and dissemination of employment and earnings data for different career paths as a means to improve the postsecondary educational choices young adults make.

In chapter 8, Cynthia Boruchowicz considers nudges as a supplement to traditional climate change policy. So-called "green nudges" are designed to help people overcome the various psychological constraints that lead them to act in individually beneficial but environmentally destructive ways. They differ from traditional tools of environmental policy (such as caps and prohibitions) in that they aim to impact people's decision-making processes without necessarily changing their economic incentives. Boruchowicz reviews several studies that assess the efficacy of green nudges and the trade-offs involved in their use, discusses how green nudges may interact with informal institutions, like social norms and culture, and examines how an institutional setting of "good" governance can better incentivize policymakers to implement effective nudges. Crucially, Boruchowicz argues, the intention-action gap in environment conservation might differ according to place of residence, exposure to specific threats, or usage of available resources. Therefore, local governments may likely have a greater chance of designing green nudge policies considering the differences of the citizens being nudged.

In chapter 9, Will Rinehart considers the privacy concerns and the related policy interventions that address that, with the growth of the Internet and social media, companies and other organizations have greater access to personal information on individuals who visit their websites and purchase their goods or services. Concerns from individuals and policymakers over what information can be retained or shared and how much control individuals have over their privacy settings have led to extensive policy debates and new regulations. Rinehart explores the effectiveness of a particular type of nudge, opt-in and opt-out mandates in privacy regulations, and examines the potential impact of these nudges on future innovation. While privacy nudges are proposed with the intention of protecting the data of individual Internet users, in practice they result in high compliance costs for Internet companies, with a disproportionate share of the burden landing on smaller firms. Furthermore, these nudges assume that rational individuals will have a particular set of preferences regarding their data privacy instead of recognizing that these preferences are highly subjective and varied. As a result, opt-in mandates should not be expected to result in Internet users being more informed about their privacy decisions.

Finally, Luis H. Lozano-Paredes, in chapter 10, examines the potential for nudges as a means to facilitate social trust, in the context of the sharing economy in various cities of Latin America. In the past several years, policymakers, academics, and other stakeholders in Latin America, such as the Inter-American Development Bank, began to explore nudging strategies related to the sharing economy in the hopes of altering the public's decision whether to embrace new sharing economy platforms. Through exploring several examples of these nudging efforts, Lozano-Parades argues that the widespread adoption of a new sharing economy arrangement is the result of an emergent order, where trust can't be "nudged" into existence via public policy. And he further extends this analysis to include the implications of the COVID-19 pandemic on the policy space in Latin America.

CONCLUSION

As a whole, this book sheds light on the degree to which paternalistic nudges in public policy can be effectively designed and implemented (or not) by policymakers in a way that accomplishes their intended goal by paying particular attention to the importance of the institutional context in which these nudges emerge. The economic institutions, political institutions, and the broader informal and cultural norms of society will influence the effectiveness of nudges. This book presents a case for policymakers to be more discerning in their attempts to use choice architecture to direct citizens to more rational decisions. Furthermore, it cautions policymakers to be careful not to fall prey to the very cognitive biases, such as optimism and overconfidence, that they use to justify these paternalistic interventions in the first place and to practice a humbler approach to nudging citizens.

REFERENCES

Abdukadirov, Sherzod, ed. 2016. *Nudge Theory in Action Behavioral Design in Policy and Markets.* New York, NY: Palgrave Macmillan.

Bastiat, Frédéric. 2011 [1850]. "That Which Is Seen, and That Which Is Not Seen." *The Bastiat Collection, second edition.* Auburn, AL: Ludwig von Mises Institute.

Boettke, Peter J. 2012. *Living Economics: Yesterday, Today, and Tomorrow.* Oakland, CA: The Independent Institute & Universidad Francisco Marroquin.

Boettke, Peter J., Christopher J. Coyne, and Peter T. Leeson. 2008. "Institutional Stickiness and the New Development Economics." *The American Journal of Economics and Sociology,* 67(2): 331–358.

Godoy, Maria. 2016. "Wheels, Pyramids and Plates: USDA's Struggles to Illustrate Good Diet." *NPR The Salt,* January 13. https://www.npr.org/sections/thesalt/201 6/01/13/462821161/illustrating-diet-advice-is-hard-heres-how-usda-has-tried-to-d o-it.

Haeffele, Stefanie, and Anne Hobson, eds. 2019. *The Need for Humility in Policymaking: Lessons from Regulatory Policy.* London: Roman & Littlefield International.

Hayek, F. A. 1945. "The Use of Knowledge in Society." *The American Economic Review,* 35(4): 519–530.

Hayek, F. A. 1988. *The Fatal Conceit.* Chicago, IL: The University of Chicago Press.

Koppl, Roger. 2018. *Expert Failure.* Cambridge, MA: Cambridge University Press.

Rizzo, Mario J., and Glen Whitman. 2019. *Escaping Paternalism: Rationality, Behavioral Economics, and Public Policy.* Cambridge, MA: Cambridge University Press.

Smith, Adam. 1982 [1759]. *The Theory of Moral Sentiments.* Edited by D. D. Raphael and A. L. Macfie. Indianapolis, IN: Liberty Fund Inc.

Thaler, Richard H., and Cass R. Sunstein. 2008. *Nudge: Improving Decisions About Health, Wealth, and Happiness.* London: Penguin Books.

Chapter 1

Irrationality Is Not Unreasonable

Behavioral Economics, Rationality, and Implications for Public Policy

Mario J. Rizzo

The key concept in all of this is rationality.[1] From the beginning, behavioral economics established itself in opposition to standard economics and especially to the standard economics postulation of economic rationality.[2] And so, the argument basically goes that people do not behave rationally. Instead, they are irrational or, as theorized more recently, boundedly rational. They are less than completely rational. And therefore, we must reassess the normative quality of what they do. Both behavioral economists and standard economists accept the concept of economic rationality as a normative standard. Standard economics says people behave rationally and they should behave rationally. Behavioral economics says people do *not* behave rationally, but they should behave rationally. Thus, while behavioral economics criticizes standard economics, they both agree that rationality is the normative criterion for evaluating individual behavior.

WHAT IS ECONOMIC RATIONALITY?

When an ordinary person who is reading policy books or articles from the behavioral perspective learns that people are not acting rationally, there is a tendency to confuse that with people not acting reasonably. However, rationality in economics is not simply about behaving reasonably. It has specific content and it is an instantiation of rationality or reasonableness more broadly conceived.

Rationality in behavioral economics and standard economics means something very specific. Let me talk about that briefly. To introduce that discussion, I have to make a distinction which I have found quite useful. A distinction was made by the philosopher John Searle (1964, 1969, 1995) who talks about two types of rules or norms: constitutive and prescriptive.

The best way to explain constitutive rules is to say that they are the rules of the game. They are the rules that define what game you are playing. So, for example, the rules of chess define the game of chess. Now, you can take a chessboard and use it to play checkers following the rules of checkers, but you are not playing chess. Some rules are constitutive of the game that you're playing. Other rules are prescriptive. They tell you how to play the game well. So, if you are playing chess, prescriptive rules tell you how to play chess well. Now, you can see when you think about the game of chess that the distinction between constitutive and prescriptive rules is not always sharp. To some extent, if you violate some of the rules of chess, you are not playing well. But if you violate a lot of the rules, then you may not be playing chess at all.

But I think for our purposes we should think about the distinction as being perhaps a little sharper than it really is. To give a clearer example of prescriptive rules, think about driving. There are rules of the road. If you are supposed to be driving on the right side of the road but you drive on the left, you are not following the rules of the road. You are still driving, but you are not driving well. If you go beyond the speed limit, you are still driving, but you are not driving safely. So, there are prescriptive rules about how to drive safely and how to drive well.

Unfortunately, the word normative, which is very popularly used in economics, sometimes means constitutive and sometimes means prescriptive. You will find economists saying the behavior of particular agents violates or does not correspond to normative behavior. What they mean is that their behavior does not correspond to the standard model of rationality. For example, if people make systematic, as opposed to random, errors they are not behaving normatively. They are supposed to make random errors if they are a rational agent, not systematic errors.

The most important conditions of economic rationality are completeness of preferences and transitivity of preferences. Now, let us examine the completeness of preferences as an axiom, or requirement, of rational behavior. Completeness means that you are able to decide between any two pairs of options, whether you prefer one to the other or are indifferent between them. However, the option of "I don't know" is not constitutive of economic rationality. Now think about that. Is it a *reasonable* requirement? When you come across things that you have never experienced before, you may not know. You may say, "Well, I have no idea which I would prefer." Part of the difficulty is that the word "preference" is often used as a synonym for "choice." Behavioral economists tend to use the word preference, and I think correctly so, as meaning that you have mental preferences and not necessarily what you *choose* to do. On the other hand, when you use preferences as a synonym for choice, then you say, "Well, if the person is constrained to choose A or B, then whatever they choose, even if they aren't familiar with A and B, is their preference." But they may choose randomly. So the failure to satisfy the axiom of completeness is not unreasonable, yet it is a requirement of economic rationality.

Now let us go back another step. Why do we have these axioms? There are more axioms besides completeness and transitivity, such as continuity and reflexivity, but they are not quite so important. Why do we have all these axioms? What function do they serve? What are these axioms of rationality about? In the nineteenth century and earlier, axioms were supposed to be self-evident propositions or those which were empirically well tested and corroborated empirically. In the twentieth century, a movement was established among mathematicians, especially a group of French mathematicians who went under the name of Nicolas Bourbaki.[3] Their task was to provide an axiomatic foundation for various branches of mathematics which were already developed. For example, they focused on an axiomatic or logical foundation for calculus, which had been developed centuries earlier, with the minimum number of axioms or assumptions necessary. Their goal was to be able to base the whole system on as few axiomatic statements as possible.

Economists got wind of this strategy and got to work on similar projects. So what projects did they have to work on? They had a notion of a utility function that was basically already established. Perhaps not in exactly the right mathematical form, but the concept was there. So they asked, what are the minimum assumptions that we need to make in order to derive a utility function? They came up with this list of axioms. Not because they thought they were realistic insofar as they conformed to actual human behavior, but because they were the necessary and sufficient assumptions to derive the utility function. And why do they want to derive utility functions? Because they found that the utility function was useful. The development of the notion of economic rationality was guided by the purpose of deriving a utility function, which was a useful tool for understanding the world. There is nothing prescriptive about the rationality assumptions. They are just a way of deriving a tool.

So that is why, in the 1950s and later, some economists, such as Milton Friedman in one way and Fritz Machlup in a somewhat different way, said that these assumptions would only prove their usefulness if the structure of which they formed the basis itself proved useful for understanding the world. However, the assumptions did not refer to any real-world agents but referred to what Machlup called "puppets" (Machlup 1967). The puppet is designed by the puppet master to have certain characteristics and to do certain things, and his function is to explain aggregate phenomena, not the behavior of real individuals.

Therefore, the rationality norms were not prescriptions about how people should behave. They were assumptions, not even about how people actually behave, but assumptions that were necessary to derive a useful tool for understanding economic phenomena. They were completely instrumental. Then, somehow along the way, some economists said, "Well, maybe they describe how people behave in some contexts." But in my mind, the worse thing is to infer is that they described how people should behave, and this leads to a major problem in economics (Whitman and Rizzo 2015).

Since I gave you an example of completeness already, let me give you just a couple of examples of why violations of other axioms might be completely reasonable behavior. This is why they should not be viewed as normative or prescriptive, in the usual sense of the words. These are both compelling examples originating with Amartya Sen (2002a,b). First, let's assume that a person has in his/her mind the following set of preferences. A large apple is preferred to an orange, and an orange is preferred to a small apple. Now, the host of a party comes by with a tray, and on the tray is a large apple and a small apple. What does the individual choose? Let's say they choose the small apple. But wait a minute. They prefer large apples to oranges to small apples. So, large apples, by the axiom of *transitivity*, are preferred to small apples. Why did they not choose the large apple? Sen says that maybe they think it is unmannerly when you have two of the same kinds of fruit. If you choose the big one, you become the guy who took the largest apple, the guy with the manners of a "pig." It is polite to choose the smaller apple. Maybe this is old-fashioned politeness, but you can relate to it. You choose the smaller apple so as not to be the pig at the party. This polite behavior, however, violates the transitivity of preferences.

Let's discuss another example, a variation of Sen's story (2002b) which I used in my most recent book (Rizzo and Whitman 2020). Imagine a sophisticated British lady. We will call her Lady Trevelyan. (I love that name, Trevelyan. There were actually many famous Lady Trevelyans in the nineteenth century, and apparently it is an important family.) So, Lady Trevelyan is told that she has a long-lost cousin named Timothy who suddenly has reappeared. Would she like to have tea with him? She says yes. She prefers having tea with him to not having tea with him. Now, later the person comes back and says, "Oh, I have another option for you. Would you like to have LSD with him instead?" She says, "No, I would not like to have LSD." By the principle of the *independence of the irrelevant alternatives*, she "should" say no LSD, but that she will have tea. However, she actually says, "No, I don't want to have tea with Timothy now either." Why did she change her mind? "Because he has displayed what kind of person he is, and I don't have tea with people like that," Lady Trevelyan declares. She has these three options now; we call that a menu. The menu conveys additional information. And now she violates this principle of the independence of the irrelevant alternatives. But the alternatives are not irrelevant because the menu conveys information. But strictly speaking, she is irrational or not completely rational.

I understand that you could read this and redescribe these situations so that they fit the rationality requirements, if you are clever enough. But the issue here is not that they can be made to fit. You can force them into the rationality requirements. You can almost always do that. The basis upon which you would do it is the reasonableness of the behavior. Once I told you the reason, you say it is reasonable, and then you try to force it back into the framework. But what enables you to do it is the insight that the behavior is reasonable, and *therefore it is really the more basic concept of reasonableness that provides the basis of the normativity.*

RATIONALITY AS A PROCESS

Let me move on to a second aspect of rationality: Rationality as a process (Rizzo and Whitman 2018). Those of you who are familiar with Austrian economics and its view of the market process will see the pretty clear analogy here. In textbooks there is the analysis of consumer behavior as a tangency or optimum between an individual's indifference curve and their budget line. This point is sometimes called in older textbooks the "equilibrium" of the individual. And I think it is a good term because it makes the analogy. The idea that a person's preferences would be consistent, transitive, and complete really represents an equilibrium condition—that is to say, a kind of causeless equilibrium where all the preferences and plans the individual has are reconciled with each other in a consistent way.

This *intra*personal equilibrium is a good analogy to the theory of perfect competition dealing with *inter*personal relationships. In the 1930s, Lionel Robbins (1969 [1935]) asked the question: Are economists confined to explaining only transitive behaviors and preferences? And he answered "no" because the assumption of transitivity requires a kind of completed internal arbitrage, whereby the person completely works out all of the inconsistencies in their behavior, and that is not necessarily going to happen completely or immediately in all cases.

Let me give an example. My self, now, is not the same as the self as I will be next year nor the same self I was last year. We live in a world in which, in a certain sense, we are not just one person but multiple people through time. Over time we change. Accordingly, the collection of these selves might be viewed analogously as a collection of several natural individuals. In this context, the arbitrage idea is very interesting because one of the forms of inconsistency that behavioral economists claim is that today I want to eat potato chips, but my future self wants me to eat more healthily. This need not be viewed as an internal inconsistency because we are dealing with the actions of different selves. Continuing with the analogy, maybe these different selves can make deals with each other. There are models which incorporate this possibility of Coasean bargains (Whitman 2006). You can make a bargain with your future self. Now, what does that mean? It means that neither self gets everything it wants. For example, the present self gets to eat potato chips once or twice a week. The future self gets the present self not to eat them five days a week. And so, the future self gets incremental health benefits while the present self gets some degree of indulgence. You see this kind of thing all the time when people diet in particular ways. They say, "Well, I follow my diet, but on Sundays I eat what I want or on my birthday I'm not going to follow my diet." They make certain exceptions. These exceptions sometimes can be viewed as cheating and weakness of will. But actually, what they often are is the glue that keeps together the intertemporal bargain between their different selves. It is not feasible for the one self to get everything and the other self to not get anything. And so, this is a kind of internal arbitrage that takes place, but it does not result in a perfect satisfaction of a single self.

Second, you might ask yourself what it takes to have completely consistent beliefs or preferences. Imagine a person having only 20 beliefs or 20 preferences. This does not seem like many. However, if you wanted to check for consistency you would have to check 190 possible pairs—that is just binary rather than examining triple or quadruple clumping of beliefs. So you would have to make at least 190 checks for 20 beliefs and preferences. Now, people have a lot more than that. So it is expensive to have completely consistent beliefs. And so, any equilibrium, even if you go through some arbitrage or consistency process, is not going to be complete. Note that Vilfredo Pareto (1971 [1906]), who invented the indifference curve system, was not unaware of that even though the recognition is left out of many textbooks. He said that the complete logical state where people know what their preferences are and know what the optimum is only occurs after a period of trial and error. It occurs in the equilibrium where people have worked through all of their errors.

HUMAN ACTION AND RATIONALITY

One of the things that behavioral economists and standard economists have in common, because they share the same normative view, is the idea that human choice is all about maximizing the utility function—a constant fixed utility function like that in the Stigler-Becker conception of neoclassical economics. But Frank Knight argued—and this is important to understand in the behavioral context—that human choice or human action is based on "the restless spirit of man, who is an aspiring rather than a desiring being" (Knight 1922, 472).[4] Now what he meant by this is that there is really an internal dynamism to human preferences. That the idea of a static utility function is appropriate only at the very moment of choice when people have already decided what they want. But in the process of deciding there is a dynamic aspect of preferences; people tend to look beyond their preferences to their underlying values which tend to conflict.

Ultimately, what Knight argued is that what people want is more and better preferences. When you satisfy your preferences, you always tend to say "Okay, so what's next now?" such as "Okay, I got my college degree, what do I do next?" There is this constant level of dissatisfaction. Thus, it is not really about a satisfaction of static preferences, but about an opportunity. The opportunity to choose things that you would never have dreamed you wanted to choose today or in the future. And behavioral economics itself, by the way, gives a lot of evidence in favor of this view. One is the so-called "hedonic treadmill." People obtain their goals, they are happy for a while, and then there is a kind of a letdown. You go back to your baseline of satisfaction and strive to achieve new goals. This is really what Knight was talking about. Satisfaction of preferences is not satisfaction in any more than a technical sense. There is no final stasis. You become unsatisfied again, you move ahead, and you get or achieve something else. People want to change aspects of their personalities and their behavior. People intentionally try to change their tastes, such as when they take music appreciation courses. People have actually been shown in some experiments to have a preference for outcomes that have an increasing trajectory of utility rather than an arbitrarily mixed set of outcomes. They want to always go up the "treadmill." Apart from the difficulties in determining what people's true preferences are, the point is, and I think Robert Sugden (2018) in his work has made this clear, providing people with opportunities to choose and not trying to nudge them in the direction of static preferences seems to be the reasonable policy.

TRUISMS IN BEHAVIORAL ECONOMICS

Behavioral economics has developed, at least in the more popular version of it, and also to some extent in the technical versions as well, a series of truisms. Such truisms include that people value weight losses more than their weight gains, that people are myopic, that people underestimate large probabilities and overestimate small probabilities, and so on.

There is, however, a dissenting psychological literature. I have spent the last seven or eight years literally going through mountains of this other literature, which you may not know about because the behavioral economists think that the only psychologists worth listening to are Daniel Kahneman (2011) and Amos Tversky and followers. The rest of the psychological discipline is largely ignored (see Rizzo and Whitman 2020).[5] Interestingly enough, Kahneman has admitted that many of the studies that he relied on turned out to have been of low statistical power (Schimmack et al. 2017) and, therefore, their results are unreliable.

In this last section, I wish to discuss briefly some of the technical problems with the biases literature. First of all, there is a real problem with generalizing the quantitative results from labs to the real world. Note that I am distinguishing quantitative from qualitative results. There are problems with the qualitative, but there are severe problems when trying to generalize quantitative results because they are difficult to reproduce and so context dependent. This problem is sometimes called lack of external validity. It is important because policy decisions oftentimes depend upon the quantitative extent of a bias. So for example, consider people having a present bias. The extent or degree to which people have present bias will affect the effectiveness of a tax that you might put on sugar or other consumption goods that are alleged to appeal to people's immediate enjoyment at the expense of long-term health. If the tax effect exceeds that of the bias then you have restrained present enjoyment too much.

Second, the literature dramatically underestimates the importance of learning, partly because the experiments do not go on for very long. Most experiments end within an hour. Real-world learning usually takes more than an hour. Experiments that have tried to capture longer-term learning frequently show that biases tend to be dramatically reduced over time (List 2003, 2011).

Another element is small-group decision-making, which is underexplored in the literature (Charness and Sutter 2012). But there are some very interesting experiments that have studied decisions made in small groups. By small groups I mean two, three, four, or possibly five people, but not more than that. What happens in small groups is oftentimes one person gets it and he then tells the other people about a mistake and nobody makes the mistake anymore. Why is small-group decision-making relevant? Because lots of important decisions that people make in real life are made in discussion with other people. They are, in effect, group decision-making. Not necessarily in a formal sense, but they get the input of other people, whether they seek counsel from family members, advisors, or whatever. What is sometimes called small-group debiasing is, I think, an extremely important element in decisions that should be further studied.

Another problem is that biases rarely have stated boundary conditions. What do I mean by that? A boundary condition tells you when under what conditions you should expect the bias to occur, or not. The problem is that behavioral experiments are usually in a sanitized environment where there is no background or context. Lacking specific circumstances, the experiment cannot tell us when the bias will occur and in what circumstances it will not occur. For example, it is sometimes claimed that people are misled by low introductory interest rates on credit card balances ("teaser rates"). Since people are imperfectly rational, it is argued, even if you tell them the interest rate is going to be higher later, they do not focus on that because they underestimate the probability that they will have unpaid balances in the future. Thus, they more or less ignore the future high rate of interest and they concentrate on the current low rate of interest.

Now, why is that? How does that fit in with the issue of boundary conditions? According to standard behavioral economics, people are supposed to underestimate high probability events. Assuming the future occurrence of unpaid balances is a high probability event, this would seem to be a relevant bias. But the research about the bias is about events external to the individual and not about the individual's own behavior. Does that research apply here? What are the general conditions under which such overestimation applies? We do not know.

Finally, I want to say something about present bias. Did you know that the latest research shows very little evidence of present bias when it comes to money transactions? Present bias is about utility and disutility (O'Donoghue and Rabin 2015). Present bias is relevant when people are undergoing a lot of trouble (disutility) today in decision-making that may have future benefits. But it is not about the preference between money today and money tomorrow. So present bias does not directly apply in any decision about saving. The easier the savings process is, the less relevant present bias will be. For example, anything that simplifies the retirement savings decision will lessen the effect of present bias.

The second thing about present bias is that present bias is about only truly immediate burdens (Balakrishnan et al. 2017). What do I mean by *immediate* burdens? You have a certain cost to incur now or very soon, like within a day or two. And the benefit that you are supposed to gain is a week or two weeks from that. It is not about longer-term decision-making.

Therefore present bias is limited to utility-calibrated burdens, and not intertemporal trade-offs of money, and to a very short time horizon. These limitations of the present bias concept suggest that it is probably one of the most overused in all of behavioral economics.

CONCLUSION

Behavioral economics has imposed an unwarranted normative structure upon the preferences and choices of individuals. It has profited from the confusion in many people's minds, including those of economists, between reasonable behavior and technically rational behavior. Much irrational or boundedly rational behavior is perfectly reasonable from a normative or prescriptive perspective. Furthermore, if you look deeply into the literature, you will find enormous deficiencies in the evidence provided for the various cognitive biases. Even when the evidence is acceptable, there are limits to the applicability of the bias and there are often countervailing tendencies that behavior economists ignore or downplay. Thus, we are by no means dealing with actual truisms. So if you are going to do policy work in this area, I think you need to take a look at the criticisms of the basic analytical structure that is being imposed upon policy analysis as well as the criticisms of the empirical evidence for irrationalities. I hope I have provided you with some skepticism, some tools, and some advice to improve your research in this area.

NOTES

1. This chapter was originally given as a lecture in October 2018 at a symposium for the development of this edited volume. A full exposition of the topics in this chapter as well as other areas and topics concerning behavioral economics and policy can be found in Rizzo and Whitman (2020).

2. See the history as told by Thaler (2015). A policy debate was launched by Thaler and Sunstein (2008) and Thaler and Sunstein (2003). Also see early critiques by Rizzo and Whitman (2009a, 2009b).

3. For more detail on Bourbaki, see https://www.britannica.com/topic/Nicolas-Bourbaki.

4. For more on this subject, see Dold and Rizzo (forthcoming).

5. In particular, see Gigerenzer (2000).

REFERENCES

Balakrishnan, Uttara, Johannes Haushofer, and Pamela Jakiela. 2020. "How Soon is Now? Evidence of Present Bias from Convex Time Budget Experiments." *Experimental Economics* 23(2): 294–321.

Charness, Gary, and Matthias Sutter. 2012. "Groups Make Better Self-Interested Decisions." *Journal of Economic Perspectives* 26(3): 157–176.

Dold, Malte, and Mario J. Rizzo. Forthcoming. "Old Chicago Against Static Welfare Economics." *Journal of Legal Studies*.

Gigerenzer, Gerd. 2000. *Adaptive Thinking: Rationality in the Real World*. Oxford: Oxford University Press.

Kahneman, Daniel. 2011. *Thinking, Fast and Slow*. New York: Macmillan.

Knight, Frank H. 1922. "Ethics and the Economic Interpretation." *The Quarterly Journal of Economics* 36(3): 454–481.

List, John A. 2003. "Does Market Experience Eliminate Market Anomalies?" *The Quarterly Journal of Economics* 118(1): 41–71.

List, John A. 2011. "Does Market Experience Eliminate Market Anomalies? The Case of Exogenous Market Experience." *American Economic Review* 101(3): 313–317.

Machlup, Fritz. 1967. "Theories of the Firm: Marginalist, Behavioral, Managerial." *The American Economic Review* 57(1): 1–33.

O'Donoghue, Ted, and Matthew Rabin. 2015. "Present Bias: Lessons Learned and to Be Learned." *American Economic Review* 105(5): 273–279.

Pareto, Vilfredo. 1971 [1906]. *Manual of Political Economy*. New York: Augustus M. Kelley.

Rizzo, Mario J., and Douglas Glen Whitman. 2009a. "Little Brother is Watching You: New Paternalism on the Slippery Slopes." *Arizona Law Review* 51(3): 685–740.

Rizzo, Mario J., and Douglas Glen Whitman. 2009b. "The Knowledge Problem of the New Paternalism." *Brigham Young University Law Review* 2009(4): 905–968.

Rizzo, Mario J., and Glen Whitman. 2018. "Rationality as a Process." *Review of Behavioral Economics* 5(3–4): 201–219.

Rizzo, Mario J., and Glen Whitman. 2020. *Escaping Paternalism: Rationality, Behavioral Economics, and Public Policy*. Cambridge: Cambridge University Press.

Robbins, Lionel. 1969 [1935]. *An Essay on the Nature and Significance of Economic Science*, 2nd edition. London: Macmillan.

Schimmack, Ulrich, Moritz Heene, and Kamini Kesavan. 2017. "Reconstruction of a Train Wreck: How Priming Research Went off the Rails." *Replicability-Index*, November 23, 2017. https://replicationindex.com/2017/02/02/reconstruction-of-a-train-wreck-how-priming-research-went-of-the-rails/.

Searle, John R. 1964. "How to Derive 'Ought' from 'Is'." *The Philosophical Review* 73: 43–58.

Searle, John R. 1969. *Speech Acts: An Essay in the Philosophy of Language*. Cambridge: Cambridge University Press.

Searle, John R. 1995. *The Construction of Social Reality*. New York: The Free Press.

Sen, Amartya K. 2002a. "Internal Consistency of Choice." In *Rationality and Freedom*, edited by Amartya Sen, 121–157. Cambridge: Harvard University Press.

Sen, Amartya K. 2002b. "Maximization and the act of choice. In *Rationality and Freedom*, edited by Amartya Sen, 158–205. Cambridge: Harvard University.

Sugden, Robert. 2018. *The Community of Advantage: A Behavioural Economist's Defence of the Market*. Oxford: Oxford University Press.

Thaler, Richard H. 2015. *Misbehaving: The Making of Behavioral Economics*. New York: WW Norton.

Thaler, Richard H., and Cass R. Sunstein. 2003. "Libertarian Paternalism." *American Economic Review* 93(2): 175–179.

Thaler, Richard H., and Cass R. Sunstein. 2008. *Nudge: Improving Decisions about Health, Wealth, and Happiness*. New Haven, CT: Yale University Press.

Whitman, Douglas Glen., and Mario J. Rizzo. (2015). "The Problematic Welfare Standards of Behavioral Paternalism." *Review of Philosophy and Psychology* 6(3): 409–425.

Whitman, Glen. 2006. "Against the New Paternalism: Internalities and the Economics of Self-Control." *Policy Analysis*, 563: 1–16. https://www.cato.org/sites/cato.org/files/pubs/pdf/pa563.pdf.

Chapter 2

What Is a Nudge?

Jeffrey Bristol

Nudges have been all the rage in political economy and applied social sciences since the publication of Thaler and Sunstein's (2009) book, *Nudge*. The idea of "choice architects" designing rules and paradigms that influence actors' decisions without the heavy hand of sanctions (called "libertarian paternalism" by Thaler and Sunstein) has captured both the popular and the academic imagination, inspiring not just a range of popular press articles (Benartzi et al. 2017; Chu 2017) but even government departments, such as the so-called "Nudge Unit" established by President Barack Obama in the United States and the Behavioural Insights Team in the United Kingdom (Vinik 2015). Based on the concepts of behavioral economics, for which Thaler won the 2017 Nobel Memorial Prize in Economic Sciences, nudges are policies intended to help individuals overcome biases in decision-making in order to achieve more optimal outcomes, as determined by the "choice architects" (or engineers) of such systems (Thaler and Sunstein 2009).

Of course, as with any prominent idea, the notion of the nudge was not immediately accepted by all parties. While many individuals hail nudges, and the behavioral economic perspective upon which they are based, as significant advances in both economics as a formal science and policy as practice, evidenced by Thaler's Nobel Prize, others remain far more skeptical. These critics often claim that nudges ignore problems associated with the imperfection of knowledge individuals, and even policymakers, face as well as question some of the fundamental assumptions of behavioral economics (see Abdukadirov 2016; Grune-Yanoff and Hertwig 2016; Leggett 2014; Wilkinson 2013; Goodwin 2012).

Nudges, Thaler and Sunstein (2009, 6) write, are "any aspect of the choice architecture that alters people's behavior in a predictable way without forbidding any options or significantly changing their economic incentives."

Unfortunately, as we will see, this definition is likely over-capacious and vague, and insufficiently describes the kind of phenomena that are best considered nudges. The goal of this chapter, therefore, is to create a cohesive definition of nudges that is neither overinclusive nor underinclusive of the phenomenon and to create a taxonomy of nudges culled from an examination of literature and implemented programs in order to gain a better understanding of nudges and their impact on broader society.

In order to accomplish this task, this chapter will be divided into two parts. The first part will consider nudges within a broad context, focusing on their uses for policy, both in the public and private sectors. I argue that nudges should refer only to the action of the government in its role as an ordering mechanism of society as a whole. Nudges, in this case, should be understood as a complement to the state's ability to alter conduct through sanctioning actions.

While many articles have focused on the use of nudges in a highly granular way, examining specific nudges as applied to specific policy problems (e.g., Dean 2018; van Kleef et al. 2018; Ho 2012; Vallgarda 2012; Dayan and Bar-Hillel 2011) or discussing nudges at a high level of theoretical abstraction (e.g., John 2018; Alemanno and Sibony 2017; Hansen 2017; Schmidt 2017; Sunstein 2014), I propose a taxonomy of nudges in the second part of this chapter. This will allow political economists and policy analysts to understand not just what nudges are and how they are used, but also how to implement nudges to their maximum effectiveness by choosing a particular kind of nudge for a particular circumstance and customizing nudges from one instance into another.

An important point this project seeks to emphasize is that nudges are, in their nature, just like any other tool of government. While they can be powerful in bringing about a desired social state, they also have unintended consequences that may enhance or subvert their original intention. While a good understanding of human psychology can help alleviate some of those concerns, it cannot overcome them due to the subjectivities of citizens and policymakers (Abdukadirov 2016, 3–4). As a result, a proper understanding of nudges emphasizes both their potential benefits and their harms. Far from being a safe, neutral, and even salutary alternative to sanctioning behavior that emphasizes the libertarian in "libertarian paternalism," nudges should be understood to present the same dangers to liberty as any other state action. In fact, they should be understood as the flip side of the coercive coin, something that buys obedience as much as it does freedom.

The coercive nature of the force of law is clear: it commands and penalizes for disobedience. The moral problem implicated here is that liberty finds few and tenuous handholds where coercion works to force people's will to conform to the legislator's own. Nudges seem to be a freer option because they leave a choice to the subject: to act in accordance with the nudge or not. However, this is not in truth a free choice for there are always penalties associated with avoiding the nudge, whether that be the extra work it takes to opt out of a system, the emotional toll it requires to disagree with authority or some other more positive sacrifice, such as the payment of a small penalty.

Either way, when we include opportunity costs in our calculations, we see that both coercive government action and nudges exert a penalty for noncompliance. While the coercive legislation exacts actual costs, the nudge exerts opportunity costs by requiring the party to engage in some positive action to avoid the nudge, thereby sacrificing resources that could have been used elsewhere, often incurring a penalty for doing something they would prefer to do and could have done free of charge had the nudge not existed. When considered from this perspective, nudges appear much less like libertarian alternatives to government coercion and begin to look more like coercion.

WHAT IS A NUDGE?

Thaler and Sunstein's (2009) definition of a nudge, which is generally used as the touchstone for most definitions of nudges, contains several important parts for understanding how nudges function. First, a nudge must be part of the "choice architecture." This means that a nudge must be part of an artificially created environment. Second, it must alter people's behavior predictably. Third, it must not forbid an option or alter a person's incentives to such a degree that the chooser is left without an actual choice (Thaler and Sunstein 2009, 6). These elements are what make the difference between a nudge and a sanction. Implicit in Thaler and Sunstein's model is that a sanction means that the designer of the "choice architecture" leaves the actor with little to no choice in their action while the nudge model simply points the way, like an arrow indicating the correct path when a road forks and allows the traveler to choose their own direction.

Given the ponderous language used by Thaler and Sunstein, unpacking exactly what a nudge is, and comparing it to both the kinds of action the authors wish to juxtapose it as well as the actions the authors endorse as nudges, will help to define a "nudge" more parsimoniously than the above. As it stands, the literature presents a wide range of examples and musings on nudges, not all of which are commensurate with each other, though the technocratic language of their description often serves to obscure this fact. After I have made a theoretical analysis of the nudge, I will attempt a synthesis by repairing and reassembling the argument in order to create our own simpler, more parsimonious definition.

The best way to begin our exploration is to examine in more detail the implicit dichotomy of action presented by Thaler and Sunstein. In their model of control, they imagine two possible ways a legislator might influence a subject.[1] The first is the classical model of positive legal action where the legislator enacts a commandment which contains a punishment that if violated, subjects the violator to a sanction which could involve either a financial/corporal penalty or a confinement. This legislation influences behavior by positing a definite penalty, theoretically forcing an individual to conform to the legislated norm. It is an active sanction.

The second is the new model of the nudge where the legislator, rather than constraining a subject through sanctions to behave, instead provides some kind of a reason to perform in a way the legislator desires either by manipulating the environment within which the subject acts or by providing a reward or goal that creates a desire within the subject to perform the given action. It is a passive incentive. Thus, two models of legislative action are proposed and juxtaposed against one another: active sanctions and passive incentives.

A closer examination reveals that this dichotomy is more fraught than this simple narrative makes it appear. If one supposes that a legislator commands and a subject follows, then the dichotomy might hold, but subjects are not simple machines that take inputs, compute them, and produce predictable, regular action. Instead, they are individuals who, while they do calculate what is and isn't in their interests, do so across a broader range of inputs, incentives, actions, desires, and other humanistic phenomena than are present in Thaler and Sunstein's implicit political-economic anthropology, a fact well explored in the public choice literature in economics as well as sociological literature on social action (e.g., Ellis 2018; Rizzo 2016; Buchanan and Tullock 1999).

In fact, if one peers deeply enough into the nudge/sanction dichotomy, it becomes clear that at a certain level all legislative actions to constrain individual behavior are nudges. Even the most criminal act is not fully prevented by laws prohibiting it, as the fact that murders occur in jurisdictions with the death penalty indicates. Individuals, driven by their personal passions, still engage with the "choice architecture" of the criminal law and decide it is in their interest (we can set aside whether it is their "best" interest) to engage in deeply criminal action. In this case, we might recast even strict criminal law into a kind of "nudge," albeit a particularly aggressive one, that tries to influence people not to kill one another (see Cornish and Clarke 2014; Newman 1997).

With this realization in mind, where do we put the dividing line between active sanctions and passive incentives? Does this remove the salience of the distinction entirely? I would argue it does not, but that it requires us to conceive the work nudges perform in a different way than Thaler and Sunstein suggest; in a way that makes nudging look more like traditional legislative action than the authors of *Nudge* might like.

It is clear that, while sanctions and nudging are similar in that they both leave the subject to choose whether or not to perform a particular action, they both influence the individual in different ways and to different degrees.[2] The active sanction is a post hoc act that seeks to penalize certain choices and deter undesired actions. The passive incentive is more often an a priori act that either changes the environment with which the actor engages or seeks to provide the actor with a structure that changes the decision-making process itself. As a result, the difference between a sanction and a nudge is not just that one is negative and the other positive, but also a temporal difference in when each occurs. Ultimately, however, the relationship between sanctioning and nudging should not be viewed as dichotomous (i.e., that one is libertarian and the other authoritarian) but that they are two sides of the same coin. Both are restrictive, but they restrict in very different ways with very different effects.

Likewise, there is the assumption that because nudges do not coerce, they are less damaging to society at large. While it is true that the damages from sanctioning on society are direct and obvious (imprisoning individuals harms the moral, social, and economic value of incarcerated persons), nudges also pose their own threat to social well-being, though the impact is less obvious.

The primary threat nudges pose to the social order comes as a result of the changes they introduce into the information-processing function of markets. As well described by Hayek (1937, 1945, 1978), one of the major functions of the market is to inform its participants about the material condition of society. Kirzner's addition to Hayek's argument is to indicate a second major function: markets by distributing information also allow entrepreneurs to discover exploitable opportunities within the market in order to provide society with previously unmet needs (Kirzner 1973, 81). Nudges run the risk of seriously distorting this mechanism by encouraging people to act in certain predetermined ways regardless of what data the market supplies. As a result, nudges introduce similar problems to economic planning (Lavoie 2015, 179–183). Indeed, nudges should be viewed not as an alternative to economic planning, but as a softer version of it.

Justice is also an important distinction to make since active sanctions are associated with crimes, or actions which violate some basic moral value while passive incentives are more likely to affect less fraught issues of health or individual benefit, there is a difference in how each is handled processually. The state seems to be more of a danger in the sanctions case because it might sanction an action unjustly, bringing undeserved moral opprobrium and physical harm. The passive incentive of a nudge, on the other hand, affects everyone equally and does not involve the same concerns of due process and unjust penalties. Of course, only a few (the criminals) suffer from the penalizing actions of the state, while many (all subjects) suffer from the constraints of the nudge.

In the end, one might wonder whether the effect on the general liberty of society is, therefore, equal between the two, the difference being the first is felt more keenly by the few and the latter more gently by the whole. The amount of control very well may be the same when considered in toto. This is not immediately obvious, however, and may explain why Thaler and Sunstein (2009) imagine the nudge as less coercive than a sanction because the sanctioning action is violent and dramatic (especially when coupled with the judicial rituals and action of the state) while the nudging action is confined to the realm of bureaucratic or legislative back-and-forth with few immediately visible repercussions.

The similarity of sanctions and incentives should not wholly undermine the idea of nudging but must be kept in mind when we think about what nudges are and how we use them. Nudges are different than sanctions. Their ability to order society in a gentler, a priori way has consequently established their use in legal and political orders. It is easier to create a program that encourages behavior than one that punishes it because there are more people willing to encourage than punish and the infrastructure is often easier to implement. In other words, far from inventing nudges, Sunstein and Thaler have simply observed and categorized something that had always been present.

The ubiquity of nudges becomes clear when we think about them within the context of our broader legal order. The state uses law as a way to engineer society (Roach Anleu 2010, 148–182; McCann 1991; Pound 1965). We see this effect most obviously in criminal law, but legal acts to shape society in other ways have long been present as well. Most obvious are legislative measures, like tax breaks or exemptions that change subjects' incentives. Such incentives are used to promote industry in certain areas or to alter consumer behavior, such as when tariffs are used to raise the price of imported goods to encourage the consumption of domestic alternatives.

Subtler, or perhaps just more overlooked, nudges have long existed with significant impact on society. Marriage law is an excellent example of such a nudge, as the government provides legal, social, and economic benefits only to couples who marry in ways the legislator deems appropriate. The laws for forming marriages, for example, ensure that American families will not be polygamous. Until very recently, the inability to marry discouraged long-term, formal unions between homosexuals. These laws also helped reinforce the ideal of the nuclear, as opposed to the extended, family living in a single household. All of these factors, when combined with the fact that one need not engage in marriage, make marriage laws a nudge under the definition presented by Thaler and Sunstein (as well as the definition developed later in this chapter).

It is clear, when viewed through this lens, that the action of nudging is as central to the work of the state as is the action of sanctioning. It is also sometimes just as coercive, even if on the surface nudges appear more voluntary. (see Table 2.1 for some common characteristics).[3]

The above statement, and much of the discussion that precedes it, makes a major assumption about nudges that Thaler and Sunstein themselves do not: namely, that the act of nudging should be considered an act that is undertaken only by the state. Indeed, Thaler and Sunstein regularly (2009, 231–238) discuss action taken by non-state actors as being nudges. I argue, however, that if nudges are primarily actions taken to shape social life in the same way as criminal law, then just as we recognize the sanctions taken by private actors as being similar, but different, to law (Hart 1994, 18–25; Austin 1832, 1–30), so too should we look at nudging actions taken by private parties as being similar to the nudging actions taken by the state, but ultimately so different in effect as to mitigate the similarity in form.

The key difference between the passive incentives provided by the state and passive incentives provided by private actors lies in the relationship between the legislator and subject versus the producer and consumer. In the former context, the contours and even the existence of the relationship are stipulated to exist by the first party and the second party has no choice but to engage with it. This means that the subject does not choose whether or not to follow the legislator's law; instead that individual is forced to do so. While in the case of the latter relationship, that between the producer and the consumer, the parties can choose voluntarily to be subject to that relationship or not. In other words, the key difference in these situations is the matter of power and authority (Hart 1994, 18–25; Austin 1832, 1–30).

Why we should consider the dynamics of power and authority in nudging relationships becomes clear when we note the similarity and even sympathy between acts of nudging and the police power granted to the state to control individual actions through sanctions. Just as the ineluctability of the relationship between state and subjects, combined with the extreme difference in power between, means that the state has absolute legal authority over the

Table 2.1   Characteristics of Sanctions and Nudges

Sanctions	*Nudges*
Penalty	Encouragement
Fear	Desire
Active state	Passive state
Post hoc	A priori
Police power	Self-control

Source: Author created.

subject, so too does the ineluctability and power differential between the state and subject make the state's ability to nudge the subject different from the producer's ability to nudge the consumer. Thus, we should consider the actions of the state nudging to be a different kind of action from the action of the producer.

Considering examples of the two relationships should help make this clear. In the case of state-provided nudges, the subject has no way of avoiding the nudging except to avoid performing the action. To use the nudge of marriage explored above, while one might avoid engaging in the institution of marriage, if one wishes to marry, one must do so as "nudged" by the state.[4] On the other hand, when one examines marriage from the perspective of voluntary associations, one can see the salient difference. Such a voluntary association would be religion.

For religious people, the church nudges marriage in a similar way to the state by defining how it can be performed, what behaviors characterize the status, and how one can exit. Unlike the relationship one has with the state, however, one can control which rules one is subject to by associating with a religious organization that aligns best with one's individual views. As a result, the Catholic church might discourage sin and adultery and promote marital stability by prohibiting divorce (it presumes), while a Protestant church sees the matter differently, allowing divorce in some situations. One's freedom to associate means that one can change denomination depending on which nudge one desires, a fact which blunts the efficacy of the nudge itself but enables choice and freedom.[5]

There is also a category problem in extending the power of nudging beyond the state. Under Thaler and Sunstein's definition, almost any action an individual takes to influence another while leaving the chooser's options open counts as a nudge. In this case, almost all human interaction becomes nudging. Advertising is a nudge. Arguments between friends and spouses might become nudges. Many interpersonal actions, such as writing a note to remind one's self to do something later, could be considered a nudge. Nudges, in other words, become so ubiquitous that they are almost synonymous with interpersonal interaction itself, making the category less useful than it might otherwise be.

Consequently, if we are to create a strong and robust definition for nudges that includes actions that should be considered nudges while excluding those that should not, we must create a new definition that differs from the one provided by Thaler and Sunstein. This definition must recognize that nudging is an action most appropriately undertaken by the state; that it involves a similar coercive power to sanctioning behavior; and that it operates to constrain an individual's action through positive reinforcement of behavior (as opposed to sanctioning actions) or by affecting the decision-making environment of the actor themselves. Consequently, I suggest that a nudge be understood as being any action taken by the state that incentivizes individuals to make certain choices over others or that creates or changes someone or something's identity or socio-environmental situation.

TAXONOMY

The previous discussion should not imply that nudges are an inappropriate exercise of state authority any more than the use of sanctions to enforce criminal law should be viewed as such. It should, however, highlight the need to consider the use of nudges carefully, at least as carefully as criminal sanctions. For far from benign elements of libertarianism, nudges are as paternalistic as any other exercise of government power. Nudges must be understood, categorized, and analytically considered in order to understand how and when to use them to influence subjects' behavior.

This categorization parallels the categorization of criminal sanctions. We can divide sanctions into imprisonment, capital/corporal punishment, fines, property seizure, and other categories (e.g., Zaibert 2006, 96–126; Cohen 2005, 26–37). These categories allow us to consider which sanctions to apply in a given situation as well as to moderate the state's use of coercive influence and prevent disproportionate punishment. Likewise, we need a similar way to discuss state-provided nudges; a taxonomy of nudges, if you will.

Such a taxonomy aims to serve two functions. First, to better elucidate how nudges work and the different effects they have on subjects. By specifying and describing the kinds of nudges that are available to decisionmakers, this chapter fills in a major gap in the literature. Most of the research focuses on nudges as a general concept or on the implementation of particular nudges. While both are necessary, they tend to neglect how nudges differ from one another, both in kind and effect. The first treats nudges as if they were all the same kind of action, making it difficult to distinguish whether one kind or another might be more or less coercive, while the second ignores all nudges but those under immediate consideration, resulting in the impression that all nudges are either alike or that nudges are unique and, thus, incapable of being grouped into higher categories.

By devising categories of nudges, we can consider which nudges are most effective and when it is most suitable to enact them. We can also explore whether some nudges are beyond the pale of consideration. A similar inquiry in criminal law is that of capital/corporal punishment, a category of crime which countries are generally phasing out *in toto* as being unacceptable in moral terms (and part of which, the corporal element, has long been removed in almost every countries' penal regime). If we did not have the category of capital punishment, however, it is unlikely we could have a conversation around whether or not such kinds of punishment are appropriate or not. Instead, we would return to a time before the theorization of criminal penalties, when fines (especially when viewed as blood money) and capital/corporal punishment were considered of a similar kind. It would consequently be impossible to argue whether one was more acceptable than the other without condemning or redeeming both in the same breath.

The second is to allow legislators to create better, more tailored nudges that can effectively accomplish the desired effects with minimum collateral consequences. It is an unfortunate truth about all human organizations, whether corporations, states, and so on, that any action they take will have unforeseen effects. This is a result of the inadequacy of human understanding and knowledge. Indeed, social interactions involve so many variables that it is impossible to know all of the details necessary to engineer a given social effect and because it is impossible to know the known unknowns and the unknown unknowns that may arise from any given action (see Hayek 1945). Even if such knowledge were available, a legislator would still be incapable of making the calculations necessary to predict the behavior and responses of each individual actor to the given stimulus of the nudge. The result is that one cannot ever know what the full scope of a nudging action will be.

With these warnings in mind, it is best for the legislator to proceed with caution because any given nudge will be unpredictably libertarian or paternalist depending on the actors and the situation. As a result, a more narrowly tailored and carefully constructed nudge is to be preferred to broader and more encompassing ones. Having a taxonomy of available nudges will help accomplish this goal by ensuring not only that the appropriate kind of nudge can be selected for the given situation, but also that if none of the nudges apply, the decisionmaker might realize that the situation is one where a nudge is simply not appropriate.

To this end, I propose ten varieties of nudges based on an exploration of the existing literature: (1) default (opt-in/opt-out), (2) choice design (arrangement of options), (3) building (arrangement of physical space), (4) dissuading (raising costs), (5) incentives, (6) information provision, (7) goal/target creation, (8) stimulus provision, (9) directions, and (10) rights/duties transfer (see Table 2.2). Each operates in a slightly different way and has slightly different effect. I should note here that this is not an exhaustive list and that there are likely nudges that either bridge two categories or exist outside of them entirely. I will describe each kind of nudge below, giving examples and discussing how they might be used to obtain the legislator's aims as well as the potential negative effects on individual liberty and society more broadly.

Default

A default consists of either opt-in or opt-out choices, depending on what is being nudged, though, for reasons we will see below, the opt-out default is the most common nudge. Changing default positions means changing the initial situation the actor faces. One of the most prominent examples is a proposal for retirement savings plans (e.g., Yan and Yates 2019; Benartzi and Thaler 2013). Normally, employees are required to opt-in to such plans rather than being automatically enrolled and required to opt out if the individual desires not to participate. This is an opt-in default. Proponents of changing the default state argue that making retirement plans opt-out (requiring employers and employees to automatically to contribute a certain amount of the employee's income to the plan unless told otherwise), rather than opt-in, would increase savings rates and ensure more workers are well prepared for retirement (e.g., Benartzi and Thaler 2013; Thaler and Sunstein 2009, 132).

Since not being involved in a plan initially is the normal state of the world, programs whose normal state are opt-outs are less often a concern for nudge theory. Consequently, these situations are rarer and most nudges consist of

Table 2.2   Types of Nudges

Type	Definition	Example
Default	Changing the initial position of an actor	Opt-out retirement plans
Choice design	Altering actor's choices	School cafeteria food options
Building	Altering the physical environment to induce preference	Urban planning that promotes walking
Dissuading	Raising the costs of an action to dissuade actors	Pigouvian taxes
Incentives	Providing a reward when actor engages in desired action	Tax credits for electric vehicles
Information provision	Providing information about the action in question with the aim of affecting behavior	Health warnings on packages of cigarettes
Goal/target creation	Providing actor with a desired end-state	Presidential Fitness Test
Stimulus provision	Providing a prompt to encourage a given action	Using red or yellow colors to induce a state of caution
Directions	Providing instructions for how to perform an action	Directions for handling nuclear waste
Rights/duties Transfer	Imposition of rights or duties on actors to cover the consequences of a given action	Assignment of fiduciary duties

Source: Author created.

changing the default from an opt-in to opt-out. There are some exceptions to this rule, however. Examples of natural opt-outs include the emancipation of minors from parental control (a child is automatically under the supervision of their parents unless they take decided action to opt out of that relationship), renunciation of state benefits (including citizenship), and the exiting of other relationships where participation rather than withdrawal is considered the natural state. These are extreme and unusual situations, however, and tend not to be amenable to nudging.

Defaults are probably the most powerful and intuitive of the nudges as they effect the most direct change on the actor. Instead of providing them with a choice or incentive, the default position actually changes the actor's world directly by forcing them into a state they would not otherwise occupy. The power of this nudge is particularly acute if the choice involves something complicated and high stakes. A retirement account is a particularly good example since financial matters are both incredibly important to one's life and often very difficult to understand. In such a case, both opting-in and opting-out present challenges: an individual may be so paralyzed by the importance of the decision and/or its complexities that they make no move to opt in. On the other hand, if the opt-out is defaulted, that same individual may feel powerless to change the state of affairs even though it may not be the financially prudent state for them at the time. As a result of the complexity of the issue, the individual may feel incompetent or even unable to second-guess the authority of the legislator and might presume that, given the authority of the legislator, they know best and their preferences should be followed. In other words, the choice is really no choice at all. The power of this dilemma is made more acute by the fact that, in most cases, these nudges typically deal with complex and highly important issues more often than trivial ones, though in the latter case the insignificance of the issue may also prevent the actor from changing the default state out of apathy, inattention, or both (Foster 2017, 69–77; Prabhakar 2017, 452–454).

Default nudges are particularly powerful actions. They have the ability to influence actors in ways the actors themselves may not even realize if they are not made aware that their choice environment has changed. Likewise, these opt-out options may deprive individuals of resources they assumed they may otherwise have had. In the case of savings plans, for example, the opt-in may cause the employee to take home less money than they would otherwise have assumed they would. This can have negative influences on their freedom to act if they fail to consider the reduction in their immediately available income or have alternative future plans to those envisioned by the savings plan. It might also alter their ability to create tailor-made solutions for their own life by dissuading the individual from researching options on their own or altering the contribution level or composition that presented in the default option.

As a result, default nudges affect actors' decisions, not only in terms of their direct investment and freedom of choice but also in terms of opportunity costs and possibly reducing net savings advantages to nil or negative numbers (Beshears et al. 2017, 1–4; Law et al. 2011, 25–27).

Choice Design

Choice design involves manipulating the actor's options. This form of nudge can be either (1) presenting an actor with a range of options when previously there was none or (2) altering the order in which options an individual is presented with the aim of affecting the individual's decision-making. Choice design involves greater or lesser manipulation of the actor's decision-making depending on the individual circumstances. Some choice design nudges can be drastic. For example, there is a debate about whether unhealthy foods should be available to children in schools (see Datar and Nicosia 2012; Story et al. 2006). Since children in schools are a captive population, the removal of the choice to eat certain items means the items are either available or they are not. While students may circumvent the choice design regime by bringing food from home or leaving campus, this creates hurdles (such as the need to plan ahead or to have transportation) that make such options difficult to procure relative to others. In such an example, the legislator has a great deal of control over the available options and, thus, individual behavior.

While the previous example is about limiting and controlling options and consequent behavior, choice design can also alter choice structure through the intentional arrangement of options. On a very simple level, this might involve providing specific answers to a question (such as a multiple-choice question) on a form rather than leaving respondents to write their own answers in a blank space on the form. This type of choice design can be more or less constraining depending on whether the actor can only choose only the choices provided or is able to provide a unique solution tailor-made to their own personal situation. An example is the healthcare exchange established by President Obama under the Patient Protection and Affordable Care Act which gathers together all the suitable healthcare plans available in one place to facilitate user access rather than requiring those looking for insurance to research and compile plans on their own from various private websites.

Choice design can be far more liberal in the freedom it provides the actor from the legislator's influence than defaults, but precisely how liberal depends on the environmental and choice constraints: if the actor is allowed total freedom and choice design focuses on the arrangement and order of the options to select, the nudge is relatively weak and liberal; if the actor is heavily constrained in their ability to choose and act and choice design removes some options entirely, then the nudge is quite constraining and restrictive. It

should always be borne in mind, however, that as with default choice manipulation, even a weak choice design nudge is not without its own manipulative
context that can persuade an actor's choice beyond the intention of the nudge.
As a result, even with an open choice scheme that includes both the preferred
and unpreferred options from the choice architect, the actor may (even sub-
consciously) ignore that freedom in favor of the presumed reliability of any
preapproved or preferred options.

Building

Building is the companion of choice design, but in the physical environment.
Bench rails serve as an excellent example of building nudges. Bench rails
are protruding devices placed on benches and other flat surfaces that prevent
homeless people from using them as beds or prevent individuals from riding
over them with skateboards or bikes. Changing physical space can be a powerful inducement or restraint to perform certain acts. Altering physical space
is a particularly powerful way of influencing people's behavior, as it forces
them to move and interact differently than they might otherwise, constraining certain behaviors while encouraging others. Architects and city designers
have been engaging in these forms of nudges for decades (see Tzoulas et al.
2007; Frumkin et al. 2004, 90–108; Barnett 1974). In addition to restrictive
nudges, they use a variety of building nudges to promote health and well-
being, such as adding bike lines and placing buildings in such a way as to
promote walking (Cimino 2018).

   In this way, building nudges are powerful nudges, for if a road does not
lead an individual to a particular location, it is possible the individual may not
be able to go there. On the other hand, building nudges can be very expensive and sometimes difficult to implement. Moreover, while building nudges
give the illusion of control because they allow the legislator to manipulate
physical space, actors can resist such manipulations through concerted action.
Desire lines, or paths people create as shortcuts between two points that often
bypass established walkways, are an example of such behavior that counter
the impacts of these nudges (Smith 2018, 2986–2991).

   Despite the possibility of their circumvention and the expense of the construction, building nudges can be very effective in altering behavior both by
altering landscapes and by making choosing alternatives to the legislator's
design either extremely difficult or practically impossible. In building nudges
there is often a direct relationship between the difficulty of constructing the
nudge and its effectiveness in shaping individual behavior. A nudge that is
expensive and highly developed, such as the layout of a building, the patterns
of roads, or other aspects of physical space, tend to be very effective at channeling certain behaviors in a given direction by making the desired behavior
either the only possible action or the only action that can be taken without

great difficulty. There is likely a direct correlation between the investment of labor and expense that goes into a building nudge and its level of coercion. Laying a sidewalk is a relatively easy task as far as construction is concerned and these forms of building are the most easily circumvented. Constructing large infrastructure projects like public transit or multifamily housing is an example of nudges that are ineluctably powerful, but also require an immense expenditure of resources to construct.

Dissuading

Dissuading involves raising the cost of a given action sufficiently high that individuals are unlikely to engage in the behavior the legislator wishes to restrict. Of all the nudges, this type is perhaps the clearest act of compulsion on behalf of the legislator and can sometimes look like coercion. An example is the debate about the nature of fines: are fines intended to be a punishment for behavior or to function as a tax upon it (see O'Malley 2009, 72–77; Becker 1974, 24–33)? The indefiniteness of fines becomes clear when thinking about other financial dissuaders such as sin taxes, taxes aimed to reduce consumption of unhealthy items like soda, or Pigouvian taxes, financial burdens which serve the purpose of dissuading an individual from engaging in a certain behavior. While such taxes may be aimed at altering behavior, they can also be viewed as simply taxes upon activity the government wishes to monetize and may be set low enough to increase revenues while not sufficiently dissuading behavior.

Despite this ambiguity, dissuading nudges are perhaps the simplest and most straightforward of all nudge types to implement. Unlike many of the other forms of nudges described in this chapter, dissuading nudges are quite straightforward in their operation: the legislator enacts a cost, either monetary or otherwise, on an action that they seek to discourage. There is no need to implement a wide-ranging program, to construct facilities, or engage in new governmental activities.

Dissuading nudges is also malleable: they can be scaled to be highly effective if the cost of the action is higher than any benefits that could be derived from it. Alternatively, dissuading nudges can be relatively light in their effect if the cost of the action is low compared to its expected benefit. The difficulty in this calibration lies in the knowledge problem: it is hard, if not impossible, for the legislator to be able to know the correct level for dissuasion. Worse, depending on the heterogeneity of the population, no such level might exist.

Incentives

Incentives involve some kind of reward, monetary or otherwise, distributed when an actor engages in the desired behavior. Incentives attempt to nudge behavior by giving individuals a reason for engaging in certain actions and, thus, leave an option for people to behave counter to the nudge, but to do so at an opportunity cost to themselves.

Like dissuading nudges, the tax regime is replete with incentives. Both credits and deductions serve as incentive-based nudges. In this way, charitable donations, children, marriage, and a whole range of different activities are encouraged by tax breaks. Incentive regimes also exist to support recycling, such as payments at bottle drops, rebates for purchasing environmentally safe cars, and so on.

Incentives potentially involve less restriction on the freedom to act than dissuading nudges, since an individual is not discouraged from taking an action they might wish to do but rather rewarded for taking other actions approved by the legislator. Incentives are relatively weak because they do not require the same trade-off calculus as dissuading. Instead, the cost built into incentives comes largely as a result of opportunity costs, which may not be a primary factor in one's mental decision-making framework. Incentives, however, still might disrupt an individual's autonomous decision-making by convincing them to take actions they may otherwise not have performed, and, consequently, may have coercive power. The greater the incentive, the greater the coercion.

Information Provision

Information provision includes providing any kind of information concerning the action in question. This type of nudge has the potential to be among the least invasive of the actor's freedom of choice, depending on how it is utilized. Perhaps the most ubiquitous form of information provision encountered is nutritional information on food products, done with the idea that informed consumers will be better able to choose healthy food options to promote physical well-being (Garretson and Burton 2000, 223–225; Keller et al. 1997, 265–268).

Information provision is often utilized in conjunction with other nudges, often gaining its coercive impact from the effects of related nudges. Posting health warnings on cigarette packages is an example of a combination of information provision and dissuasion. Analytically, information provision tends to be neutral in and of itself but gains its efficacy through the positive or negative valence of the message conveyed. The health warnings on a cigarette package (or the even more ubiquitous warnings from California about carcinogens found on nearly every product in the United States, it seems) carry the legislators' hopes that people will note the dangers inherent in the product and avoid their use. For example, in Europe cigarette packages now contain graphic pictures of diseased organs (Tobacco Products Directive 2014/40/

EU). This is information provision in that it shows the purchaser what their bodies could look like, but it contains no real informational content. It seems to exist largely for the shock value inherent in the image, and, thus, can also be considered a dissuading nudge. Consequently, the distinction between a simple provision of information and other nudges lies in the way the information is provided.

Other forms of information provision have to do with informing individuals of other nudges that might be in place, including dissuading and incentives. An example of this includes signs warning individuals about increased liability if certain activities are undertaken (such as "swim at your own risk" signs that let potential swimmers know that not only is swimming in this area potentially risky but the property owner is not responsible for their safety or liable if they incur injuries).

Information provision tends to be among the least invasive nudges because of its usually neutral position in terms of action. While providing information does imply a position the government takes, which like in the case of defaults and choice design can be read as an endorsement, this is not inevitable and may often be considered to be relatively weak. This is because information provision typically seeks generally to inform the actor as to their environment rather than attempting to direct the actor's behavior toward a particular goal, which is the case with most nudges.

Goal/Target Creation

Goal or target creation is similar to incentives, where a desired action is articulated but, unlike incentives, there is not a corresponding reward. In goal/target creation, the actor is provided with a particular end-state that the legislator believes is desirable with the hope that individuals will then seek to accomplish the goal. This type of nudge is often accomplished through information provision. The food pyramid, for example, provides both information about the kinds of food one should eat and goals in terms of balance and caloric intake that an individual should meet (USDA 1996). The combination of these two nudges allows individuals to know why they should monitor their food consumption and what their consumption (the goal) should include.

Goal/target creation can also be used as a form of social manipulation. By creating goals or targets, even sometimes without incentives, a legislator might encourage a form of competition among citizens. Signs around workplaces, for example, that show how many days a factory has been accident-free, are commonly used to see how long one can persist without an accident and, implicitly, whether one can beat the longest, previously held record. These forms of nudges can be effective both on an individual level, where the individual competes against their past performance, and on a group level, where individuals or the group competes against others to achieve some goal.

Goal/target creation, like information provision, is a relatively innocuous form of nudging. Its primary effect is to act on predispositions which already exist in the personalities of those being nudged, and so works only to the extent the actors are willing to engage with the goals of the legislator. Actors are consequently free to avoid these nudges if they so desire. When these nudges serve to induce competition, they may be somewhat more coercive, but only insofar as the individuals are persuaded by competition. If people find no value in the competition, then the nudge will fail. The infamous Presidential Fitness Test, which had an element of peer competition for fitness, is an example of a nudge that failed as the participants generally did not compete as expected (Whitehead and Corbin 1991; 14–15). It might have succeeded, however, if the goal had been created or implemented in a more effective manner (Wiersma and Sherman 2008).

Stimulus Provision

Stimulus provision is similar to goal/target creation, except that instead of focusing an actor's attention on the end-state, it provides a prompt for action. Education programs emphasizing STEM programs for girls are examples of a stimulus provision that attempts to increase the number of women who become scientists (see Mosatche et al. 2013). These nudges include providing girls with toys that involve manipulation and construction, focused math lessons, and other forms of encouragement to follow math- and science-intensive fields. They do so without requiring the girls to enter into any agreements to pursue studies in these fields, but, instead, are based upon the belief that providing toys and learning opportunities to girls at a young age will increase their desires to become scientists or pursue other careers in STEM.

Perhaps the most common stimulus provisions are prompts for engaging in certain behaviors to which we learn to respond. Bells alerting us to the arrival of a train, warning noises broadcast before the opening of doors, or tornado sirens signaling a need to shelter-in-place are all examples of simple stimulus provisions intended to provoke a basic response in the actor toward a particular goal. These stimuli present a problem, however, in that they must usually be taught and learned. Consequently, these nudges are heavily reliant on socialization, an effective bureaucracy that communicates to individuals how to respond, and actors who are both willing and able to learn how to respond to stimuli.

Some stimuli are, of course, not reliant on training and may unconsciously impact individuals, like encouraging girls to pursue STEM fields, or can rely on already learned cultural habits, such as the use of colors to induce moods

(Bellizzi and Hite 1992, 60–62; Hale and Strickland 1976). Signs indicating dangers are often colored yellow or red, which signals a need to be alert.

Stimulus provision is relatively low in terms of its intrusiveness on freedom of action unless the actor is highly habituated to the stimulus, which is unlikely given the difficulty of creating reflexive action. Environments can be shaped to help develop such stimuli, however, and so this is a nudge that can often be used in conjunction with building. Subway and train stations, for example, have many stimuli with which people interact, such as lights and sounds. These stations can be designed to help maximize such warnings by enhancing their acoustic, having lights clearly visible indicating whether it is safe to board or not, or simply being designed to facilitate the efficient movement of passengers through the space (Durmisevic and Sariyildiz 2001, 22–23; Edwards 1996, 93–99). Physical spaces might be designed so that when a stimulus excites a group, the actual movement patterns of the space reduce the actors' level of energy or dissipates it over time so that a careful balance might be maintained. Perhaps the most famous example of this is a nudge used on animals rather than people: the slaughterhouses for cattle designed by Temple Grandin are indirect and circuitously built so as to deny cows a view of the slaughterhouse floor and soothe their nerves by forcing them to walk a long distance before the slaughter takes place (Grandin 2014). Prisons are also a built environment where space is manipulated to create similar levels of control among people, isolating, calming, or otherwise controlling them to create a more manageable population (Fowler 2015).

Directions

Directions are relatively straightforward nudges. They simply comprise instructions to the actor on how to engage in a particular behavior. There are many examples of rules from regulatory agencies, ranging from rules on how to handle nuclear waste down (e.g., 10 CF 20.2002) to food sanitation guidelines issued by a local government (e.g., Chapter 64E-11, Florida Administrative Code). Directions are a powerful tool for nudging and their efficacy can range from merely suggestive to compulsory, depending on how strict the liability regime is that enforces them. Directions might be structured so that failure to follow them means increased liability for individuals injured as a result of the lapse in compliance. Alternatively, a governmental organization may promulgate a directions regime in the form of best practices, which means that the convening authority is simply putting the weight of its experience and influence behind particular ordinances without the threat of punishment. If the consequence is complete liability for anything that goes wrong, then the nudge is quite heavy-handed. If there are no consequences, however, then directions are simply another form of recommendation which people may accept or ignore as they will.

Rights or Duties Transfer

Rights or duties transfer is similar to directions, in that they shift liability. With transfers, the legislator prescribes a regime where individuals bear certain rights or duties vis-à-vis other actors when involved in the legislated action. The intention behind this structure is to ensure that the encumbered entities take care in their actions or the privileged entities are given deference by others, emboldening them to act. Rights or duties transfers are powerful nudges which operate with legal power. Since they do not create sanctionable actions in and of themselves, however, they are not criminal penalties. The government cannot itself sanction an individual for a violation of a right or duty transfer; instead a private action brought by a non-state actor is required to realize their compulsive power. Examples include many state laws establishing rules of liability for engaging in certain activities. In many states with ski resorts, for example, have a law that uphill skiers are liable for injuries incurred by those downhill (e.g., The Colorado Ski Safety Act, Colorado Revised Statutes, § 33-44-109(2)). This transfer of liability ensures that uphill skiers take more care to avoid downhill skiers than vice versa, encouraging more careful behavior than they might otherwise exercise. Consequently, these transfers should be considered nudges rather than sanctions.

A fiduciary requirement is an example of a duty transfer. In the case of a rule promulgated by the Department of Labor under the Obama administration, financial advisers are considered fiduciaries of their clients, meaning practically that if they made an investment that was in the best interests of someone other than their client, the adviser would be liable and open to a lawsuit (Department of Labor 2019). This rule was a nudge in that it set a standard of behavior that was not subject to criminal sanctions and did not seek to exercise direct control of the power of the state over advisers, but instead allowed other actors to hold the violator accountable via lawsuits.

Rights transfers operate somewhat differently. A right transfer means shifting a property right, or the ownership and use of a resource. These rights can serve to promote activity within the economy in relation to certain goods. An example of these types of nudges is patent. Patents, by granting a short-term property right (or monopoly of use) over an invention, attempt to induce inventors to create new goods and services (Lunn 1985, 423). Likewise, one of the core principles behind the idea of a natural monopoly is that, in certain sectors, only the guarantee of a sole right of exploitation will drive revenue high enough to make business viable (Sharkey 1983, 1–11).

A legislator might also transfer the right to benefit from a particular action. The right to sue is an example that is commonly used in the context of antitrust and civil rights, where private individuals who are better positioned to apprehend breaches of these laws are given standing to sue and collect damages instead of the state. Thus a person whose civil rights are being violated can sue on either their own behalf or on the behalf of others, if they can prove standing, and a person suffering from antitrust violations can sue to collect damages and receive an injunction against the offender, both of which would not be allowable if not permitted by specific statutory grants of authority. Using the concept of "private attorneys general," the legislator can transfer the right to sue in certain circumstances from the state to private actors, allowing those actors both the ability to remedy harms to themselves and to benefit from engaging in police action and, thus, providing incentives to certain actors to engage in an activity the legislator deems desirable (Meltzer 1988, 249–52).

Duty transfers can be highly coercive, especially if they create a relationship of liability between parties that previously had none. In such cases where lawsuits are likely, these new duties radically alter the behavior of the actor incurring the liability. Of course, in cases where lawsuits are unlikely to occur, for whatever reason, such duty transfers are less effective. Rights transfers are far less coercive because they are only effective when an individual is already willing to engage in the behavior the legislator desires to encourage and, as a result, are likely only to result in modifying actions that may already be underway.

CONCLUSION

This chapter has attempted to introduce a new definition of and categorization for nudges. Nudges, properly considered, have a strong relationship to state control and should be viewed as the flip side of the state's coercive sanctioning power. In both, the state is acting in order to promote particular patterns of behavior.

Nudges are often treated as if they are a new innovation, having been invented with the rise of behavioral economics. However, nudges are not new and have been in existence since the rise of politics. It is true that nudges are likely more prominent now than they have been in the past, but that is probably a result of the increasing power of the state. While earlier periods saw less effective enforcement of criminal laws due to a less efficient bureaucracy and police force, an increased and more effective bureaucracy allows for more opportunities for the state to engage in all sorts of activities, including nudges.

Along these lines, this chapter attempts to build a taxonomy of nudges in order to better appreciate the increased options that the state has to engage in nudging behavior. Nudges exist in a wider variety than do criminal punishments and as such are harder to categorize, especially when they are often combined in order to increase effectiveness. Yet they may likely form the predominant work of the contemporary state. Some nudges may be more effective the more resources are devoted to them. In other cases, nudges, especially those that rely on society's adoption of them, may have very little relation in terms of effectiveness to the resources expended toward their realization.

Nudges, in other words, are a dynamic and highly developed repertoire of state action that complements criminal sanctions. Without nudges, a state would find itself unable to fulfill completely the governance role expected by modern constituents. However, nudges are an exercise of power like all other actions by the state and should be understood as such. Far from being the act of a neutral, beneficent authority, they can be coercive. This does not mean that nudges should never be used, but it does mean their use should be circumscribed and considered just as the government's punishment of criminals is circumscribed and considered. Indeed, since nudges can impact the whole populace rather than just the narrow band of lawbreakers, they might call for even higher levels of caution and examination.

NOTES

1. I use the term "legislator" and "subject" in this chapter to describe the relations between the individual who enact state action: those who crafting nudges (legislator) and those upon whom the state acts (subjects). Since subjects are subjected to the actions of legislators in both criminal law and nudging actions equally, using the term legislator to describe the builders of nudges rather than the euphemistic "choice architects" clarifies the fact that these actors are engaged in a project of power which constrains the actions of those upon whom the rule operates.

2. There is an implicit assumption in Thaler and Sunstein's (2009) reasoning (it is in fact a first principle without which their model is unsupportable) that the passive incentive action is less efficient at driving an individual to the legislator's preference than an active sanction. As we shall see below, this assumption may not always hold true.

3. One could also flip this around: marital laws and taxes have a heavy hand that many people would say discount them from being nudges, but we can look at many criminal laws whose penalties are lax or not properly enforced, such as speeding tickets or laws against jay-walking, disturbing the peace, which do not count as nudges under the Thaler and Sunstein (2009) definition, but still seem to act in a similar way when considered from the perspective of the subject's choice calculus. In other words, if there are strong nudges, there are also weak sanctions.

4. Indeed, one can wonder if a totalitarian state can possess nudges, or, perhaps put in a better way, is not everything in a totalitarian state one overwhelming nudge?

This shows the similarity between nudging and coercive action, for in totalitarianism, where everything is under the supervision of the state, a kind of singularity is reached where all laws are both nudges in that they prescribe certain actions, and crimes in that they proscribe certain actions, providing both rewards for their fulfillment and penalties for their rupture simultaneously. Returning to the temporal difference between nudges and sanctions above, we see this again demonstrated, for under such regimes the state directs action both before it is taken as well as intervening afterward to ensure that individual action conforms to official purpose by monitoring individual action with stipulations and punishments.

5. Of course, one can rightly point out that it is not so easy to change religious denominations to fit one's desire for marital arrangements since there is much more that goes into choosing one's religious affiliation than marital rules. This is true, though it does not stop people from changing denominations for this very reason. Regardless, one can still view this as a strong private association. If we take a much weaker association, say the kind of cereal one buys, we can see how weak the power of the nudge really is in relationships of voluntary association. It is unlikely that the cereal company will have much ability to bind an individual to its choice constraints.

REFERENCES

Abdukadirov, Sherzod. 2016. "Introduction: Regulation versus Technology as Tools of Behavior Change." In *Nudge Theory in Action: Behavioral Design in Policies and Markets*, edited by Sherzod Abdukadirov, 1–12. Bassingstoke, UK: Palgrave Macmillan.

Alemanno, Alberto, and Anne-Lise Sibony. 2017. *Nudge and the Law: A European Perspective*. Portland: Hart Publishing.

Austin, J. 1832. *The Province of Jurisprudence Determined*. London: John Murray.

Barnett, J. 1974. *Urban Design as Public Policy*. New York: McGraw Hill.

Bellizzi, J., and R. Hite. 1992. "Environmental Color, Consumer Feelings and Purchase Likelihood." *Psychology & Marketing* 9(5): 347–363.

Benartzi, Shlomo, John Beshears, Katherine L. Milkman, Cass R. Sunstein and Richard H. Thaler. 2017, August 11. "Governments Are Trying to Nudge Us Into better Behavior. Is It Working?" *Washington Post*. https://www.washingtonpost.com/news/wonk/wp/2017/08/11/governments-are-trying-to-nudge-us-into-better-behavior-is-it-working/.

Benartzi, S., and R. Thaler. 2013. "Behavioral Economics and the Retirement Savings Crisis," *Science* 339(6124): 1152–1153.

Becker, G. 1974. "Crime and Punishment: An Economic Approach." In *Essays in the Economics of Crime and Punishment*, edited by G. Becker and W. Landes, 27–36. New York: Columbia University Press.

Beshears, J., J. Choi, D. Laibson, B. Madrian, and W. Skimmyhorn. 2017. "Borrowing to Save? The Impact of Automatic Enrollment on Debt. Working Paper." https://scholar.harvard.edu/files/laibson/files/total_savings_impact_2017_12_06.pdf.

Buchanan, James M., and Gordan Tullock. 1999. *The Calculus of Consent.* Indianapolis, IN: Liberty Fund, Inc.

Chu, Be. 2017, October 9. "What Is 'Nudge Theory' and Why Should We Care? Explaining Richard Thaler's Nobel Economics Prize-Winning Concept." *Independent.* https://www.independent.co.uk/news/business/analysis-and-features/nudge-theory-richard-thaler-meaning-explanation-what-is-it-nobel-economics-priz e-winner-2017-a7990461.html.

Cimino, S. 2018. "Designing for Healthy Decisions." *AIA Architect.* https ://www.architectmagazine.com/aia-architect/aiafeature/designing-for-healthy -decisions_o.

Cohen, S. 2005. *Visions of Social Control: Crime, Punishment and Classification.* Cambridge, UK: Polity Press.

Cornish, D., and R. Clarke. 1986. "Introduction." In *The Reasoning Criminal: Rational Choice Perspectives on Offending*, edited by Derek Cornish and Ronald Clark, 1–18. New Brunswick, CT: Transaction Publishers.

Datar, A., and N. Nicosia. 2012. "Junk Food in Schools and Childhood Obesity." *Journal of Policy Analysis and Management* 21(2): 312–337.

Dayan, E., and M. Bar-Hillel. 2011. "Nudge to Nobesity II: Menu Positions Influence Food Orders." *Judgment and Decision Making* 6(4): 333–342.

Dean, N. 2018. "Feel the Nudge." *Nature Energy* 3: 616–630.

Department of Labor. 2019. "Conflict of Interest Final Rule." https://www.dol.gov/agencies/ebsa/laws-and-regulations/rules-and-regulations/completed-rulemaking/1210-AB32-2.

Durmisevic, S., and S. Sariyildiz. 2001. "A Systematic Quality Assessment of Underground Spaces—Public Transport Stations." *Cities* 18(1): 13–23.

Edwards, B. 1996. *The Modern Station: New Approaches to Railway Architecture.* New York: Taylor & Francis.

Ellis, R. 2018. *Culture Matters.* New York: Taylor & Francis.

Foster, L. 2017. "Young People and Attitudes towards Pension Planning." *Social Policy and Society* 16(1): 65–80.

Fowler, Megan. 2015. "The Human Factor in Prison Design: Contrasting Prison Architecture in the United States and Scandinavia." In *103rd ACSA Annual Proceedings: The Expanding Periphery and the Migrating Center.* https://www.acs a-arch.org/chapter/the-human-factor-in-prison-design-contrasting-prison-architec ture-in-the-united-states-and-scandinavia/.

Frumkin, H., L. Frank, and R. Jackson. 2004. *Urban Sprawl and Public Health: Designing, Planning and Building for Healthy Communities.* Washington, DC.: Island Press.

Garretson, J., and S. Burton. 2000. "Effects of Nutrition Fact Panel values, Nutrition Claims, and Health Claims on Consumer Attitudes, Perceptions of Disease-Related Risks and Trust." *Journal of Public Policy and Marketing* 19(2): 213–227.

Goodwin, T. 2012. "Why We Should Reject 'Nudge.'" *Politics* 32(2): 85–92.

Grandin, Temple. 2014. "A Whole Systems Approach to Assessing Animal Welfare During Handling and Restraint." In *Livestock Handling and Transport.* Boston, MA: CABI.

Grune-Yanoff, T., and R. Hertwig. 2016. "Nudge versus Boost: How Coherent are Policy and Theory?" *Minds & Machines* 26: 149–183.

Hale, D., and B. Strickland. 1976. "Induction of Mood States and their Effect on Cognitive and Social Behaviors." *Journal of Consulting and Clinical Psychology* 44(1): 155–186.

Hansen, P. 2017. "The Definition of Nudge and Libertarian Paternalism: Does the Hand Fit the Glove?" *European Journal of Risk Regulation* 7(1): 155–174.

Hart, A. 1994. *The Concept of Law*. Oxford, UK: Clarendon Press.

Hayek, F. A. 1937. "Economics and Knowledge." *Economica* 4: 33–54.

Hayek, F. A. 1945. "The Use of Knowledge in Society." *American Economic Review* 35: 519–530.

Hayek, F. A. 1978. "Competition as a Discovery Procedure," In *New Studies in Philosophy, Politics, Economics and the History of Ideas*. Chicago, IL: University of Chicago Press.

Ho, D. 2012. "Fudging the Nudge: Information Disclosure and Restaurant Grading." *Yale Law Journal* 122: 574–688.

John, P. 2018. *How Far to Nudge: Assessing Behavioral Public Policy*. Northampton, MA: Edward Elgar Publishing, Inc.

Keller, S., M. Landry, J. Olson, A. Velliquette, S. Burton, and J. Craig Andrews. 1997. "Effects of Nutrition Package Claims, Nutrition Fact Panels, and Motivation to Process Nutrition Information on Consumer Product Evaluations." *Journal of Public Policy and Marketing* 16(2): 256–269.

Kirzner, I. M. 1973. *Competition and Entrepreneurship*. Chicago, IL: University of Chicago Press.

Lavoie, Don C. 2015. *Rivalry and Central Planning: The Socialist Calculation Debate Reconsidered*. Arlington: Mercatus Center at George Mason University.

Law, D., G. Scobie, and L. Meehan. 2011. "KiwiSaver: An Initial Evaluation of the Impact on Retirement Saving." Working Paper. https://treasury.govt.nz/publicatio ns/wp/kiwisaver-initial-evaluation-impact-retirement-saving-html.

Leggett, W. 2014. "The Politics of Behaviour Change: Nudge, Neoliberalism, and the State." *Policy & Politics* 42(1): 3–19.

Lunn, J. 1985. "The Roles of Property Rights and Market Power in Appropriating Innovative Output." *The Journal of Legal Studies* 14(2): 423–433.

McCann, M. W. 1991. "Legal Mobilization and Social Reform Movements: Notes on Theory and Its Application." *Studies in Law, Politics, and Society* 11: 225–254.

Meltzer, D. 1988. "Deterring Constitutional Violations by Law Enforcement Officials: Plaintiffs and Defendants as Private Attorneys General." *Columbia Law Review* 88: 247–328.

Mosatche, H. S., S. Matloff-Nieves, L. Kekelis, and E. K. Lawner. "Effective STEM Programs for Adolescent Girls: Three Approaches and Many Lessons Learned." *Afterschool Matters*. https://files.eric.ed.gov/fulltext/EJ1003839.pdf.

Newman, G. 1997. "Introduction: Towards a Theory of Situational Crime Prevention." In *Rational Choice and Situational Crime Prevention*, edited by Graeme Newman, Ronald V. Clarke and Shlomo Shoham, 1–22. New York: Routledge.

O'Malley, P. 2009. "Theorizing Fines." *Punishment and Society* 11(1): 67–83.

Prabhakar, R. 2017. "Why Do People Opt-Out or not Opt-Out of Automatic Enrollment? A Focus Group Study of Automatic Enrollment into a Workplace Pension in the United Kingdom." *Journal of European Social Policy* 27(5): 447–457.

Pound, R. 1965. "Contemporary Juristic Theory." In *Introduction to Jurisprudence*, edited by D. Lloyd. London: Steven and Sons.

Rizzo, M. 2016. "The Four Pillars of Behavioral Paternalism." In *Nudge Theory in Action: Behavioral Design in Policies and Markets*, edited by Sherzod Abdukadirov. Bassingstoke, UK: Palgrave Macmillan.

Roach Anleu, S. 2010. *Law and Social Change*. London: Sage Publications.

Schmidt, A. 2017. "The Power to Nudge." *American Political Science Review* 111(2): 404–417.

Sharkey, W. 1983. *The Theory of Natural Monopoly*. Cambridge, UK: Cambridge University Press.

Smith, N., and P. Walters. 2018. Desire Lines and Defensive Architecture in Modern Urban Environments. *Urban Studies* 55(13): 2980–2995.

Story, M., K. Kaphingst, and S. French. 2006. "The Role of Schools in Obesity Prevention." *The Future of Children* 16(1): 109–142.

Sunstein, C. 2014. *Why Nudge?: The Politics of Libertarian Paternalism*. New Haven, CT: Yale University Press.

Thaler, R. H., and C. R. Sunstein. 2009. *Nudge*. New York: Penguin Group.

Tzoulas, K., K. Korpela, S. Venn, V. Yli-Pelkonen, A. Kazmierczak, J. Niemela, and P. James. 2004. "Promoting Ecosystem and Human Health in Urban Areas Using Green Infrastructure: A Literature Review." *Landscape and Urban Planning* 81(3): 167–178.

USDA. 1996. "The Food Guide Pyramid." https://www.cnpp.usda.gov/sites/default/files/archived_projects/FGPPamphlet.pdf.

Vallgarda, S. 2012. "Nudge-A New and Better Way to Improve Health?" *Health Policy* 104(2): 200–203.

Van Kleef, E., K. Seijdell, M. Vingerhoeds, R. de Wijk, and H. van Trijp. 2018. "The Effect of a Default-Based Nudge on the Choice of Whole-Wheat Bread." *Appetite* 121:179–185.

Vinik, D. 2015, October 15. *Obama's Effort to 'Nudge' America*. https://www.politico.com/agenda/story/2015/10/obamas-effort-to-nudge-america-000276.

Whitehead, J., and C. Corbin. 1991. "Effects of Fitness Test Type, Teacher, and Gender on Exercise Intrinsic Motivation and Physical Self-Worth." *Journal of School Health* 61(1): 11–16.

Wiersma, L., and C. Sherman. 2008. "The Responsible Use of Youth Fitness Testing to Enhance Student Motivation, Enjoyment and Performance." *Measurement in Physical Education and Exercise Science* 12: 167–183.

Wilkinson, T. 2013. "Nudging and Manipulation." *Political Studies* 61(2): 341–355.

Yan, H., and J. Yates. 2019. "Improving Acceptability of Nudges: Learning from Attitudes towards Opt-In and Opt-Out Policies." *Judgment and Decision Making* 14(1): 26–39.

Zaibert, L. 2006. *Punishment and Retribution*. New York: Routledge.

Chapter 3

Why Nudges Should Be
Local and Decentralized

Katarina Hall

Everyone has made decisions that they regret, as well as decisions that bring about unintended consequences. We know that we should be saving money but instead choose to purchase a new pair of shoes that we do not really need. We forget to take the vitamins we bought in our attempt to be healthy. We know that we should be eating more fruits and vegetables instead of fast food, yet we still choose fast food. We procrastinate instead of completing an assignment even though we know the deadline is approaching soon. Sometimes we choose to do those things that are not beneficial, even though we know it. This is simply a part of life.

Behavioral science has picked up on the kinds of actions people make that do not help them achieve their well-being. Our decisions, however, can be changed to lead to better outcomes simply by manipulating the decision-making environment. In doing so, people can be motivated to choose the best (or a better) outcome. The use of behavioral science can be seen throughout our daily life. Marketing campaigns aim to change behavior to get customers to buy their products. Clothing stores put their trendiest clothes on display in order to attract people to buy them. Supermarkets organize their displays and layouts in order to get people to purchase certain items they may not have otherwise. These are just a few of the countless examples that businesses use in order to change people's purchasing behavior.

Similarly, public policy has picked up on the lessons of behavioral science and regulations are being designed to move people toward picking an option that leads to increased well-being. These regulations are called nudge policies. Similar to how traditional regulations aim to reduce the harm that individuals cause to themselves and to others, nudge policies aim to fix individual failures or promote the general welfare of society (Sunstein 2014). While traditional regulation changes people's behavior by coercing them into acting a certain way, this new kind of policy claims that it does not. Nudge policy only suggests that people should act a certain way, without forbidding any other possible choices. This is one of the reasons why nudge policies have become so popular as of late, with many preferring nudging over other kinds of policy strategies.

While nudge policies have been studied and critiqued, many questions surrounding them have been left unaddressed. This chapter attempts to address one such question: what is the best institutional setting for a nudge?

The chapter starts with a review of the literature surrounding nudge policies, focusing on several of the main critiques of nudge policy. Then the next section analyzes some of the challenges that nudge policy faces and how they could be mitigated at the local level, including knowledge problems, incentive issues, costs of bureaucracy, voter misrepresentation, and flexibility. The final section concludes.

USING NUDGE POLICY

People are not always rational. They have behavioral biases that prevent them from making decisions that maximize their welfare and sometimes even make them act against their own self-interest. These biases can include hyperbolic discounting, lack of willpower, hot and cold states, automatic thinking, status quo, and inconsistency, among others (Thaler and Sunstein 2008). Knowing that we are prone to these kinds of irrational behaviors, there are ways to try to change our behavior in order to make up for the loss of well-being that we experience when choosing inadequate options.

Choice architects are those who intentionally try to influence the behavior of others by shaping the choices that people make. According to Yeung (2016), there are three major forms of choice architecture: coercion, inducements, and nudges. First, coercion is when choice architects get people to behave in certain ways by establishing some kind of negative consequence when they fail to act in the desired way. Second, inducements involve a choice architect getting people to act by rewarding them for performing the desired action. Finally, nudges are used to get people to act in the desired way by designing their choices in a way that makes them pick the outcome that the choice architect deems most beneficial. While coercion and inducements have been used for a long time in government and nudges have been used in the market, Thaler and Sunstein are credited for bringing the idea of nudges into public policy.

A nudge, as described by Thaler and Sunstein (2008, 6), is "any aspect of choice architecture that alters people's behavior in a predictable way without forbidding them any option or changing their economic incentives."

The overall goal of nudges is to maximize the well-being of the population. According to their theory, nudge policies are used by policymakers to help reduce the negative impacts of biases in different areas of people's lives, such as wealth or health, or to promote some kind of social outcome.

An important aspect of nudge policies is that they are different from mandates or other kinds of coercive regulation: they, supposedly, still allow people the freedom to not follow the policy without any major consequence or cost (Sunstein 2003). Nudge policies, in essence, allow people to make their own choices and are just a way to get people to achieve the outcomes they truly want regardless of their biases (Lepenies and Malecka 2015). In this sense, nudge policies claim to preserve individual liberty and freedom of choice (Sunstein 2003; Yeung 2016). As Sunstein (2014, 583) puts it, nudges are "liberty-preserving approaches that steer people in particular directions, but allows them to go their own way." It is by this logic that Thaler and Sunstein (2008) name these policies as "libertarian paternalism," for they are policies steering people in a direction but attempt to preserve freedom.

Thaler and Sunstein (2003) believe that choice architecture is inevitable. Most aspects of life, whether it is the design of a room, the way that products are laid out in a store, or how questions are framed, are already set to a default nudge. For example, in a supermarket, the way employees lay out the food has an effect on its consumers, regardless of whether or not it is their intention to affect their purchasing behavior. This implies that nudges are going to happen no matter what (Vallier 2018). Since people will be nudged to certain behaviors inevitably, Thaler and Sunstein (2008) believe that we should take advantage of this and design nudges that will improve people's well-being instead of causing them harm.

Policies can implement nudges in several ways, including disseminating information, such as nutrition facts or calorie counts; setting defaults for overdraft protection, automatic enrollment of retirement savings, health-care enrollment, or auto-renewal of subscriptions; framing designs, such as framing questions or texts a certain way; using social norms to discourage behavior; simplifying processes by removing paperwork or steps; reminders, such as a text reminder for doctor's appointments or an alarm to take a pill; or warnings, such as those seen on cigarette boxes warning against cancer. Other examples are found in Sunstein (2014) and Thaler and Sunstein (2008). Furthermore, these nudges can be implemented in several different policy areas and in various different forms. In healthcare, for example, there are nudges trying to solve all kinds of problems from weight loss encouragement and calorie counts to chronic disease management and HIV prevention. Nudges are also used to promote healthier eating habits: nudges that reduce portion size, alter the assortment of foods, provide descriptive labels, alter the visibility of choices, and so on (Sunstein 2014).

The responses to nudge policies are wide and varied. The following are some of the debates and arguments against nudging found in the academic and policy literature. Some critics argue that the concept of a nudge lacks clarity (Wilkinson 2013) and that sometimes this lack of clarity blurs the line between the definition of a nudge, a mandate, and a prohibition. Others argue that nudges are not ethical. Viscusi and Gayer (2015), Lusk (2014), and Hasnas (2016) argue that cognitive biases are not a sound justification for government intervention in personal lives or the economy. Codagnone et al. (2014) contend that nudges prevent people from deciding among all possible choices. Grüne-Yanoff (2012) claims that the limited choices presented in nudges limit people's freedom. Viscusi and Gayer (2015) argue that nudges dismiss individual choices. According to Koopman and Ghei (2013), reducing choices restricts innovation and solutions that address the same problems that come from the private market. Furthermore, they argue that restricting choices lead agents to make more expensive decisions. Therefore, limiting choice imposes a cost on people. Following this line of thought, Lepenies and Malecka (2015) describe nudges as intrusive policies.

One of the most popular critiques comes from the apparent contradiction of the concept of libertarian paternalism. Thaler and Sunstein (2003) argue that a policy is paternalistic if its objective is to influence the choices of agents in order to make them better off. Because traditional paternalism involves restricting someone's freedom, Thaler and Sunstein (2008) prefer libertarian paternalism since it does not coerce but leaves options open to those being nudged. However, critics argue that there is no significant difference between traditional paternalism and libertarian paternalism. The main reason for their criticism of libertarian paternalism stems from two main ideas: (1) any kind of paternalism—libertarian or not—is coercive in nature, and (2) the nature of libertarianism makes it free of any kind of coercion to individuals.

Hasnas (2016) states that nudges are coercive because they try to improve the behavior of those influenced by nudges, whether they want to do so or not. This means that nudgers have an objective standard of how they want people to act. Improving people's behavior implies that the nudgers know how people should live their lives (Lusk 2014). Koopman and Ghei (2013) claim that a nudge imposes someone else's optimal choice over people's own choice in order to prevent them from making what the nudgers deem are less-than-optimal decisions. In this way, the nudger imposes their preferences on the rest of society (Lusk 2014) and disregards the individual preferences of those being nudged (Lepenies and Malecka 2015). There is no problem when a nudger's optimal choice is the same as the nudgee's choice. But when the nudger's optimal choice is different from the nudgee's, then he is imposing his own conception of good choices (Hasnas 2016). Furthermore, Abdukadirov (2016b) explains how experts can fail to determine the optimal choice and end up making it harder for nudgees to make decisions because they are presented with options that are not targeted to them. To overcome this obstacle, Lepenies and Malecka (2015) contend that policymakers and politicians should not choose nudge objectives alone but, instead, they should be chosen democratically. Others argue that government nudges are fine as long as they are not paternalistic. According to Abdukadirov et al. (2016), non-paternalistic nudges do not impose an optimal choice on agents but only make it easier for agents to make choices that will advance their interests. Furthermore, they claim that non-paternalistic nudges tend to have fewer negative consequences to agents and reduce the risk of misdiagnosing agent biases.

Sunstein (2014) claims that any official nudge should be transparent, not covert. He follows by saying that the people affected by the nudge should be able to review the policy. Yet critics also argue that nudges are implemented nonvoluntarily and are used without the knowledge of many people (Yeung 2016), ultimately violating their freedom. Hasnas (2016) also claims that nudges can be unethically deceptive because they are implemented without informing or obtaining consent from the public.

Another popular criticism addresses the question, "who nudges the nudgers?" Experts and policymakers are also subjected to the same kind of biases as the population they are trying to nudge (Abdukadirov et al. 2016; Viscusi and Gayer 2015; Lusk 2015; Marlow 2016). Koopman and Ghei (2013) claim that policymakers might be biased to pick nudges that solve small, short-term risks, instead of more important, large-term risks. Abdukadirov and Marlow (2012) argue that people assume that policymakers are acting rationally when designing nudges. However, they fail to take into account their own potential irrationality. A study by Berggren (2011) shows the cognitive biases of policymakers have been unaccounted for in behavioral economics. He found that 95.5 percent of articles addressing nudge policies did not analyze the possibility that policymakers are also subjected to biases.

Much of the academic discussion surrounding nudges deals with the concept of nudges, the ethics of nudging, and criticisms of nudging. However, very little focus has been given to the institutional setting in which nudges are carried out. Of the existing studies dealing with the institutional setting of nudges, most focus on the difference between market nudges and government nudges, which ultimately deal with two different kinds of institutions. Some nudges happen extralegally, meaning that they do not need political support to be implemented or are not part of a legislature. Others, however, are legal and require the support of the government and its functions (Lepenies and Malecka 2015). Glaeser (2006) argues that government nudges are more costly than private nudges because agents have more incentives to overcome biases than the government. Part of his reasoning for this is because he contends that the market process provides more opportunities and information to correct errors, contrary to the government. Beggs (2016) advances that private nudges can be rent-seeking since companies are trying to get agents to buy their products, while government nudges could be socially efficient because they are aimed toward activities that have public goods characteristics. Another study deals with the institutional consequences of nudge policies. Lepenies and Malecka (2015) argue that nudges affect and, ultimately, shape legal and political institutional structures. The difference between nudges at different levels of government seems to be underemphasized in the literature. Abdukadirov (2016b) makes a distinction between the process of designing nudges at the federal level versus nudges at the state and local level. However, the distinction between federal and local nudges was not the main aim of the study.

SHOULD NUDGES BE LOCAL?

Many of the challenges associated with nudge policies are mitigated—and sometimes even solved—when nudges are applied at the local levels of government. The reason for this is that local governments tend to be more decentralized and polycentric, compared to federal governments, which tend to be more centralized and monocentric. Decentralized and polycentric governments are characterized by having multiple decision-making centers that are independent yet related to each other. Monocentric orders, on the other hand, tend to centralize power with a single decisionmaker and there are multiple hierarchical levels. The former type allows local governments to have more access to local knowledge and individual preferences, less bureaucracy, incentives that are aligned with the public, and more adaptability and flexibility.

Knowledge Problems

Nudge policies are meant to be designed with the agent in mind. In order to design an effective nudge policy, policymakers would need to gather information about agents and the environment they live in. However, as F. A. Hayek famously articulated, no single person possesses all of the relevant information on the diverse and varied preferences across society. This information, along with the other data needed for economic calculation, does not exist in one place but is instead dispersed among several individuals (Hayek 1945). This is because individuals possess only bits of information and, in some cases, that information that is contradictory to what someone else knows. Furthermore, there is some information that we cannot even articulate and is tacit (Polanyi 1958, Lavoie 1986). Therefore, there is no individual or institution that possesses all of the information needed. In the market, this knowledge is channeled and utilized through the mechanisms of property rights, prices, and profit and loss; centralized government, however, does not have the mechanisms that filter knowledge and signal social progress. Nudgers, in short, do not possess the knowledge needed to design paternalistic policies such as nudges (Rizzo and Whitman 2008). Even if policymakers had all of the knowledge of the past and the present, as well as knowledge of specific situations, they would still not be able to find the most profitable and effective policy (Alchian 2006).

Sunstein (2015) claims that when people's choices are not taken into account when designing policies, they experience a reduction in their welfare. If no knowledge exists in a concentrated form, how are policymakers supposed to define a nudge policy that is based on the optimal choices of the agents? In order to craft nudge policies, policymakers require at least two kinds of knowledge, each of which is hard to collect: knowledge about the biases affecting individual choices and knowledge about the preferences of the population. However, as explained in the next sections, the costs of collecting this knowledge can be diminished by focusing on local knowledge instead of broad, general knowledge.

Bias Knowledge

Not being able to tailor nudges to specific people makes it hard to come up with an optimal policy. In order to craft the best nudge possible, policymakers need to know the biases that are affecting their target population. Yet, behavioral science is not complete. There is no comprehensive theory that describes exactly what biases people have, why people behave in certain ways, or why people have one preference over another (Abdukadirov 2016b). Therefore, it is up to policymakers to gather this knowledge. Gathering the knowledge needed to determine biases, however, is hard to access and costly to gather. First of all, not every individual is subjected to the same bias. Gender, age, locality, aptitude, culture, and cognitive mindsets all affect behavior differently (Rizzo and Whitman 2008). It is the policymaker's task to adapt the policy to the population distribution of the bias, not just to a single case of individual biases (Rizzo and Whitman 2008).

Policymakers do not only need to know the bias that is affecting agent choices, but they also need to know the extent of the bias (Abdukadirov et al. 2016). Different sizes of biases require different degrees of intervention (Rizzo and Whitman 2008). Overestimating or underestimating the effect of the bias can reduce the welfare of the population (Rizzo and Whitman 2008). Overestimating biases can lead to excessive regulation, correcting for behavior that does not need to be corrected, while underestimating biases can lead to not enough intervention, leaving the people who should be affected by the policy unaffected.

Knowledge of the Preferences of the Population

Nudges are supposed to provide the best outcome for the majority of individuals. Nudge policies assume that the majority of the population has clear preferences of what their optimal outcome should be (Willis 2012) and that those who have other preferences will simply not follow the nudge. Rizzo and Whitman (2008) state that policymakers must know the preference of the agents in order to know how to best help general welfare. To do so, they need a baseline of preferences. Identifying the correct preference is imperative for nudge policies; if policymakers mistakenly identify preferences, they can harm the individuals affected by them (Lepenies and Malecka 2015).

There are several problems that policymakers encounter when trying to find out the true preferences of a very large population. White (2016) argues that it is impossible for policymakers to know the interests of all of those who are nudged. While policymakers might have some idea of the general goals that people might want to achieve, such as better health or more safety, they do not know the interest of any particular individual or population. The true preferences of the population are not revealed simply by the choices they make (Rizzo and Whitman 2008). Most of the information is local and tacit. Most of the time people also have difficulty establishing concrete preferences, their opinions are constantly changing, and they value different things at different points of their life. Overall, their preferences are inconsistent; while some goals are desirable outcomes to many, such as increased wealth and improved health, people have different ideas of what each of these constitutes and how to attain them. Furthermore, White (2016) claims that these interests are combined with other important objectives for each individual in complex ways. Policymakers have no way of knowing how each of these individual's objectives are related to each other.

Gathering Information Locally

The knowledge of biases and preferences differ from time to time, place to place, and situation to situation. Hayek called this kind of knowledge only known by the "man on the spot" (Hayek 1945). By this term, he meant all of the knowledge that has to do with a particular time and particular place and particular individual. Knowledge that no one else would know unless they are in the same specific situation. People who use nudges are not the same as those who design them (Abdukadirov 2016b). Therefore, nudgers need to get information about the environment and each situation in order for nudges to work properly.

In other words, many of the problems are contextual and depend on the environmental factors influencing the person deciding on whether to follow the nudge or not. Since this information changes from person to person and place to place, gathering this information is difficult and costly, especially when the information is spread over a large area and a large population (Oates 2006).

If we compare the information gathering process between local government and central government, it is evident that central government nudges will necessarily have a harder time gathering the information of time and place since they are affecting various localities and millions of people. Meanwhile, local governments tend to affect one single municipality or neighborhood. Hayek (1945) claimed that the way to ensure that the knowledge of the man on the spot is used and acquired appropriately is through decentralization. In a decentralized system, governments tend to be smaller and the population they are serving is also smaller, making it easier and less costly to gather this information. Similarly, Oates (2006) claims that local governments are better positioned to implement public services that match the preferences and circumstances of their public. Oates (2006) also claims that by providing a uniform policy throughout many localities, the welfare gains according to time and place are lost (Oates 2006). Furthermore, nudges only work for a segment of the population when the populations are too large (Lusk 2014). When nudges are uniformly implemented at the federal or state level, policymakers are assuming that most of the population is affected by the same biases and share the same preferences. Energy efficiency regulations in the United States, for example, show what happens when nudges are implemented uniformly throughout a population and when knowledge of time and place is not taken into account. These regulations restrict how much energy consumer products can use in order to nudge people into consuming less energy. However, Miller and Mannix (2016) found that these regulations do not conserve as much energy as they intend to. They also found that these regulations impose extra costs on low-income consumers. The problem with these regulations is that policymakers assumed that the population of consumers was homogeneous, and they would all react to the nudges in the same way. Ultimately, this led them to misrepresent their consumer preferences, and therefore led them to apply a regulation that was not effective on the population.

The same argument can be applied to other kinds of policies. A further look into disaster-relief policies shows how knowledge problems can be mitigated by decentralization and efforts at the local level (Grube and Storr 2014). Centralized relief policies sometimes fail because they face similar

challenges that central government nudges face, including knowledge problems. Disaster-relief policymakers need information about the displaced
residents and the conditions of a neighborhood. They need to know when
residents plan to come back to an area or what goods and services are running
in a neighborhood, among other things. In order to do so, policymakers need
to collect the information about the preferences of the residents, the situation
of the neighborhood, the resources needed, and the best way to allocate them
(Storr and Haeffele-Balch 2021). Yet, government officials often lack knowledge and the means to obtain it. Collecting the data is not a small task, yet
central governments need this information to ensure recovery from disasters.
Sobel and Leeson's (2006) analysis of FEMA's disaster relief after Hurricane
Katrina in 2005 shows how FEMA did not have access to the information
needed to allocate resources where they were needed the most, resulting in a
delayed recovery of many communities.

On the contrary, local actors—or entrepreneurs in their words—who took
matters into their own hands were the ones who helped communities rebound
(Storr et al. 2015). Entrepreneurs were successful in this case because they
focused on the particular circumstances of their own locality, instead of trying to solve all of the areas affected by a disaster at once. In contrast to the
central government, entrepreneurs had knowledge of their neighborhood and
its residents. They did not have to make extra efforts to collect the information in order to implement the best solution to the disaster. This allowed them
to rapidly determine the goods and services that each community needed,
and thereby, facilitating their recovery. Taking these examples into account,
nudge policies similarly would more likely be tailored to the biases and preferences of the population when applied locally.

Incentive Issues and Voter Misrepresentation

Nudges necessarily involve a choice architect deciding what is best for the
population (Abdukadirov et al. 2016). A major concern of nudge policy is
that policymakers might be replacing the judgment of individuals with their
own ideals of what constitutes welfare. Rizzo and Whitman (2008) claim that
if policymakers are lacking the information necessary to craft nudge policies,
they tend to substitute their own preferences for those of the population. When
policymakers do this, the nudge policy might not be wealth maximizing.

Tullock (1969) claims that the more layers there are between the voters
and the government action, the more likely it is that bureaucrats substitute
their own preferences into the process. This would mean that if nudges were
designed and applied by a local government, there would be fewer opportunities for policymakers to substitute their preferences for that of the nudgees.
Furthermore, if policymakers are local, in the sense that they are living in

and working in the community that they are regulating, then they do not have the incentives to substitute their own preferences into the process. Contrary to politicians that are further away from where the regulation is being implemented, local politicians might have a larger vested interest in the community and might have similar preferences with the community they reside in. This vested interest provides them with stronger incentives to choose welfare-maximizing nudges.

Policymakers, however, might also have ulterior motives for nudging society toward their desired outcomes. Many times, policymakers do not have the incentive to choose the optimal choice for the agent (Abdukadirov et al. 2016). According to Lepenies and Malecka (2015), nudges can be used to achieve policy goals that are not related to the population's well-being. Yeung (2016) argues that nudges are problematic and prone to abuse. Sometimes the incentives of the policymaker directly conflict with the preference of the agent (Abdukadirov et al. 2016). Paternalism can be abused by governments in order to increase their power or to respond to special interests (Glaeser 2006; Abdukadirov and Marlow 2012). Hasnas (2016), as well as Viscusi and Gayer (2015), argues that policymakers could misuse nudges to enhance their regulatory control or favor special interests instead of the general welfare.

Returning to the Hurricane Katrina example, Chamlee-Wright and Storr (2010) found that government officials had other interests besides those of the victims. Instead of aiming for the well-being of the population hurt by the hurricane, Leeson (2006) claims that FEMA incentivizes to delay actions in order to prevent criticism that could arise from its mistakes. Furthermore, politicians involved sought to enhance their political careers by acquiring more votes and larger budgets instead of a hasty recovery of the affected communities. In this sense, the policymaker's incentives were not aligned with the public. However, local actors did have an incentive to see their communities rebound and it was through their efforts that communities recovered from the disaster.

Tullock demonstrated how it is easier for local government policies to be influenced by the preferences of the community through a simple example. He claims that voter influence at the national level is very low since the average citizen is one single voter out of millions. Yet, in small or local governments, the voter's influence is higher since the population is smaller and more connected. Tullock stresses how citizens have more influence over smaller units of government. When this happens, you can expect the government unit to fit the preferences of the citizens (Tullock 1969). The more influence citizens have on their policymaker and the more the policymaker relies on their vote, the more likely the policymaker will adopt policies for the well-being of the community.

When the policymaker is closer to the community it is regulating, the more likely it is for nudges to match the voter's preference. The government could be considered effective when it responds to people's desires more accurately (Tullock 2005). According to Tullock (2005), in places with larger populations the variety of preferences is too much for the government to implement a single policy causing less efficiency in government regulations. Government is less likely to address everyone's preferences if there are many differences among voters. Therefore, at the local level, it is easier to address the preferences of the community since the number of people residing in it is less than at the federal or state level.

The Costs of Bureaucracy

Williamson (1967) claims that there is a trade-off between information distribution and the number of hierarchical levels in an organization; adding more levels removes those supervising the project from the knowledge needed for the operation of the project itself. Buchanan (1999) defines cost as that which an individual gives up when making a decision. According to him, individuals make decisions by weighing the utility of each alternative against its cost. However, when nudges are implemented by central governments, politicians and policymakers are often far removed from the benefits obtained by nudges. Therefore, policymakers implement nudges that are based on their own personal estimates of the costs instead of those of the population. In studying firms, Williamson (1967) finds that in large organizations the decisionmakers are more likely to be living in imaginary worlds. He claims this is so because those at the top of an organization have their own idea of what is happening in other areas of the organization, and many times it is very different from what is really going on. The same can be said of government bureaucracy.

For example, in disaster recovery policy, people tend to believe that the central government is the best organization equipped to help prevent disasters or recover from them once they have happened. The argument behind this is that the government has the resources to help areas that were struck by disasters, the capacity to provide the public goods needed, and the manpower to get this done (Storr et al. 2015). However, the central government is not always the best way to address disaster relief. In fact, in many cases bureaucratic intervention might hinder the recovery of an affected area (Storr et al. 2015). In fact, a closer look at FEMA's disaster relief after Hurricane Katrina shows how one of the main problems that hindered the recovery of the area was layered bureaucracy (Sobel and Leeson 2006). FEMA itself is a large bureaucracy, but it is also nested within the Department of Homeland Security. This created additional layers of people involved in the decision-making process, thereby stalling any action. Furthermore, the decisionmakers for the disaster recovery policies were far away from the problems caused by the disaster. What worked in the case of the recovery of Hurricane Katrina was a decentralized and polycentric approach led by local actors (Storr et al. 2015).

Not only does a large bureaucracy create distance between policymakers and voters, but it also creates noise (Tullock 1969). This noise can cause the information to be transmitted incorrectly or to even be lost among the multiple layers of bureaucrats. On the other hand, if we have a decentralized governance system and fewer layers of bureaucracy, the information does not have to be transmitted through so many layers and the information is more likely to stay intact while transmitted from individual to individual (Tullock 2005).

According to Leeson (2006), the benefits that the government provides have to be larger than the costs it incurs. Yet when the public goods provided by the government are offered to a large population, the cost to provide the goods increases. Taking this argument into account, we can say that centralized government tends to be costlier when implementing policies at a large scale. As an exaggerated example, Leeson (2006) provides a thought experiment: a government that rules over the whole world's population would be far more costly than a local government. Because the population of the world is so heterogeneous and the bureaucracy of the government is so far removed from the population, the organizational costs of government and enforcement costs of policies would be much more expensive than at local levels.

Finally, the more the levels of government needed to approve and implement a nudge, the slower the process of implementing a policy becomes. Abdukadirov (2016b) goes over the process to get nudges approved at the federal level and at the local level. Federal nudges have to start in Congress and then go through a series of other government agencies to get approved. Compared to the process of nudging at the federal level, the one at the local level tends to be simpler and can vary from municipality to municipality. Abdukadirov (2016b) makes the process clear with two examples, each at a different level of government. At the federal level, he discusses a provision in the Affordable Care Act that required places with a certain number of vending machines to add calorie counts next to each item being sold. Even though this nudge sounds relatively simple, it took almost seven years to go through the whole process and get approved. On the other hand, Abdukadirov (2016b) shows how nudges at the local level can take half the amount of time to get approved than at the federal level. He uses the example of New York City's ban on large-sized sodas. The regulation was proposed in June 2012. By September, it had already been approved to go into effect the following March. That is less than one year in the approval process. This example shows how at the municipal level the process for getting nudges approved can be much faster.

According to Tullock (1969), costs increase when there is more bureaucracy. But if this is fragmented into smaller units, then costs will decrease. One way to lower the costs of bureaucracy is to fragment government into smaller units that act in a decentralized manner. A benefit of having nudges implemented at the local level is that it allows different localities to compete with one another (Tullock 2005). When a nudge is implemented by the central government, citizens do not have much of a vote or say on whether they agree with the policy or not. However, at the local level, citizens who are not happy with the policy decision can exit the locality and move to another one that better suits their needs or preferences. According to Tiebout (1956), allowing localities to compete can lead to the optimal provisions of public goods due to competitive pressures among local governments. Furthermore, he claims that as more communities offer options and more variation between them exists, agents will have a greater ability to choose and find a community that suits their preferences. This same argument can be applied to nudge policies. If several municipalities offer different nudges, or different variations of nudges, and compete with each other, individuals are more likely to find a locality that provides the nudges that they prefer. Furthermore, according to Oates (2006), a decentralized sector in which the competition between jurisdictions takes place can cause policymakers to promote the welfare of their constituents.

Lack of Adaptability and Flexibility

Nudging policies are based only on a select amount of nudge literature (Lepenies and Malecka 2015). The literature usually presents case studies of tested nudges which seem to be replicable in other places. Yet the evidence of nudging is still contradictory. Some papers find evidence of nudges that work extremely well, while others find evidence of them not working. In examining weight loss nudges, Marlow (2016) finds that the results of the success of the nudges are inconclusive. Rendell (2014) also found mixed results when analyzing whether calorie labeling has an effect on the number of calories ordered. Wilson et al. (2016) find that different nudges promoting healthier food and drink choices do not have consistent effects. They argue that while some nudges have extremely positive results, similar nudges in other places had no effect.

Willis (2012), for example, examines whether the success of one kind of default nudge in one area can be replicated in other areas. With the success of defaults in retirement savings, she tests whether these kinds of nudges can be replicated in other areas, particularly in checking account overdraft coverage.

Willis (2012) finds that the policy is not as effective in overdraft coverage because the defaults could be slippery and more customers were opting out of the nudge. This, in effect, signaled that the aim of the default was not being met and agent preferences were not well established beforehand.

As the example above shows, it is of primary importance to test the nudge implementing policies. As we have seen in previous sections, many nudges might not work because they lack an understanding of the behavior or the people in question. Sunstein (2019) believes that this is why it is important to test the behavioral hypothesis. Sunstein (2014) also claims that nudges should rely on evidence. Testing can show how some nudge policies sound like good ideas but do not actually work. Similarly, it can show that a variation of the nudge is more efficient than the original nudge (Sunstein 2014).

A problem with testing nudge policies is that nudges are tested in artificial environments, where people might act differently from real life (Lusk 2014). If the setting in a lab is different from people's day-to-day lives, then policy-makers can assume the wrong biases or the wrong outcomes, and ultimately, lead to ineffective policies (Abdukadirov 2016b).

For example, Walmsley et al. (2018) examined whether choice architecture influenced agents to purchase more fruits and vegetables at a university grocery store. They conducted two different interventions from 2012 to 2017, in which they arranged the food in two different ways to see if they had an effect on the purchase of fruits and vegetables. Originally, fruits and vegetables were in the back of the store. The first intervention moved the fruits and vegetables from the back of the store to a shelf near the entrance of the store. The second intervention kept the fruits and vegetables in the same place but put them inside a chiller cabinet that had less visibility. The results found that both interventions had increased the sales of fruits and vegetables compared to the baseline. However, they also found that the first intervention sold more fruits and vegetables than the second intervention.

It was fairly easy to measure the difference in sales between the two interventions, but it may not lead to the same results in other locations. Now imagine if this was a nation-wide policy. You would have to conduct the same test in more university grocery stores and compare the results in order to claim that the nudge does indeed work universally. Having a study made in a significant number of stores not only raises the cost of the tests (observers, displays, and chillers) but it also requires processing more data. On the other hand, having a nudge at a local level—such as a university grocery store—allows for a fairly easy test to determine whether the nudge has an effect or not.

Furthermore, if nudges are implemented locally, that would mean that policymakers can more easily respond to errors and change the nudge if it is not working. At a local level, nudge policies cover a narrower scope of the population. If an adjustment has to be made to a nudge policy, it would be easier and less costly to adjust at a local level, since it affects a small population and there is less bureaucracy involved in the change. Local nudges, in this sense, are more flexible. Nudges at the federal level, however, require more time and effort to adjust since they affect a larger population and involve several government offices since they are applied to the country as a whole. Ultimately, this makes federal-level nudges more rigid and less likely to adapt.

CONCLUSION

The problems that nudge policies face are not unique by any means. For example, disaster-relief policies also face many of the same challenges as nudge policies: knowledge problems, incentive issues, large bureaucratic hierarchies, and rigidity in the system. Yet the relevant literature shows how many of these problems were also mitigated by decentralization and efforts at the local level (Grube and Storr 2014). When we contrast the two approaches to disaster relief, we see that the central government tends to be monocentric and centralized. The decisionmakers for these policies are at the top of bureaucratic hierarchies and far away from the problems caused by the disaster. The bureaucratic hierarchy is composed of multiple overlapping layers and multiple decisionmakers, making it harder to reach decisions. In contrast, the approach of multiple local entrepreneurs helping their community is decentralized and polycentric. Local agents have access to local knowledge, can act without requiring the permission of other actors, can easily fix errors, and tend to address the needs of the population. Similar to how disaster-relief policy can mitigate many of these problems by implementing a polycentric, decentralized approach, nudge policy can also mitigate knowledge problems, incentive issues and voter misrepresentation, bureaucracy, and rigidity by implementing nudges at the local level.

This chapter does not intend to claim that all federal and centralized nudges are bad, nor that all local nudges are effective. Each nudge policy should be examined on its own, evaluating where it was imposed, its target population, and its results. Take for example the New York City soda ban: it was a local level nudge policy that failed. In order to nudge New Yorkers into having healthier diets, the Bloomberg Administration tried to ban stores from selling sodas larger than 16 ounces in 2013. While this nudge was not actually passed, it would have faced similar problems as a large-scale nudge. Assume that New York City's large soda ban was implemented. This ban would affect all of the city's residents, even those who have enough self-control to not order sodas, those that are healthy and have no craving for soda, or those who do not even like sodas. Assuming that all of the residents of New York City have the same bias toward large sodas only reduced the number of agent choices and their welfare.

The aim of this chapter is to point out that some of the challenges that are present in nudge policy, as well as in other policy areas, can be mitigated when implemented in a decentralized, polycentric system. Local nudges tend to overcome knowledge problems, incentive issues, costs of bureaucracy, voter misrepresentation, and rigidity better than nudges that are implemented at the federal level.

REFERENCES

Abdukadirov, Sherzod, ed. 2016a. *Nudge Theory in Action Behavioral Design in Policy and Markets*. New York, NY: Palgrave Macmillan.

Abdukadirov, Sherzod. 2016b. "Who Should Nudge?" In *Nudge Theory in Action: Behavioral Design in Policy and Markets*, edited by Sherzod Abdukadirov, 151–191. New York, NY: Palgrave Macmillan.

Abdukadirov, Sherzod, David Wille, and Scott P. King. 2016. "Taking Paternalism Out of Nudge: The Case of Medication Nonadherence Among Patients with Chronic Conditions." *Mercatus Center at George Mason University Working Paper.*

Abdukadirov, Sherzod, and Michael L. Marlow. 2012. "Can Behavioral Economics Combat Obesity?" *Regulation* 35, no. 2: 14–18.

Alchian, Armen A. 2006. *The Collected Works of Armen A. Alchian. Choice and Cost under Uncertainty.* Indianapolis, IN: Liberty Fund, Inc.

Beggs, Jodi M. 2016. "Private sector nudging: The good, the bad, and the uncertain." In *Nudge Theory in Action: Behavioral Design in Policy and Markets*, edited by Sherzod Abdukadirov, 125–178. New York, NY: Palgrave Macmillan.

Berggren, Niclas. 2012. "Time for Behavioral Political Economy? An Analysis of Articles in Behavioral Economics." *The Review of Austrian Economics* 25: 199–221.

Buchanan, James M. 1999. *Cost and Choice: An Inquiry in Economic Theory.* Indianapolis, IN: Liberty Fund, Inc.

Chamlee-Wright, Emily, and Virgil Henry Storr. 2010. "Expectations of Government's Response to Disaster." *Public Choice* 144: 253–274.

Codagnone, Cristiano, Giuseppe Alessandro Veltri, Francisco Lupiáñez-Villanueva, and Francesco Bogliacino. 2014. "The Challenges and Opportunities of 'Nudging.'" *Journal of Epidemiology and Community Health* 68, no. 10: 909–911.

Glaeser, Edward. 2006. "Paternalism and Psychology." *The University of Chicago Law Review* 73, no. 1: 133–156.

Grube, Laura, and Virgil Henry Storr. 2014. "The Capacity for Self-Governance and Post Disaster Resiliency." *The Review of Austrian Economics* 27, no. 3: 301–324.

Grüne-Yanoff, Till. 2012. "Old Wine in New Casks: Libertarian Paternalism Still Violates Liberal Principles." *Social Choice and Welfare* 38, no. 4: 635–645.

Hasnas, John. 2016. "Some Noodging About Nudging: Four Questions About Libertarian Paternalism." *Georgetown Journal of Law & Public Policy* 14: 645–662.

Hayek, F. A. 1945. "The Use of Knowledge in Society." *The American Economic Review* 35, no. 4: 519–530.

Koopman, Christopher, and Nita Ghei. 2013. "Behavioral Economics, Consumer Choice, and Regulatory Agencies." *Economic Perspectives*. Arlington, VA: Mercatus Center at George Mason University.

Lavoie, Don. 1986. "The Market as a Procedure for Discovery and Conveyance of Inarticulate Knowledge." *Comparative Economic Studies* 28: 1–19.

Lepenies, Robert, and Magdalena Małecka. 2015. "The Institutional Consequences of Nudging—Nudges, Politics, and the Law." *Review of Philosophy and Psychology* 6, no. 3: 427–437.

Leeson, Peter T. 2006. "Efficient Anarchy." *Public Choice* 130: 41–53.

Lusk, Jayson L. 2014. "Are You Smart Enough to Know What to Eat? A Critique of Behavioural Economics as Justification for Regulation." *European Review of Agricultural Economics* 41, no. 3: 355–373.

Lusk, Jayson L. 2015. "The Rise of Nudge and the Use of Behavioral Economics in Food and Health Policy." *Mercatus on Policy Series*, December 10. Arlington, VA: Mercatus Center at George Mason University. https://www.mercatus.org/publication/rise-nudge-and-use-behavioral-economics-food-and-health-policy

Marlow, Michael. 2016. "Weight-Loss Nudges: Market Test or Government Guess?" In *Nudge Theory in Action: Behavioral Design in Policy and Markets*, edited by Sherzod Abdukadirov, 195–224. New York, NY: Palgrave Macmillan.

Miller, Sofie E., and Brian F. Mannix. 2016. "One Standard to Rule Them All: The Disparate Impact of Energy Efficiency Regulations." In *Nudge Theory in Action: Behavioral Design in Policy and Markets*, edited by Sherzod Abdukadirov, 251–287. New York, NY: Palgrave Macmillan.

Oates, Wallace E. 2006. "On the Theory and Practice of Fiscal Decentralization." *Institute for Federalism and Intergovernmental Relations Working Paper*, No. 2006-05.

Ostrom, Elinor. 2016. *Governing the Commons: The Evolution of Institutions for Collective Action.* Cambridge, UK: Cambridge University Press.

Polanyi, Michael. *Personal Knowledge: Towards a Post-critical Philosophy.* Chicago, IL: University of Chicago Press.

Rizzo, Mario J. 2016. "Behavioral Economics and Deficient Willpower: Searching for Akrasia." *Georgetown Journal of Law & Public Policy* 14: 789–806.

Rendell, Sarah Litman. 2014. "Availability of Point-of-purchase Calorie Labeling: Its Relationship to Food Purchasing Decisions." PhD Dissertation. New York, NY: Yeshiva Academic Institutional Repository.

Rizzo, Mario J., and Douglas Glen Whitman. 2008. "The Knowledge Problem of New Paternalism." *Brigham Young University Law Review* 2009: 905–968.

Shughart, William. 2011. "Disaster Relief as Bad Public Policy." *The Independent Review* 15, no. 4: 519–539.

Sober, Russel, and Leeson, Peter T. 2006. "Government's Response to Hurricane Katrina: A Public Choice Analysis." *Public Choice* 127: 55–73.

Storr, Virgin Henry, and Stefanie Haeffele-Balch. 2012. "Post-Disaster Community Recovery in Heterogeneous, Loosely Connected Communities." *Review of Social Economy* 70, no. 3: 1–20.

Storr, Virgil Henry, Stefanie Haeffele-Balch, and Laura E. Grube. 2015. *Community Revival in the Wake of Disaster: Lessons in Local Entrepreneurship.* New York, NY: Palgrave Macmillan.

Sunstein, Cass R. 2014. "Nudging: A Very Short Guide." *Journal of Consumer Policy* 37: 583–588.

Sunstein, Cass R. 2015. *Why Nudge? The Politics of Libertarian Paternalism.* New Haven, CT: Yale University Press.

Sunstein, Cass R. 2019. *How Change Happens.* Cambridge, MA: MIT Press.

Sunstein, Cass R., and Richard H. Thaler. 2003. "Libertarian Paternalism Is Not An Oxymoron." *The University of Chicago Law Review* 70, no. 4: 1159–1202.

Thaler, Richard H., and Cass R. Sunstein. 2003. "Libertarian Paternalism." *The American Economic Review* 93, no. 2: 175–179.

Thaler, Richard H., and Cass R. Sunstein. 2008. *Nudge: Improving Decisions Using the Architecture of Choice.* New Haven, CT: Yale University Press.

Tiebout, Charles M. 1956. "A Pure Theory of Local Expenditures." *The Journal of Political Economy* 64, no. 5: 416–424.

Tullock, Gordon. 1969. "Federalism: Problems of Scale." *Public Choice* 6, no. 1: 19–29.

Tullock, Gordon. 2005. *Bureaucracy.* Indianapolis, IN: Liberty Fund, Inc.

Tullock, Gordon, Gordon L. Brady, and Arthur Seldon. 2005. *Government Failure: A Primer in Public Choice.* Washington, DC: Cato Institute.

Vallier, Kevin. 2018. "On the Inevitability of Nudging." In *Nudging: Possibilities, Limitations, and Applications in European Law and Economics*, edited by Mathis, Klaus, and Avishalom Tor. New York, NY: Springer International Publishing.

Viscusi, W. Kip, and Ted Gayer. 2015. "Behavioral Public Choice: The Behavioral Paradox of Government Policy." *Harvard Journal of Law & Public Policy* 38: 973–1008.

Walmsley, Rosemary, David Jenkinson, Ian Saunders, Tony Howard, and Oyinlola Oyebode. 2018. "Choice Architecture Modifies Fruit and Vegetable Purchasing in a University Campus Grocery Store: Time Series Modelling of a Natural Experiment." *BMC Public Health* 18: 1149.

Weiner, Rachel. 2013. "The New York City Soda Ban Explained." *The Washington Post,* March 11. https://www.washingtonpost.com/news/the-fix/wp/2013/03/11/the-new-york-city-soda-ban-explained/?utm_term=.395a755ec3b5

White, Mark D. 2016. "Overview of behavioral economics and policy." In *Nudge Theory in Action: Behavioral Design in Policy and Markets*, edited by Sherzod Abdukadirov, Sherzod, 15–36. New York, NY: Palgrave Macmillan.

Wilkinson, T. M. 2013. "Thinking Harder about Nudges." *Journal of Medical Ethics* 39, no. 8: 485.

Williamson, Oliver E. 1967. "Hierarchical Control and Optimum Firm Size." *Journal of Political Economy* 75, no. 2: 123–138.

Willis, Lauren E. "When Nudges Fail: Slippery Defaults." *The University of Chicago Law Review* 80, no. 3: 1155–1229.

Wilson, Amy L., Elizabeth Buckley, Jonathan D. Buckley, and Svetlana Bogomolova. 2016. "Nudging Healthier Food and Beverage Choices through Salience and Priming. Evidence from a Systematic Review." *Food Quality and Preference* 51: 47–64.

Yeung, Karen. 2016. "The Forms and Limits of Choice Architecture as a Tool of Government." *Law & Policy* 38, no. 3: 186–210.

Chapter 4

Incentivized Migration in Colonial Contexts

The Challenge of Asymmetric Information in Public Policy Nudges

Oliver McPherson-Smith

An enduring legacy of colonial expansion in recent centuries is the persistence of economic, social, and political institutions that were fostered by foreign powers. Recent comparative economic development literature has given much focus to the way in which these institutions arose, particularly concerning the early experiences of European colonizers in climates and environments they often found to be hostile. However, little consideration has been given to the policies which enticed settlers to try their luck in the colonies. Some settlers emigrated for ideological reasons, such as the pilgrims who headed to North America to pursue their religious beliefs, while others were forced against their will, such as the convicts who were sentenced to transportation to Australia. In many cases, however, governments used incentives or choice architecture to facilitate the expansion and control of once-native-owned lands.

In the French colonies in Algeria, for example, the state employed a diverse set of economic incentives to entice settlers from both France and its neighboring countries to achieve the official goal of populating the colony. These incentives, while in no way forced potential migrants to participate, sought to "nudge" the spatial reallocation of labor from overcrowded French cities to the fields of colonial Algeria. In addition to providing the benefit of employment to individuals, these nudges sought to use choice architecture to diminish the domestic ill of unemployment, while achieving the imperial state's interest in bolstering the colonial population. Lured by the promise of opportunity and wealth in the colonies, French civilians who were ill-suited to the arduous agricultural life in Algeria were consequently nudged to try their luck in the colony—with many meeting an untimely demise. For those who survived, their state-sponsored migration to the colony served to maintain France's brutal control of the local population. Across the Atlantic Ocean, the American government similarly used choice architecture in the Civil War period to entice settlers onto once-American Indian land. The Homestead Act of 1862 harnessed the self-interest of civilians to shore up the United States' control of resource-rich territory, to the protracted detriment of its former owners.

The historical nudging of migration, particularly as a form of territorial expansion, offers a variety of contemporary implications for public policy and our understanding of colonization alike. Within the literature on comparative economic development, an exploration of the diverse motivations of governments and individuals to create settler colonies demonstrates the methodological limitations of relying solely upon regression analysis. While the use of settler mortality as an instrumental variable provides a broad illustration of the relationship between institutions and economic development, a historical analysis of the French state's efforts to facilitate migration to colonial Algeria through nudging highlights the diverse incentives of policymakers in the process of colonization. Moreover, both France's colonial nudging and the Homestead Act in the United States highlight the moral dilemma of nudging ordinary citizens to achieve a contentious policy objective. Given the unique political interests of policymakers, and their ability to exploit asymmetries in information, efforts to nudge ordinary citizens must be scrutinized due to the potential for citizens to be made party to unscrupulous policies. The integrity of a citizen's range of choices and the will to choose does not absolve policymakers of liability for the perverse outcomes of the actions they nudge. Despite the relatively recent creation of nudge-inspired government units and taskforces, the logic and use of nudging has a long and checkered history. Contemporary policymakers and citizens alike should take heed of the historic ways in which policymakers have employed the ethos of nudging to the benefit of themselves and (sometimes) the voter—albeit to the detriment of the unseen third party.

The chapter proceeds with an initial consideration of the definition and nature of nudging. The next section provides a brief history of France's colonization of Algeria and the various policies employed to achieve its imperial ambitions. The chapter then explores how France's policies to facilitate migration to colonial Algeria can be understood as an early form of nudging. Considering the impact of nudging on settler mortality in colonial Algeria, the next section questions its implications for contemporary academic discussions around the use of settler mortality data. The subsequent section explores how policies to nudge settlers were similarly used in the westward expansion of the United States. Drawing lessons from these two historical examples, the chapter offers contemporary policy implications and concludes.

WHAT IS A NUDGE?

Before considering nudges in the context of their implementation, it is imperative to explore the exact meaning of the term.[1] Nudges, as defined by Thaler and Sunstein (2009, 6), are "any aspect of the choice architecture that alters people's behavior in a predictable way without forbidding any options or significantly changing their economic incentives. To count as a nudge, the intervention must be cheap and easy to avoid. Nudges are not mandates." The parameters of this definition, however, require a little interpretation. Central to the authors' definition is the maintaining of the integrity of the potential options without penalizing *bad* choices. This is reiterated by the assertion that they "favor nudges over commands, requirements, and prohibitions" (Thaler and Sunstein 2009, 10).

However, choice architecture without "significantly changing their economic incentives" is a misnomer (Thaler and Sunstein 2009, 6). While their design aims to not penalize a *bad* choice, it does, however, alter the economic incentive in favor of a *good* choice. For example, Thaler and Sunstein (2009, 44) point to the Clocky alarm clock as a nudge that forces individuals to chase an alarm clock to silence it, thereby enhancing the incentive to get out of bed. This nudge is, in effect, a tax upon the utility one derives from *not* changing one's behavior. Similarly, Thaler and Sunstein's (2009, 46) example of not being invited to a luxurious party due to not having completed sufficient work on time raises the opportunity cost of the decision to not work. While some scholars do not consider subsidies to be a form of nudging—such as Chetty et al. (2013), Lipscomb and Schechter (2018), and Benartzi et al. (2017)—Thaler and Sunstein's (2009) party example represents a subsidy for *good* behavior (in the form of an invitation to a party), albeit in the absence of a penalty for *bad* behavior. Although Thaler and Sunstein (2009) stress that nudges do not *de jure* threaten a penalty for ignoring them, for many practical incarnations of nudges, an individual's economic incentives are, in fact, altered. Consequently, for the purpose of this study, Thaler and Sunstein's (2009, 6) aforementioned initial and most basic definition of nudging is employed, albeit without reference to changes in economic incentives.

Another central question for choice architects is how to accurately calculate the interests and preferences of citizens. Congruent with Rizzo and Whitman's (2009, 907) definition of "new paternalism," Thaler and Sunstein (2009, 5) suggest that nudging is paternalistic in its effort, "to make choices in a way that will make choosers better off, as judged by themselves." The

ability to understand the preferences of individuals is therefore crucial if policy is to be designed to help them achieve that subjective outcome. However,
Rizzo and Whitman (2009, 910) argue that, much like the *knowledge problem*
of socialist planning as identified by Hayek (1945), paternalist policymakers
lack the capacity to completely gauge the preferences of individuals. The
assumption, particularly in a diverse and multicultural society such as the
contemporary United States, that policymakers can both calculate and har-
monize the preferences of such a varied citizenry is incredibly ambitious. In
addition to questioning a central assumption of "new paternalism," Rizzo and
Whitman (2009) suggest that the absence of knowledge about an individual's
preferences will invite paternalistic policymakers to fill the void with their
own preferences.

If policymakers are prone to substituting their own preferences when faced
with uncertainty, there is thus the risk that they will use choice architecture
to achieve a self-serving, partisan, or ideological objective. This outcome
blurs the distinction between nudging and traditional paternalism. Rizzo and
Whitman (2009, 907) highlight how "old paternalism" ignores the preferences of the individual in favor of the interests of the policymaker, while
"new paternalism" seeks to base policy recommendations upon the interests
of the individual. Thaler and Sunstein (2009, 243) recognize the potential
for self-serving policymakers, who are motivated for partisan or personal
gain, to rig choice architecture in favor of a result that is contrary to the best
interests of citizens. The authors suggest transparency as an antidote to this
form of corruption and note that choice architects face an inherent level of
accountability as, "managers in the public sector have to answer to voters"
(Thaler and Sunstein 2009, 242). However, this appears to be more of an
idealized principle than a realistic solution. It would seem infeasible that the
same citizen who, according to Thaler and Sunstein (2009, 204), struggled
to choose a school for their child in North Carolina due to an overwhelming
amount of information would have the time or capacity to monitor changes
in policy across several levels of government for signs of malintent nudging.

The use of transparency and accountability to combat this form of corruption provides an inutile panacea, particularly given the routine occurrence of
asymmetric information. As a collective body of individuals, it is a benign
assumption that the policymaking corpus has access to far greater information and tools of analysis than any given citizen. In addition to the ability to
analyze technical information, government bodies have access to crucial, sensitive data. From national security intelligence to current public health information, the government has access to information that is legally prevented
from entering the public discourse. This inequality of information, however,
introduces a moral challenge for would-be nudgers. Choice architects, while
knowing that a choice is detrimental to a third party but beneficial for voters,

may nudge toward it if it aligns with the *ex-ante* preferences of voters. If voters are not privy to the damage being done to the third party, there is little incentive for partisan policymakers to nudge away from it. For example, if American policymakers have credible reason to believe that chlorofluorocarbons (CFCs, or Freon) will damage the ozone layer of the atmosphere above Australia, thus causing a higher incidence of deadly skin cancer in Australia, but this information is not widely distributed among the American voting public, would American policymakers seek to nudge away from using CFCs? And what if the production of CFCs were a key American industry and the industry was expanding, to the benefit of American job seekers? Avoiding environmental damage and the premature death of their allies down-under would likely be a preference of the compassionate American public, but partisan policymakers have no incentive to nudge away this damage until the public becomes aware of it. The fundamental challenge derived from this observation is for individuals to hold self-interested policymakers accountable when the policymakers have access to vastly more information than they do. Policymakers may struggle to calculate the preferences of individuals, but they may also seek to withhold information, lest the identified preferences of the public misalign with those of the policymakers.

NUDGES IN COLONIAL ALGERIA

Despite their relatively recent introduction into the public policy lexicon, nudges—and the multifaceted questions about their use and implications— have a lengthy history in practice. In as early as the nineteenth century in colonial Algeria, French authorities sought to use choice architecture to facilitate a mutually beneficial geographic reallocation of labor. By aiding poor French citizens in finding a job in Algeria and providing passage across the Mediterranean, French authorities sought to rid their cities of chronic unemployment while strengthening their grip on their colonial territories through a larger settler population. The implications of this policy were profound. To manage this colonial occupation, the French authorities developed the *code de l'indigénat* that relegated the indigenous population to a legally inferior status (Funes 2019). In medical terms, the influx of ill-prepared soldiers and settlers created a desperate need for medical solutions to newly encountered diseases. The results, such as the use of quinine to treat malaria, were groundbreaking and were replicated across the globe. In terms of governance, the nudging of settlers demonstrates the propensity of primarily self-interested policymakers to utilize choice architecture to achieve their own objective, irrespective of the significant personal cost and high mortality that persisted among settlers.

These nudges also call into question our understanding of the causes of settler mortality during European colonial expansion and suggest that settler mortality was not the make-or-break factor which drove policies of European settlement. It also illustrates the willingness of policymakers to nudge individuals into becoming third parties to the brutal and repressive subjugation of the subaltern Algerian population. The use of choice architecture by pro-colonial policymakers gives reason to question the ability of citizens to hold the government accountable, particularly when it purports to use nudging in pursuit of the best interests of the citizenry.

The French were, however, not the first colonial occupiers of the Algerian coast. Following attempts to control various territories along the southern Mediterranean by Spain and Portugal, it was the Ottomans who last held the coastal territories of Oran and Algiers before the enduring French invasion of 1830, which made the North African possession one of the geographically closest colonies to a European metropole. Through the constitution of 1848, France officially integrated its Algerian territories with the mainland by declaring them as three *départments*. After more than a century of colonial occupation, French rule was brought to an end with the Évian Accords of 1962, with approximately one million residents of European descent fleeing the country (Savarese 2016).

The growth of the European community in Algeria, often known as the *Pied Noirs*, developed across the full breadth of France's occupation. The first settlers departed France in 1830, before official colonization began in 1838 (Blais and Deprest 2012). The rationale for France's colonial ambitions in Algeria mirrored those of its European neighbors, albeit with unique French characteristics. During a period of sustained competition for colonial influence across the globe, many in France viewed the absorption of Algeria as vital for the country's international standing. In 1841, Tocqueville (2002, 5), for example, wrote that, "if we could come to hold this coast of Africa firmly and peacefully, our influence in the general affairs of the world would be greatly increased . . . if these positions do not remain in our hands, they will pass into those of another people of Europe. If they are not for us, they will be against us."

In addition to the more commonplace motivations for colonization, such as an additional source of natural resources and labor, the Algerian colony was seen as particularly sensitive to national interests due to the potential of other European powers usurping control of it. Moreover, there was also an ideological rationale of France's colonial ambitions. French politicians espoused ideas of racial superiority, evident in former Prime Minister Jules Ferry's declaration in 1885, that "the higher races have a right over the lower races . . . they have a duty to civilize the inferior races" (Assemblée Nationale 2019, NP). This notion of superiority was embodied in a policy of assimilation which sought to conform the indigenous peoples with French culture. These two objectives are evident in the work of Prévost-Paradol (1868, 416), who suggested, "May that day soon come when our fellow-citizens . . . will establish finally that Mediterranean empire that will be not only a satisfaction for our pride, but will also certainly be in the future development of the world." Buoyed by economic, geopolitical, and ideological interests, the French state had a multifaceted interest in pursuing policies that would maintain its control of Algeria. In addition to these motivations, the early years of settlement were facilitated by advances in transportation technology. It initially took 10 days to make the sea journey; however, by 1838, and the advent of frequent steamer ships, the journey took between two to three days to reach the Algerian coast. From three trips a month in 1830, there were up to five return trips a week by the end of the decade (Blais and Deprest 2012).

To fulfill its colonial ambitions, the French state utilized a variety of policies to bolster the settler population in Algeria. Some settlers were forcibly transported, such as those who were transferred to colonial prisons. The law of January 24, 1850, for example, designated Algeria as a destination for penal transportation and, in February of that year, the steam frigates *L'Asmodée* and *Gomer* transported over 400 prisoners from the cities of Cherbourg and Brest to be incarcerated at the Casbah of Bône (Barbançon 2008). Almost half of this first cohort were political prisoners, and many of them were sentenced to forced labor. However, there was also early recognition that economic incentives could also be used to facilitate the growth of the colony. In his 1841 essay entitled "Work on Algeria," Tocqueville (2002, 35) argues that, "it is necessary to build a golden bridge to those who go to Africa." Advocating for the use of economic incentives, such as a reduction of trade barriers on Algerian products, to foster the colony's growth, Tocqueville suggests that, "The lure of gain and affluence will soon attract as many settlers to the Massif and the Mitidja as you wish" Tocqueville (2002, 35).[2]

While politicians at the height of the French government saw the growth of the colony as an opportunity to expand France's geopolitical presence, local metropolitan politicians saw the chance to alleviate their constituencies of social and economic challenges through the use of nudges. Consequently, according to Sessions (2011, 265), "almost immediately . . . French officials, especially in large towns, began to dream of sending the poor and unemployed to Algiers." Across the breadth of the state in metropolitan France, politicians and bureaucrats sought to facilitate the passage of settlers to Algeria in the first decades of the French occupation by engaging in choice architecture. These would-be workers were not mandated to emigrate, nor were they taxed for remaining in place; however, they were provided both transport to and lodging in Marseille or Toulon, before embarking on a state-funded journey across the Mediterranean (Blais and Deprest 2012). In addition to subsidizing the passage to Algeria, the French state also sought to entice future settlers with the promise of employment, higher wages, or land. An 1844 Ministry of the Interior investigation found that the respondents' motivating factors for emigration to Algeria were, *inter alia*, "government assistance, including free passages . . . land concessions, and official promises of higher wages" (Sessions 2011, 300). Once, across the Mediterranean, in an effort to entice settlers to remain in Algeria, officials sought to recruit Catholic clergy in the early years of French rule. By providing an ecclesiastical community, the local officials hoped that emigrants "would have less of an incentive to return to France or elsewhere in Europe" (Francis 2015, 2).

Despite the vision of Algeria as a bucolic land of untapped agricultural opportunity, the overwhelming majority of French settler recruits were unprepared for the work that lay ahead of them. Seventy-five percent of those offered subsidized passage to Algeria in the 1840s were not hardy agricultural workers—but migrants from French urban areas. According to Sessions (2011, 298), local government officials "were charged with publicizing the "advantages" offered to migrants, and it was in administrative centers that placards, migrant handbooks, and prefectoral circulars would have been most visible," as opposed to their rural counterparts. Furthermore, for other migrants, the chance of a new life in Algeria represented an escape path from conflict and poverty in neighboring continental European countries. Barclay et al. (2018) note that some migrants to Algeria were refugees from the German annexation of Alsace-Lorraine in 1871 and, given their high standing in the homeland, went on to become some of the most privileged in the Algerian colonies. Alternatively, Pervillé (1997) highlights that many settlers who sought wealth and opportunity were from countries such as Italy and Spain. While the swell of non-French migrants helped to populate the colony, it posed a potential national security challenge due to the vast number of people from rival European powers who may have remained sympathetic to their country of origin in a potential future conflict. In response to this influx, the law of June 26, 1889, created a policy of immediate naturalization, whereby any child born in Algeria to European parents was to be considered a French citizen with equal rights. By giving these settler families significant equity in the French imperial project, this development marked a significant change of policy, as Balch (1909) suggests that access to French citizenship prior to 1889 was fiercely guarded. While Pervillé (1997) characterizes this policy of naturalization as a defensive mechanism, it was clearly not a policy of deterrence for potential non-French settlers as it afforded them increased rights and opportunities within the French colony.

Faced with an ill-suited population in a foreign climate, public health proved a challenge for French colonial authorities in Algeria. Curtin (1989) provides a thorough image of the hostile climate that the first European settlers and soldiers faced. Medical reports from 1847 suggest that the mortality rate for soldiers in Algeria was seven times that of their colleagues stationed in France. Rather than discouraging settlement, this high mortality rate provoked public outrage, and demands that authorities find a solution. Curtin (1989, 56) notes, "In Algeria, the high death rates of settlers brought a sense of crisis and a demand for public action and public spending similar to that of the West Indies and greater than in France itself." The quality of the water supply, for example, was a focal point of infrastructural upgrade and renewal. Similarly, in response to diseases such as malaria, the use of quinine as a treatment was pioneered in Algeria by the French army doctor François Maillot. The acclimatization of the European population to life in Algeria, no doubt aided through medical and scientific advances, resulted in a dramatic fall in mortality; "from 78 per thousand in the first five years of conquest (1831–35) to 15 per thousand in the late 1860s (1863–69)" (Curtin 1989, 30).

The decrease in death was so dramatic that envious British officials were dispatched to Algeria to learn of the French secret to success, such that it could be replicated in the British colonies. These emissaries produced the 1866 account, the "Report on the causes of reduced mortality in the French Army serving in Algeria," which detailed, among other things, the aggressive strategies employed to stymie the spread of syphilis across the colonial population (Acton 1972). Furthermore, the advances of public health in the French colonies must also be placed in a broader context. While tuberculosis was responsible for only seven percent of military deaths in Algeria in the 1840s, in as late as the 1860s it was responsible for 22 percent of military deaths in France (Curtin 1989, 76). Although the colonial climate proved a challenge in many respects, it also provided an escape from the common diseases of France. The early years of colonization were marked by an extremely high mortality rate; however, this did not deter the creation of a settler colony. Additional resources were afforded by the metropole, and advances in science and medicine made the public health of the Algerian colony the envy of the rest of the colonial world.

Despite the initial medical challenges, the success of the French government's efforts to increase migration to the Algerian colony is clear. As a result of these policies of facilitated migration, Sessions (2011, 290) suggests that French migration to Algeria in the nineteenth century was as high as French migration to the United States during that time. Furthermore, the colonial population in Algeria for the first 60 years of its history grew at the same pace as the colonial population of Australia in its first 60 years. Rather than a far-away, extractive colony, Algeria became a tourist destination in the decades following the French conquest. Blais and Deprest (2012), for example, highlight how French tourists were enticed to cross the Mediterranean due to the increase in steamboat traffic, and the marketing of the Algerian landscape as being likened to that of the south-eastern French region of Provence. By 1863, even British travelers were making the voyage across the Mediterranean for tourism. Rogers (1865) notes that, at that time, settlers on state-subsidized passages were confined to the lower decks, so as to not displease the paying tourists. Although the nomenclature of nudging is a relatively recent development, nudges were fundamental to the growth of the French colonial population in Algeria in the nineteenth century.

FACILITATED FRENCH MIGRATION AS NUDGES

Employing a modified version of Thaler and Sunstein's (2009, 6) initial definition of nudging being "any aspect of the choice architecture that alters people's behavior in a predictable way without forbidding any options . . . To count as a nudge, the intervention must be cheap and easy to avoid. Nudges are not mandates," France's efforts to bolster its colonial population constitute a policy of multifaceted nudging. As previously discussed, the creation of subsidies, particularly in the absence of mandates, is congruent with this definition. Unlike the transportation of criminals to the Algerian colony, the provision of free transport, higher wages, or legal benefits (such as the acquisition of French citizenship) constitutes a nudge-based subsidy. This nudge utilized choice architecture to facilitate a predictable change in behavior, while also allowing the urban poor to simply ignore the opportunity and continue their behavior at no additional cost. The policy also bears resemblance to what Thaler and Sunstein (2009) call "channeling" and "feedback and information" nudges. Channeling occurs when an action is deemed desirable by a third party, and so an individual is provided with overt and subliminal reminders to carry out the action, or information on how to carry out the action. According to Thaler and Sunstein (2009, 72), "often we can do more to facilitate good behavior by removing some small obstacle than by trying to shove people in some direction." Similarly, providing feedback and information is a nudge in which individuals are made overtly aware of factual information that may alter their decisions. For example, Thaler and Sunstein (2009, 192), citing Jin and Leslie (2003), highlight how mandatory visible restaurant hygiene grading in Los Angeles both made patrons more conscious of the risks of poor food hygiene, and incentivized restaurants to ameliorate their cleanliness.

France's urban poor thus faced a veritable buffet of choices from which to better their lot in the mid-nineteenth century. The choice to take up employment in the recently established Algerian colony, in the eyes of the state, aligned both the interests of the unemployed as well as policymakers. The decision to remain in France was not penalized; however, the opportunity cost of doing so was raised. Through subsidizing the voyage across the Mediterranean, policymakers sought to nudge, or channel, migrants to make the journey. Similarly, government officials played a crucial role in connecting would-be settlers with opportunities in Algeria, and their actions represent an incarnation of a feedback and information nudge.

Unfortunately for the Algerians, however, these nudges did not consider their preferences. The increased settler population was just one of the many policies which sought to shore up France's extractive and discriminatory colonization of North Africa. From land dispossession to an inferior legal status, the strength of the French colonial administration allowed the state to systematically disadvantage the native population. The ability to holistically calculate the preferences of any single individual remains a central challenge to any effort to nudge, and thus it would be near impossible that the French state had gauged the contentment of the migrants to be party to such a punitive colonial regime.[3] Consequently, these nudges sought to harness the self-interest of some of the poorest and most downtrodden in French society to pursue an official policy of external repression. While the benefits of a better job in Algeria were keenly advertised by the state, the wholesale and systematic disruption of the Algerian way of life was undoubtedly omitted. The efforts to nudge colonial migration thus made the most desperate in French society party to a punitive imperial occupation.

NUDGING SETTLER MORTALITY

France's nudging of potential settlers had a clear impact on the mortality rate of the Algerian colony. However, it did not deter the state's successful efforts to bolster its colonial population. This decision poses profound ramifications for contemporary efforts to understand the development of colonial institutions. In seeking to explain the similarity of Algeria's long-run economic performance with other former colonies in the global south, authors such as Acemoglu et al. (2001) have utilized colonial settler mortality as an instrumental variable for the quality of broad, long-run social and political institutions. However, if a high settler mortality rate did not deter the establishment of a settler colony, as was the case in colonial Algeria, the link between mortality and institutional quality appears tenuous.

Acemoglu et al.'s (2001) seminal paper uses European settler mortality to gauge the relative ease or difficulty of colonization which, in turn, is described as a deciding factor in the type of institutions that colonizers fostered. The authors contend that the tenets of these institutions have persisted until today, and thus have affected long-run national-level measurements of economic prosperity. Explicitly building upon the work of their predecessors,

Acemoglu et al. (2001, 1372) highlight the unique contribution of their work, as they "are not aware of others who have pointed out the link between settler mortality and institutions." For example, the authors cite, and seek to build upon, Young's (1994) exploration of the persistence of colonial institutions. Furthermore, they also respond to authors such as Diamond (1999) who have suggested that climate or distance from the equator is correlated with economic performance. Thus, the role of settler mortality in their argument is crucial. This argument, however, has not been unanimously accepted, particularly due to the authors' practical methodology. Albouy (2012), for example, highlights how, despite purportedly using the instrumental variable of settler mortality, Acemoglu et al. (2001) rather utilize the mortality rates of soldiers, bishops, sailors, and laborers, sometimes even when data on the mortality rate of the actual settler population is available. Furthermore, Albouy (2012, 3060) draws acute awareness to the authors' creative use of assigning mortality rates to neighboring countries and benchmarking, noting that, "out of 64 countries in the sample, only 28 countries have mortality rates that originate from within their own borders."

The history of nudging in colonial Algeria suggests, conversely, that historical flaws may be embedded in the assumptions of Acemoglu et al. (2001). Despite the diversity of policy which embodied over 500 years of European colonial rule across five continents, Acemoglu et al. (2001, 1373) waste little time in establishing the purported primacy of settler mortality as a determining factor in the creation of settlements, suggesting that, "there is little doubt that mortality rates were a key determinant of European settlements." The French experience in Algeria, however, suggests that the contrary is also true. Despite having a settler mortality rate more than four times greater than the United States,[4] the French state was adamant about fostering a colonial settlement on the southern shore of the Mediterranean through a process of incentivized migration. Rather than being deterred by the high mortality rate, French officials continued to send the poorest and ill-suited urbanites to the colony. Conversely, while there was initial public concern over the high mortality rate, it was met with demands for greater salutary funding. Had the French state not nudged the voyage of the poorest and ill-suited French migrants, the settler mortality rate would have likely been lower.

The nudges to settle the French colony of Algeria, thus, elucidate two significant conclusions in light of this line of research. The first being that many French settlers were self-selecting due to the incentives they faced and may have been particularly ill-suited to the challenging life of agriculture in Algeria. This poor suitability resulted in an inflated settler mortality rate *by design*, rather than by climactic coincidence. Second, the persistence of the nudges suggests that the French state was not deterred by the deaths of its citizens abroad. While these observations do not question the extractive nature of Algeria's colonial institutions, they demonstrate that there is not an irrefutable inverse link between initial settler mortality and the propensity of policymakers to pursue colonial settlement. Although Algeria represents just one country among the 64 that Acemoglu et al. (2001) analyze, the inapplicability of their assumptions gives reason to reconsider whether the other countries fit within their conceptualization of colonial history.

PREDATORY NUDGING IN THE UNITED STATES

While the nudges in favor of increasing the colonial population in Algeria benefited both the state and the migrants that did not perish, this gain was at the expense of the domestic Algerian population. However, nudges which made ordinary citizens party to broader repressive and punitive policies were not only contained to colonial Algeria, with examples found in many diverse contexts. The Homestead Act 1862, for example, provided a legal mechanism for settlers in the United States to occupy and gain ownership rights to government land.[5] While this policy appears benign in principle, it was used to settle land which was acquired from American Indian[6] communities under duress. Although the Homestead Act's primary purpose was to spread agricultural settlement across the American West, it was also employed in tandem with persistent efforts to appropriate land from indigenous communities and bring that land under the irrefutable control of the U.S. government. Much like in Algeria, the self-interest of individuals was harnessed to achieve a government objective that significantly caused detriment to a third party, the ramifications of which most likely would not have been known to the individuals themselves.[7]

American Indian communities are some of the most deprived in modern American society. With reference to the broader population of the United States, American Indians today suffer from, "lower life expectancy . . . inadequate education, [and] disproportionate poverty" (Indian Health Service 2018, NP). The arrival of Europeans to the North American continent, and often the militaristic inferiority of the American Indians, resulted in the implementation of a variety of violent and discriminatory policies which contributed to these disparate outcomes. The historic malice of these government policies was formally recognized by the U.S. Congress in 2010, in which the government formally, "apologizes on behalf of the people of the United States to all Native Peoples for the many instances of violence, maltreatment, and neglect inflicted on Native Peoples by citizens of the United States" (Department of Defense Appropriations Act 2010, Sec. 8113 (a) (4)).

One of the maltreatments inflicted upon American Indians was the diverse and continued ways in which they were displaced from their traditional lands.

The Homestead Act of 1862 enabled some 270 million acres of land to be transferred from government to private ownership, constituting roughly 10 percent of the territory of the United States today (Potter and Schamel 1997). The requirements to claim 160 acres of land were to be the head of a household or at least 21 years old, a U.S. citizen or someone who had applied for citizenship, and to have not fought against the United States. After five years of residence and proof of having ameliorated the land, ownership could be acquired by paying a nominal fee. Edlefsen (2018, 5) notes that the homesteading process was remarkably progressive for its time, with women and African Americans eligible to participate in the program.

The Homestead Act constitutes a nudge, as it seeks to entice individuals to take a certain action without penalizing those who do not. Potential homesteaders could choose to remain in their previous dwelling, or to purchase a home elsewhere, without being compelled to take up the government's offer of land. While recognizing the difficulty in measuring both a given individual's preferences and interests, it may be said that acquiring a home through homesteading, particularly for those who lacked the financial capital or ability to acquire a line of credit, represents an effort to fulfill some of their interests and preferences.

Despite the Homestead Act's racial and gender progressivism, it also provided a mechanism by which the U.S. government could establish control over territory that was incrementally absorbed from American Indian communities. With settlers establishing themselves on the newly acquired land, the government would have both greater interest and manpower in protecting the land from American Indian efforts to reclaim it. The use of the Homestead Act in tandem with predatory land policies is evident in the history of South Dakota. According to the Fort Laramie Treaty of 1868, the territory to the west of the Mississippi River in what is now the state of South Dakota was recognized as the Great Sioux Reservation. However, the discovery of gold in the westernmost part of that territory, the Black Hills, led to the Great Sioux War of 1876 and the consequential annexation of the Black Hills by the United States government. Under the guise of the Homestead Act, settlers were nudged to settle on the land that had until recently been central to the local American Indian livelihood.

The impact of the Homestead Act upon the American Indian population was replicated across the American West. Edlefsen (2018, 11) notes that while around 19–20 percent of land acquired through the Homestead Act was in Oklahoma, North Dakota, and South Dakota, "prior to 1862, most of that land was under the ownership of American Indians and thus was not available for whites to claim or own." It would be inaccurate to attribute this dispossession solely to the malevolence of the state, as private homesteaders had previously advocated for access to indigenous land. Efforts by would-be homesteaders in Oklahoma, for example, to access restricted American Indian lands contributed to the eventual opening of the Unassigned Lands to settlement, and the consequent Land Rush of 1889.[8]

The Homestead Act provided a streamlined method through which would-be settlers were incentivized to settle on land that was dispossessed from American Indian communities. It remains to be known how many of those who utilized the Homestead Act were aware of the previous American Indian ownership of the land they were attempting to settle. Furthermore, it would have been irregular or uncommon that the detrimental impact of this disposition upon indigenous communities was made aware to the potential settlers. Consequentially, the Homestead Act made ordinary citizens third parties to the dispossession of American Indians, which no doubt played an adverse role in the social and economic development of American Indian communities.

PUBLIC POLICY IMPLICATIONS

As illustrated by the aforementioned examples, nudging offers an effective mechanism by which to mobilize a willing public, albeit with a variety of moral questions. The government, due to its unparalleled role in society, must fundamentally take responsibility for the outcomes toward which it nudges. Similarly, as with any expression of government power, policymakers must be held accountable, particularly when there are incentives for self-interest to supersede the interests of others. Instances of asymmetric information pose a particular challenge to this accountability and question the benevolence of a policy mechanism which can facilitate such abuses.

The two examples elucidated within this chapter offer similar, albeit distinct, cases of the willful obfuscation of asymmetric information in pursuit of nudging. In the example from the United States, fundamental information is omitted from the public discourse. The Homestead Act provided would-be settlers to acquire land but did not make a principle of disclosing how that land was forcefully acquired from the indigenous population. Putting aside the moral issue of using taxpayer money to encourage the consumption of a good acquired by questionable means, the fact that nudging works fine without seeking to disclose this potentially preference-altering information should be of cause for concern for consumers.

France's colonial nudging moreover illustrates how both the unseen third party and those being nudged can suffer due to this fundamental imbalance in power. A significant risk of nudging is the propensity of it to become coercive, particularly when there are vested interests in the outcome but little concern for the public cost (Rizzo and Whitman 2009, 713). Similarly, this can also occur when the justification of a previous policy, such as the geopolitical rationale for colonization, is utilized to justify an increasingly coercive policy of exploiting informational asymmetries to nudge migration. While nudging colonial migration may appear to have been mutually beneficial and mutually agreed upon by both the individuals and the state, there is reason to suggest it may have been coercive. For the urban poor in France, the option to migrate to Algeria was always a free choice—however, that "choice" may have been the sole visible avenue out of poverty and squalor in the metropole. The fact remains that the poor were enticed with the lure of wealth, but ultimately faced a vicious mortality rate and became an accessory to a regime that was discriminatory and cruel for the indigenous peoples.

A central condition of nudging is that no choice is made significantly more difficult or costly, irrespective of changes in opportunity cost. The moral implications of this condition are profound, particularly when, as we have seen, government nudges ordinary citizens to reach questionable, broader policy objectives. Is the government responsible for the negative outcomes it facilitates? Proponents of nudging may argue to the contrary, as individuals choose to involve themselves in the given policy and are not forced to make a *good, benign,* or *bad* choice. Others, however, would argue that government is responsible for the outcome of any choice it facilitates, particularly when the rationale for nudging is based on the premise that expert nudge architects have access to more information, intelligence, and time to evaluate a decision than any individual citizen. Maintaining the integrity of choice does not absolve the government of responsibility. If the government were not to be held liable, the implication would be that individuals who, as described by Thaler and Sunstein (2009), already lack sufficient time or capacity to make challenging yet routine decisions, must thoroughly investigate the potential third-party implications of the action they are being nudged to undertake.

It is not unreasonable to say that this is infeasible for most. On the contrary, much of the rationale for government intervention is to provide information to which the average citizen is not privy. The U.S. Food and Drug Administration (FDA), for example, carries out the technical and costly testing of pharmaceuticals so that consumers do not have to. Government advocacy carries a clear signal to individuals that it is safe, beneficial or, at the very least, not harmful. Consequently, it is logically incongruent that Thaler and Sunstein (2009, 242) would suggest that individuals should perhaps be more vigilant of private sector nudging than that of public actors. The public sector has a mandate to provide social goods, or at least not harm citizens, but is controlled by self-interested actors. The private sector, conversely, makes no qualms about being self-interested; for most companies in America, any social benefit achieved through business is secondary to profit. Consequently, most Americans do not look to business leaders for an indication of the *right* thing to do but may look to community leaders who take up political or bureaucratic office. Being warned that businesses might not always have the public's best interest in mind is trite, but such warnings about officials from the Environmental Protection Agency or Department of Veterans Affairs would surprise most. Aside from its unique right to being the sole legitimate user of force, the government thus holds a special place in our society, and cannot be held to the same standard as private actors— particularly when it is enabled to carry out its actions with taxpayer money and with information that remains legally excluded from the public domain. Consequently, if we can accept the unique role of government in society, and that government ultimately bears responsibility for its actions, there can be little excuse for ignorance of the results of government intervention—including nudging.

The profoundly deleterious effects of the French and American states' nudging should furthermore serve as a stark example of how democracies and regimes whose institutions permit debate and dissent can nonetheless arrive at such policies. According to Mises (1949, 193), democracies "cannot prevent majorities from falling victim to erroneous ideas and from adopting inappropriate policies which not only fail to realize the ends aimed at but result in disaster." The state's rational ignorance of the costs of its policies upon the indigenous peoples, for example, constitutes one such inappropriate policy that resulted in disaster. According to Downs (1957, 146), for both citizens and policymakers alike, "It is always rational to perform any act if its marginal return is larger than its marginal cost." Given that the marginal benefit to policymakers of colonial expansion was significantly higher than the cost of assessing the impact of expansion upon the indigenous peoples, policymakers may have been incentivized to remain *rationally ignorant* of the full effects of their nudging policies. If, as Rizzo and Whitman (2009, 910) have highlighted, policymakers are prone to substituting their own preferences into nudges when they cannot determine those of the public, and the state is incentivized to remain ignorant of the costs it inflicts upon a third party, it is little surprise that nudging can serve as a tool of what Tocqueville (1835, 410) called the "tyranny of the majority."

While this chapter has employed some of the most egregious examples to illustrate the pitfalls of nudging, this method offers several insights. The logic and implications of nudging have a long history, and were not created with the publishing of Thaler and Sunstein's (2009) *Nudge*. Consequently, the recent flurry of nudge-inspired government taskforces and units should not be interpreted as an effort to give wind to the sails of the latest economic innovation, but rather upholding the mantle of an established form of public policy with a questionable history. Policymakers in these organizations would be wise to familiarize themselves with the historic uses of their *raison d'être*. These most egregious incarnations of nudges were, after all, carried out with the enlightened fervor of the pursuit of then-fashionable "advances" in public policy.

The two examples of this chapter—colonial Algeria and the Civil War era of the United States—illustrate that the misguidance which fueled these policies was not limited to one society, language, or culture. Furthermore, there is little to preclude the exploitation of asymmetric information within nudging in contemporary society. For example, if a policymaker advocated for automatic enrollment in the local public primary school, as it would entitle the school to greater government funding, would it be popular? Education is often seen as a public good and so this nudge might be popular, even among those who opt for private education. But what if that funding were at the direct expense of the neighboring public school? And what if that neighboring school was the only educational opportunity for families in that impoverished suburb? If the government were to take up the onus of nudging citizens, citizens should be made aware of the costs of such nudges. Without doing so, citizens' selections of choices are impaired by the omission of information. If we can accept that government bears ultimate responsibility for the actions it facilitates, and policymakers are prone to acting out of self-interest, it is imperative that efforts to nudge be scrutinized and subject to transparency. If said transparency cannot be achieved, there is serious reason to consider whether such a form of government intervention should be encouraged.

CONCLUSION

Nudging offers a unique method by which the government can seek to achieve the fulfillment of both the interests of the individual citizen and the broader, national interest. The achievement of that ambition, however, is challenged by a variety of factors. The ability to holistically evaluate the preferences of individuals poses a significant stumbling block for the creation of nudge-inspired public policy. Furthermore, an examination of historical efforts to use nudge-based policies in both colonial Algeria and the Civil War era of the United States illustrates the potential informational asymmetries between policymakers and individuals. When nudges exploit that asymmetry, individuals can be made party to policies which are punitive and deleterious for both themselves and third parties. An analysis of the French government's efforts to nudge colonial settlers also gives cause to reconsider some of the assumptions behind the use of settler mortality data as an instrumental variable for institutional quality, particularly as French policymakers did not abate their efforts to nudge settlers despite the enduring colonial fatalities. Moreover, the potential for exploiting information asymmetries evokes the question of where liability lies when nudges generate perverse outcomes. Given the role of government in modern society, this chapter makes the case the state is liable for the outcomes of nudging in public policy, and thus policymakers and citizens alike should give thorough consideration to the use of nudges.

NOTES

1. See Bristol (2020) for a discussion on the challenges of defining and classifying nudges, including those that utilize incentives.
2. Massif and the Mitidja are areas in northern Algeria.
3. While it may be possible that the preferences of some of the French urban poor aligned with the pro-colonization agenda of French lawmakers, and the deliberate detriment caused to the indigenous population, no effort was made to assess whether this was indeed the case for all of the settlers. Congruent with Rizzo and Whitman's (2009, 910) assessment, the French state filled this factual void with the preferences of its own lawmakers.
4. According to "Appendix Table 2A—Data on Mortality" in Acemoglu, Johnson, and Robinson (2001, 1398).
5. Roberts (2015) similarly identifies parallels between the contemporary elite discourse of territorial expansion in colonial Algeria and the United States' western frontier.
6. As per the U.S. census, the term "American Indian" is used to refer to the diverse indigenous peoples of the United States.
7. Much like in the Algerian case, it is possible that the preferences and views of American policymakers toward American Indians were also held by a portion of the settler population. However, there is no guarantee that these views—particularly on complex topics such as race during the Civil War—were held consistently across the entire settler population.
8. See *The Leavenworth Times* (1889) for a contemporary account.

REFERENCES

Acemoglu, Daron, Simon Johnson, and James A. Robinson. 2001. "The Colonial Origins of Comparative Development: An Empirical Investigation." *American Economic Review* 91(5): 1369–1401.

Acton, William. 1972. *Prostitution, Considered in Its Moral, Social and Sanitary Aspects*. Cass Library of Victorian Times, No. 9. London: Cass.

Albouy, David Y. 2012. "The Colonial Origins of Comparative Development: An Empirical Investigation: Comment." *American Economic Review* 102(6): 3059–3076.

Assemblée Nationale. 2019. "*Jules Ferry (1885) : Les Fondements de la Politique Coloniale* (28 juillet 1885)." http://www2.assemblee-nationale.fr/decouvrir-l-ass emblee/histoire/grands-discours-parlementaires/jules-ferry-28-juillet-1885

Balch, Thomas Willing. 1909. "French Colonization in North Africa." *The American Political Science Review* 3(4): 539–551.

Barbançon, Louis-José. 2008. "Les Transportés de 1848 (Statistiques, Analyse, Commentaires)." *Criminocorpus* (blog). January 1, 2008. http://journals.openediti on.org.ezp-prod1.hul.harvard.edu/criminocorpus/148.

Barclay, Fiona, Charlotte Ann Chopin, and Martin Evans. 2018. "Introduction: Settler Colonialism and French Algeria." *Settler Colonial Studies* 8(2): 115–130.

Benartzi, Shlomo, John Beshears, Katherine L. Milkman, Cass R. Sunstein, Richard H. Thaler, Maya Shankar, Will Tucker-Ray, William J. Congdon, and Steven Galing. 2017. "Should Governments Invest More in Nudging?" *Psychological Science* 28(8): 1041–1055.

Blais, Hélène, and Florence Deprest. 2012. "The Mediterranean, a Territory between France and Colonial Algeria: Imperial Constructions." *European Review of History: Revue Europeenne d'histoire* 19(1): 33–57.

Chetty, Raj, John N. Friedman, Soren Leth-Petersen, Torben Heien Nielsen, and Tore Olsen. 2013. "Subsidies Vs. Nudges: Which Policies Increase Saving the Most?" *Center for Retirement Research at Boston University* 13(3): 1–7. https://crr.bc.edu /wp-content/uploads/2013/03/IB_13-3-508.pdf.

Curtin, Philip D. 1989. *Death by Migration: Europe's Encounter with the Tropical World in the Nineteenth Century.* New York: Cambridge University Press.

Department of Defense Appropriations Act, H.R. 3326, 111th Cong. (2010) (enacted).

Diamond, Jared M. 1999. *Guns, Germs, and Steel: The Fates of Human Societies.* New York: W.W. Norton.

Downs, Anthony. 1957. "An Economic Theory of Political Action in a Democracy." *Journal of Political Economy* 65(2): 135–150.

Edlefsen, David. 2018. "How the West Was Claimed: The Homestead Act and the General Allotment Act." Working Paper for the Western Political Science Association Conference. http://www.wpsanet.org/papers/docs/WPSA_HtWwC.pdf.

Francis, Kyle. 2015. "Civilizing Settlers: Catholic Missionaries and the Colonial State in French Algeria, 1830–1914." Unpublished PhD Dissertation. The City University of New York.

Funes, Nathalie. 2019. "Code de l'indigénat Dans Les Colonies : Un Siècle de Répression." *L'Obs*, February 24, 2019. https://www.nouvelobs.com/monde/afr ique/20190221.OBS0653/code-de-l-indigenat-dans-les-colonies-un-siecle-de-re pression.html.

Hayek, F. A. 1945. "The Use of Knowledge in Society." *The American Economic Review* 35(4): 519–530.

Indian Health Service. 2018. "Disparities | Fact Sheets." *Newsroom.* April 2018. https ://www.ihs.gov/newsroom/factsheets/disparities/.

Jin, G. Z., and P. Leslie. 2003. "The Effect of Information on Product Quality: Evidence from Restaurant Hygiene Grade Cards." *The Quarterly Journal of Economics* 118(2): 409–451.

Lipscomb, Molly, and Laura Schechter. 2018. "Subsidies versus Mental Accounting Nudges: Harnessing Mobile Payment Systems to Improve Sanitation." *Journal of Development Economics* 135(November): 235–254.

Mises, Ludwig von. 1949. *Human Action: A Treatise on Economics*. Auburn, Alabama: Ludwig von Mises Institute.

Pervillé, Guy. 1997. "La Politique Algérienne de La France, de 1830 à 1962." *Le Genre Humain*, September, 27–37.

Potter, Lee Ann, and Wynell Schamel. 1997. "The Homestead Act of 1862." *Social Education* 61(6): 359–364.

Prévost-Paradol, Lucien-Anatole. 1868. *La France Nouvelle*. Paris: Librairie Nouvelle.

Rizzo, Mario J., and Douglas Glen Whitman. 2009. "The Knowledge Problem of New Paternalism." *BYU Law Review* 2009(4): 905–968.

Roberts, Timothy Mason. 2015. "The Role of French Algeria in American Expansion during the Early Republic." *The Journal of the Western Society for French History* 43.

Rogers, G. Albert. 1865. *A Winter in Algeria*. London: Sampson Low, Son, and Marston.

Savarese, Eric. 2016. "The Pieds-Noirs and French Political Life, 1962–2015." In *Vertriebene and Pieds-Noirs in Postwar Germany and France Comparative Perspectives*, edited by Manuel Borutta and Jan C Jansen. London: Palgrave Macmillan.

Sessions, Jennifer E. 2011. *By Sword and Plow: France and the Conquest of Algeria*. Ithaca, NY: Cornell University Press.

Thaler, Richard H., and Cass R. Sunstein. 2009. *Nudge: Improving Decisions about Health, Wealth, and Happiness*. Revised and expanded edition. New York: Penguin Books.

The Leavenworth Times. 1889. "Boomers Eager to Settle Oklahoma," March 22, 1889. https://www.newspapers.com/newspage/78565424/.

Tocqueville, Alexis de. 1835. *Democracy in America: Historical-Critical Edition of De La Démocratie En Amérique*. Edited by Eduardo Nolla and James T. Schleifer. Bilingual French-English edition. Indianapolis: Liberty Fund.

Tocqueville, Alexis de. 2002. *Travail sur l'Algérie*. Classiques des Sciences Sociales. Chicoutimi: J.-M. Tremblay.

Young, Crawford. 1994. *The African Colonial State in Comparative Perspective*. New Haven: Yale University Press.

Chapter 5

Nudge, Nations, and Cultural Change

The Process of Identity Formation in Singapore

Erin Dunne

For Thaler and Sunstein, "nudges" are policy actions that change an individual's choices or behaviors without "forbidding any options" and in a way that is "easy and cheap to avoid" (2009, 6). In the classic example of arranging food in the cafeteria line to put fruit or vegetables first, the goal is to prompt individual actors to select healthier items. In Thaler and Sunstein (2009) as well as subsequent literature in behavioral economics, the analysis almost always ends with that individual choice. But changes in individual habits, such as choosing an apple over a cupcake, often ultimately shift self-perception and identity. For example, "I'm eating an apple" could easily become "I'm someone who makes healthy choices" to—on a broader, social level—"we are the sort of people who make healthy choices" or "preferring apples over cupcakes is *normal*" (see Chaiken and Baldwin 1981; Goldstein and Cialdini 2007). In behavioral economics, these social consequences of nudges and how they impact norms, culture, and beliefs have been largely unexplored. This chapter addresses this gap in existing literature, outlining how nudges fit into models of entrepreneurial-driven social and institutional change and applying this framework to assess nudges in their most alarming form: state-sponsored culture change.

This underdeveloped line of inquiry has fruitful implications for understanding the mechanisms through which entrepreneurial "choice architects" pursue institutional changes rather than simply influencing individual actors. As national governments increasingly adopt nudge theory (Afif 2017) to accomplish political and social objectives, it is critical to understand how nudges interact on a social and institutional level. For critics of nudge theory, the potential consequences for interventions, especially from state actors, are tantamount to authoritarian social engineering and contrary to freedom and liberty (Thaler and Sunstein 2009, 242–244; Mitchell 2005). On a social level, nudging as a tool to foster identity and change beliefs raises serious questions about ethics, liberty, and self-governance. This is especially true when nudging becomes an instrument of top-down culture creation and national identity formation; that is, nation-building.

Those concerns are well founded. History is littered with the sometimes murderous and often destructive consequences of governments and companies pushing groups of people to act in certain ways by playing into the worst aspects of human psychology (Akerlof and Shiller 2015; Clendinnen 2002; Scull et al. 2016). As disheartening as that reality is—about both the intentions of governments and their success at mobilizing people for their ends— studying the successes and failures of institutions engaged in these efforts offers a more complex view of both the extent of control by elite actors and the power of those subjected to their nudges.

Using elements of Singapore's relatively recent and well-documented nation-building efforts as case studies, this chapter analyzes the intentions and outcomes of various Singaporean government efforts to nudge the country's diverse and initially fragmented population toward a distinct Singaporean identity (see also Keating 2018). In Singapore, government "nudges" were deliberately constructed not only to shift individual behavior but also to shape social identity and perception. As I will show, the success of nudges—both in changing individual behavior and group identity—is largely determined by buy-in from the nudged population and its preexisting inclinations to accept (or reject) the nudge offered. This assessment means that attempts to create culture (or more narrowly defined social change) are acts of coproduction by elites (acting as choice architects) *and* the nudged population. In essence, this line of inquiry addresses the question at the heart of both the critiques and praises of nudge theory: Does it work?

This chapter first examines the literature on the relationship between culture, institutions, entrepreneurship, and the interdisciplinary study of nations and nationalism. I then develop a theoretical foundation to understand how nudges act on individual and group behavior. After a brief overview of Singaporean history, I offer several case studies demonstrating how nudges function in the context of nation-building. I conclude with a discussion of the utility of nudges and their social consequences.

AN ECONOMIC VIEW OF INSTITUTIONAL
AND CULTURAL CHANGE

Thaler and Sunstein argue that "[w]orkplaces, corporate boards, universities, religious organizations, clubs, and even families might be able to use, and benefit from, small exercises in libertarian paternalism" (2009, 252). The implication is that nudges are beneficial on an institutional level—shaping culture, boosting functionality, and changing social behaviors. In the private sector, human resources staff and business consultants have incorporated behavioral economic insights to improve corporate culture, increase productivity, enhance corporate compliance efforts, and effect other behavioral changes among employees. As two McKinsey & Company employees explained in a company blog post, "Rather than being seen as a tool on its own, behavioral science is rather a turbo-charger for efforts on cultural change and corporate transformation, or a support tool for more effective processes" (Güntner and Sperling 2017, n.p.).

Previous research on institutional and cultural change offers significant insights into the function of such attempted shifts in social behavior, identity, and beliefs, and the likelihood of success or failure. To examine these implications, however, it is first useful to lay out working definitions of culture and institutions.

North defines institutions as "the humanly devised constraints that structure human interaction. They are made up of formal constraints (e.g., rules, laws, constitutions), informal constraints (e.g., norms of behavior, convention, and self-imposed codes of conduct), and their enforcement characteristics" (1994, 360). For North, institutions are "the rules of the game" and include the informal constraints, which he describes as "the heritage which we call culture" (1990, 37). Subsequent studies have made clear that culture and institutions can function in similar ways, but that culture—composed of beliefs, norms, heritage, and other factors—is much more complex.

Culture, for example, is not only a set of rules but also a form of social capital with far-reaching effects. Putnam's study of regional Italian governments led him to hypothesize that modern differences in civic functionality were related to experience (or lack thereof) as a medieval city-state (1993). Putnam suggests that this experience precipitated cultural developments of traits (such as trust, cooperation, and participation) that impact modern civic institutions. Guiso, Sapienza, and Zingales tested Putnam's hypothesis and confirmed, through quantitative measures of civic life, that social capital in modern Italian cities correlates with their medieval predecessors' experiences as independent city-states (2016). Culture is not simply an informal set of "rules of the game" governing interactions, but also a form of social capital, a determinant of future development that results from coproduction with formal institutions (Alesina and Giuliano 2015). Additional research supports these findings, showing that institutional shifts can create cultural shifts that become generationally transmitted traits. Alesina and Fuchs-Schündeln (2007) demonstrated this in their study of the impact of communism on generational social beliefs and immigrant communities (2007).

Culture is thus a complex variable of economic analysis that, as Storr explains, plays "a direct role in influencing how institutions come to be understood and experienced" (2012, 89). To understand that role and the dynamic process of cultural change, Storr—building on Max Weber's view of "the nature of economic life in a society as being partially the result of the economic attitudes and values that exist in that society"—proposed a research agenda that "attempted to identify the origins and to trace out the effects of those attitudes and values" (2012, 83). In addition to placing attitudes and values in conversation with economics, this approach to culture necessarily sees the interaction between formal institutions and identity, beliefs, or values as one of continuous, but not boundless, change. To draw on North's work on institutions, cultural change is "path dependent" (1990) but, as Storr reminds us, "not static" (2012, 50). Simply put, for both culture and institutions, history matters.

That foundational thesis has been subsequently developed within economics. Of particular importance is Boettke, Coyne, and Lesson's work to answer *how* history matters. As they explain, "stickiness" and the success of institutional change are tied to preexisting indigenous orders (behaviors, relationships, and institutions that are socially created rather than imposed). Institutions or institutional changes imposed by outsiders without incorporating indigenous institutions are thus unlikely to be credible or workable to local agents and thus unlikely to succeed (2008, 353–354).

Boettke, Coyne, and Lesson's work is applicable to the success of nudging as a tool to shift culture and identity (2008). Indeed, that the success of future changes would necessarily be limited by past experience fits well with John's articulation of culture as a constitution which offers a framework for cultural development and change (2015). According to John, culture, like constitutions, arises spontaneously and provides a framework within which decisions are made and understood. As John explains, "the reason culture is like a constitution is because culture represents a shared *pattern* of meanings against which the actions of others can be interpreted" (2015, 234). In other words, institutional changes can be understood and incorporated against a cultural framework. This is because, although not explicitly articulated by John, constitutions offer a mechanism for change—so long as the framework is not violated. This conclusion points to a similar limit on institutional change that Boettke, Coyne, and Lesson's work does: enduring cultural change is possible only within the bounds of existing historical, and by extension, institutional, and cultural frameworks (2008).

This idea can be applied to economic change as well. As Lavoie and Chamlee-Wright explain:

> All rational deliberation takes place within cultural parameters. What serves as an incentive for somebody depends on what the person wants. What seems

rational depends on the prevailing culture's understanding of things. Culture is not another factor to be considered in addition to rational incentives, it is the underlying meaning of the specific context of any rational choice. (2000, 42)

Thus, it would seem that for nudge, or indeed any program of social change to be successful, it cannot offer—at least immediately—a truly radical departure from the past nor violate existing cultural and social norms.

Drawing on this literature, I borrow the definitions established by Alesina and Giuliano with culture meaning "values and beliefs (one could say informal rules)" and institutions meaning "formal institutions" (2015, 902). This definition establishes culture as a complex web of interactions while also recognizing similarities between formal and informal institutions. Additionally, I adopt Storr's Weberian approach to understand how culture and institutions came to develop as they did. Using this foundation, I build off existing literature on the likelihood of cultural or institutional change, and I demonstrate that attempts to make such change through nudges—on an individual and social level—are likewise subject to constraints.

THE ENTREPRENEURIAL CHOICE ARCHITECT

Entrepreneurs drive change. In the market, Austrian theories of entrepreneurship—particularly as developed by Schumpeter (1943) and Kirzner (1973)—offer models for how individuals foster development and growth. Schumpeter explains that entrepreneurship is "creative destruction" or the constant process of mutation and revolution from within (1943, 83). Utilizing new combinations, Schumpeter's entrepreneur drives economic development by "reform[ing] or revolutioniz[ing] the pattern of production" (1976, 132). Kirzner's entrepreneur is alert to ignorance and notices the useful opportunities that are overlooked or unexploited (1973, 15–16).

In noncommercial settings, as North notes, the driver of institutional change is similarly the "individual entrepreneur" (1990, 83) or "ideological entrepreneur" who can change people's beliefs as a necessary component of changing "the rules of the game." In developing this concept, Storr applied Austrian theories of entrepreneurship to explain the various processes by which people can seek to influence other people's ideas, values, and behavior (2011). Storr explains:

A Kirznerian ideological entrepreneur would be alert to opportunities to advance an existing ideology that people in a particular place want but do not yet know about (i.e., to engage in ideological arbitrage). He would be alert to opportunities to sell a new ideology that better explains the world than existing ideologies. Similarly, a Schumpeterian ideological entrepreneur would be a bold innovator who created new conceptions of how the world works or combined and presented existing models of how the world works in new ways (i.e., to promote ideological development). He would work to capture the ideological marketplace, competing fiercely against other ideological entrepreneurs as well as against the weight of existing public opinion and conventions. (2011, 107–108)

A separate but related body of literature develops the idea of "social entrepreneurship," defined as "innovative, social value creating activity that can occur within or across the non-profit, business, or government sectors" (Austin et al. 2006, 2). Swedberg uses Schumpeter's concept of entrepreneurship to explain how social entrepreneurs produce social change through creativity (2006). As Chamlee-Wright and Storr explain, social entrepreneurs play a key role in post-disaster community redevelopment and were instrumental in solving the collective action problem, serving as activists and advocates, organizing outreach and "directly assisting in rebuilding efforts and providing essential services" (2010, 153). These findings have similar applications in community development or nation-building.

Entrepreneurship in nonmarket settings, like the institutional change it precipitates, is limited. Chamlee-Wright and Myers demonstrate that the success of social entrepreneurs is partially dependent on their status and reputation (2008). Social entrepreneurship is also limited by path dependence. Existing institutions constrain would-be social entrepreneurs and their actions (Chamlee-Wright and Storr 2010, 159–161).

The relationship between social or ideological change and institutional change, however, is a two-way street. North observes that people "obey the rules" even when "an individualistic calculus would have them do otherwise" (1981, 46). In other words, people still follow the rules even when they could get away with breaking them. To successfully alter "the rules of the game" (i.e., causing institutional change) thus requires ideological change "if the new institutional structure is to stick" (Storr 2011, 103). Put differently, ideological shifts, "follow, co-evolve with, or precipitate" institutional change (Storr 2011, 103).

Thaler and Sunstein's "choice architects" (2009) fit within this framework and are subject to same limitations of ideological or social entrepreneurs. Choice architects use behavioral insights (new, creatively applied combinations and alertness to previously underutilized human behaviors) to drive the actions and choices of the nudged population and thus further a particular goal or goals (Thaler and Sunstein 2009, 3). The entrepreneurial choice architect thereby prompts institutional and social change.

NATION-BUILDING AND INSTITUTIONAL CHANGE

Sunstein hints at the application of nudges in nation-building, writing that

> [t]he history of freedom-respecting nations is full of changes in choice architecture that have been motivated by an aspiration to realize the highest and most enduring of national ideals. In moving closer to those ideals, new nudges, and new forms of choice architecture, will prove indispensable. (2015, 450)

Modifying choice architecture to achieve "national ideals" fits well with North's ideological entrepreneur as developed in the previous section.

Indeed, among the examples of ideological entrepreneurs cited by North are the U.S. Founding Fathers (1981, 121). In his development of North's idea, Storr offers another political example, citing the development of the Bahamian Progressive Liberal Party and their success in achieving ideological change (2011, 112–113). Storr is careful to point out that ideological entrepreneurs are not always a positive influence: "Hitler, for instance, was an ideological entrepreneur who was alert to the growing feeling of alienation amongst his countrymen and convinced many of them that in order for their nation to reach its destiny they needed to launch a world war and to being systematically killing millions of Jews" (Storr 2011, 113). For the ideological or social entrepreneur, nationalism is fertile ground for change.

While previous studies offer a framework for understanding the relationship between culture, formal institutions, and entrepreneurs in relation to social change, the application of these concepts to nationalism and the processes of nation-building are underdeveloped.

Modern theory on nations and nationalism rejects the notion of a "natural" world order premised on political entities (i.e., states) that map on to defined populations bound together by common beliefs, culture, and history (i.e., nations). Thus, nation-states and both their formal institutions and shared culture, beliefs, and identity are dynamic and subject to entrepreneurial change.

In other words, nations do not simply exist but must be created. Anderson described nations as "imagined communities" implying a deliberate act of imagining and purposeful construction, not accident or happenstance (1983). Hobsbawm's work similarly examined the creation of traditions, often considered "immutable" fixtures of a culture, demonstrating that these "timeless" practices were often created relatively recently rather than inherited from antiquity (1983). Gellner's functionalist approach to nations—positing that nations developed in response to the post-Industrial Revolution needs of cities with diverse populations and requiring rapid retraining—further emphasized that modern national identity is developed rather than innate or intrinsic (1983).

All of these conceptions of nationalism, however, "impl[y] the conscious act on behalf of elites in generating a common culture that is supportive of the political system" (Ortmann 2009, 25). As elites engage in this conscious community-generating activity of ideological and social entrepreneurship, however, they rely on existing frameworks of identity, reworked and articulated as needed to reflect new political realities. Or, as Smith explains, "nationalists cannot, and do not, create nations *ex nihilo*" (1996, 108).

For Smith, then, "the 'nation' is not, as we see, built up only through the provision of 'infrastructures' and 'institutions,' as 'nation-building' theories assumed, but derives from the central fund of culture and symbolism and mythology provided by shared historical experiences" (1986, 258). Nations, viewed through this lens, are the result of existing social and political factors which cause a group of individuals to develop a distinct identity that claims the right of self-determination or nationhood. Often, existing factors such as shared language, religion, and common origin stories form the building blocks of a nation. To borrow North's (1981) terminology, the result is a sort of national path dependence that, as Boettke, Coyne, and Lesson (2008) might put it, must be built on the "stickiness" of indigenous institutions.

Smith also posits that even nation-states that attempt to transcend distinctions among ethnic groups (which he terms *ethnies*) are still bound by them. Smith explains that immigrant nations, such as the United States, saw an initial ethic core that "assumed cultural primacy" and built institutions with the original *ethnie* transforming itself "into a broader political community" (1986, 259). This cultural transformation thus enables a polyethnic nation-state based on civic or territorial nationalism as opposed to ethnic or genea-logical nationalism (Smith 1988, 9–10).

Ethnic nationalism, and its primordial conception of exclusive identity, and civic nationalism, based on shared citizenship and political institutions, have clear differences. It would be an oversimplification, however, to categorize most nations as falling into purely one category or the other. Instead, most modern nation-states are the result of a merging of civic and ethnic nationalism that attempts to use preexisting cultural and social bonds to reinforce the legitimacy of a geographically defined nation-state. This means that even ethnic nationalism is based to some extent on fabricated identity that reinforces the territorial and political claims of the state (Weber 1976; Harrison 2001). For these constructs to be successful, citizens must gain a shared understanding of the value of the institutions of state and a recognition of each other as legitimate citizens. Since these bonds may not be readily apparent, they must be fostered or created.

Further, because the legitimacy of a government in a world of nation-states is predicated on the representation of a "nation" (Lemay-Hébert 2009), states

seek to maintain, enhance, or create the shared social understanding necessary for cohesive identity (Leifer 1972, 1). In other words, social cohesion is
developed by both building interdependence and fostering enough commonality to have a degree of uniformity.[1]

Social cohesion is clearly useful. Storr and Chamlee-Wright, for example,
demonstrate that common narratives are a form of social capital that enables
groups to better function internally and with other institutions (2011).
Although their study focuses on specific communities in the context of disaster recovery, there are clear analogues to nation-building in communication,
trust, and a sense of shared purpose. As Wang explains, nation-building
begins almost as soon as a state forms and political leaders work to solidify
their government through various policies that both give "power of the state"
and create common aspirations for newly minted citizens (2005, 13).

These shared aspirations and narratives can be divided into two distinct
forms derived from Gellner's "makeshift, temporary definitions" of a nation:
an internal sense of commonality and an external sense of being different that
sets the nation apart from all others (1983, 7). The first form, internal identity,
focuses on the creation of a shared identity among citizens, allowing for the
emergence of a coherent and interconnected society despite ethnic and cultural differences—or, in other words, gives meaning to the national "we." The
second form, external identity, allows the nation to appear as a distinct entity,
sometimes explained as a brand (van Ham 2001; Anholt 2006). Achieving
both internal and external identities is critical to a successful nation-state for
achieving both internal and external legitimacies.[2]

Identity formation, from state or other institutional actors, requires investment in formal and informal institutions. For example, theaters, school systems, literacy, religion, and language, are all institutions and systems that
facilitate "a density of linguistic or cultural ties enabling a higher degree of
social communication within the group than beyond it" (Hroch 1996, 79).
Just as a nation-state can invest in its formal political institutions (i.e., government, courts, and laws) and physical infrastructure, a nation can invest in
cultural institutions with the goal of fostering and developing identity among
its citizens.[3]

Here is where the social or ideological entrepreneur, often a state actor,
finds new ways to innovate and successfully win converts for the "national
identity." For the nationalist and entrepreneurial choice architect, government policies can enhance or create elements of shared identity, which in
turn will enhance the legitimacy of the nation-state. Given this context, the
use of nudge as a tool to modify culture and identity must be considered both
in terms of the means with which nudges may be employed and its potential
effects on social change, especially when the change sought contradicts existing intuitions of culture.

INDIVIDUAL AND GROUP-ORIENTED NUDGES

To examine nudges as a tool of social and individual change, I posit that nudges may be classified into two interrelated categories: individual-oriented nudges and group-oriented nudges.

Individual-oriented nudges primarily aim to change the behavior of an individual, without explicitly aiming to change group culture. Group-oriented nudges, by contrast, aim to shift individuals' beliefs regarding their relationship to the group, thereby shifting social norms and culture. More specifically, individual-oriented nudges aim to shift individual behavior within, to borrow North's framing, the existing formal and informal "rules of the game." Group-oriented nudges instead aim to rewrite some of those "rules" creating cultural or institutional change (also see chapter 8 for more on group-oriented nudges).

Institutional actors (i.e., social or ideological entrepreneurs) often employ individual and group-oriented nudges in tandem. This makes sense. Publicly directed attempts to modify specific social behaviors must include individual-oriented efforts. For those efforts to be considered within the framework of nation-building and the necessary sociocultural transformation that process entails, nudges must also be group-oriented, meaning they are defined by group change rather than individual change.

Even some of Thaler and Sunstein's favorite examples are not so much about individual betterment but about advancing broader social objectives (2009). As Lepenies and Malecka warn, "an ulterior motive is to make policy more efficient and achieve states of affairs that are socially desirable in the eyes of nudging advocates, such as, for example, public health" (2015, 3). This applies even to the classic example of flies etched on urinals at Amsterdam's Schipol airport. As Yeung explains, "the benefits arising from spillage reduction in Schipol airport urinals accrue not to those whose aim is thereby improved, but to subsequent travelers who encounter clean facilities" (2012, 124). Still, the flies etched on urinals are an individual-oriented nudge designed to modify individual behavior.

Now consider the hypothetical imposition of fines for spillage. This nudge would affect individuals, but yet would still be group-oriented, as it would aim to socialize the acceptable behavior of not making a mess. It is still a choice; no one is forcing an individual to accept spillage as bad, but the nudge to consider it so is readily apparent. Laws—and rules and regulations more generally—are designed not only to shape individual behavior but to impact underlying attitudes and even perceived morality (Bilz and Nadler 2014, 241). Such socialization cannot be an individual change alone but must also operate in a social context.

Within this example, it is clear that individual and group-oriented nudges can work in concert and that fines or other penalties need not be imposed to socialize beliefs. Indeed, successfully enacting the individual-oriented nudge combined with messaging invoking common ownership or shaming may well yield the same result. Using this model of individual and group-oriented nudges operating within nation-building public campaigns, this chapter will show how nudges impact culture and assess their effectiveness at doing so.

NUDGING, PROPAGANDA, AND NATIONAL MYTHMAKING

Storr explains that "winning converts in the ideological marketplace" is comparable to "winning customers in the commercial sphere" (2011, 109). In the context of nation-building, Storr's "converts" then would be those who buy in to considering themselves members of a nation. Although advertising clearly has noncommercial applications (churches and other nonprofits routinely promote their events and services, for instance), marketing a particular ideology or belief is often considered propaganda. Propaganda, however, is an imprecise term that has been applied to public diplomacy, soft power, the rise of nationalism, and even the study of history as reinforcing a world of artificially bounded nation-states (Marsden 2000). Although propaganda is not unjustly seen as a sinister tool of fascism, it is worth considering what we mean by propaganda in the context of ideological entrepreneurs looking for converts.

The ideological marketplace is fundamentally different from the commercial sphere (Hirschman 1983). Regardless of institutional similarities, buying into one ideology, such as religion or national identity, often forecloses on even considering another. In the commercial sphere, this is generally not the case. Moreover, ideology—unlike commercial goods—is not merely something to have, but something *to be*. Ideololgy determines how we understand and interact with the market, society, and ourselves writ large.

Despite these differences, advertising in both the ideological and commercial spheres falls squarely within the definition of nudge offered by Sunstein and Thaler, as it "alters people's behavior in a predictable way without forbidding any options or significantly changing economic incentives" (2009, 6). Thaler and Sunstein include noncommercial advertising within their framework of nudge as demonstrated by their example of the "Don't Mess with Texas" campaign against littering (2009, 64–65). And, although Sunstein views propaganda as bad, he also places it explicitly within the category of nudges. As he writes: "Groups or nations that are committed to violence sometimes enlist nudges in their cause, often in the form of propaganda, which can be counted as a (bad) kind of nudge" (Sunstein 2015, 420).

Moreover, modern nudge theory—and the field of public relations (see Tye 2002)—can generally be thought of as the direct successor of Bernays' 1928 work, *Propaganda*, which is best described as the synthesis of psychological manipulation and tools of public communication. As Bernays explains, "the conscious and intelligent manipulation of the organized habits and opinions of the masses is an important element in democratic society . . . [w]e are governed, our minds are molded, our tastes formed, our ideas suggested, largely by men we have never heard of" (1928, 9).

Bernays put his insights to work in ways that preyed on the darker side of the same psychological manipulation championed by Thaler and Sunstein. When tobacco companies wanted to promote smoking among women, for example, Bernays famously cast cigarettes as "torches of freedom" after orchestrating a publicity stunt of New York City debutantes, cigarettes in hand, marching in the Fifth Avenue in the Easter Parade (2011 Diggs-Brown, 48). Brilliant, manipulative and certainly a nudge meant to change individual actions and social conceptions about women smoking—and, of course, serve the economic interest of tobacco companies.

While Thaler and Sunstein focus on the less sweeping implications of nudges, Bernays' work posits not only that that manipulation in the public and commercial sector is inevitable but that it is necessary for a smoothly functioning society. As Bernays puts it, a "vast number of human beings must cooperate in this manner if they are to live together as a smoothly functioning society" (1928, 9). North's (1981, 121) ideological entrepreneurs, ranging from religious figures (such as Rabbi Meir, Jesus of Nazareth, Saul of Tarsus, and Mohammed) to the U.S. Founding Fathers, would likely agree with Bernays. Indeed, as I explored in previous sections, shared myths and beliefs are the foundations of modern nations and social cohesion more generally. Although Thaler and Sunstein attempt to separate good nudges from evil (2009, 242–244), rarely are the actions of choice architects—or the lines between advertising, manipulation, and propaganda—so clearly divided (Raftopoulou and Hogg 2010).

THE CASE OF SINGAPORE

Singapore, as a distinct entity, was born when Sir Stamford Raffles arrived on the island at the tip of modern-day Malaysia in 1819 and decided that it was an excellent location for a new British port (Kathirithamby-Wells 1969, 48–49). Raffles had made a good bet, and as a port, Singapore prospered, attracting a diverse array of immigrants to the lucrative commercial hub.

Despite its success, the multiethnic, multilingual city of Indians, Malays, Chinese, and Europeans developed little in the way of shared culture or identity and the colonial administration was more concerned with commerce and the day-to-day running of the port than community building.

Singapore's more recent past has similarly provided little opportunity for the development of unifying historical bonds that Smith highlights as instrumental to the success of a future nation-state (1986). In 1942, the entire Malay Peninsula and Singapore fell to Imperial Japan. Following the surrender of Allied forces in Singapore, the island was left under brutal Japanese occupation punctuated with massacres of civilians and deadly forced labor (Kwok 2015). By the time the island was liberated in 1945, its infrastructure had largely been destroyed and its institutions of government gutted, leading to immediate and violent chaos. Even after British authorities returned to the island, food shortages, disease, and uncontrollable crime mixed with rising anti-colonial sentiment aimed at the British (Turnbull 1989, 214). As British authority waned, new social and political tensions emerged among the island's Chinese, Malay, Indian, and European populations, culminating in a series of violent race riots fermented in part by accusations that the island's ethnically Chinese population harbored sympathies for the Communist government in mainland China (Spector 1956).

After Singapore gained independence from the United Kingdom in 1958, the People's Action Party emerged as an electoral winner and set out to address persistent postwar social and economic ills through economic investment and free trade, workforce training, infrastructure development, the adoption of English as a national common language, the consolidation of labor unions, and an elaborate and comprehensive public housing and public healthcare systems (Beng 2011, 273–277).

Singapore's leaders also firmly believed that the island could not survive without integration with Malaya, and the island unified with the peninsula in 1963. That arrangement, however, proved short-lived, largely due to ethnic tensions, often resulting in violence (Leifer 1964). In 1965, Singapore was ejected from the Federation of Malaya, leaving Singapore again on its own, without a clearly defined national identity or a shared history on which to build one as well as persistent challenges of unemployment, ethnic tensions, scarce housing, and lacking public resources. With these new challenges, the People's Action Party set out to create Singapore as a modern nation-state while addressing the problems facing the island's population (see Ortmann 2009, 24).

Developing national identity in a multiethnic state also required fostering common narratives and shared social understanding. These government efforts often took the form of public campaigns, defined as "a government initiated and inspired movement which has an organized and formal course of action, used with the intent of arousing public awareness and influencing public behavior" (Tham 1986, 41). Speaking about two decades after Singapore's abrupt and unwanted independence, Prime Minister Lee Kuan Yew explained during his National Day speech in 1986:

> I say without the slightest remorse that we wouldn't be here, we would not have made the economic progress if we had not intervened on very personal matters. Who your neighbor is, how you live, the noise you make, how you spit or where you spit, or what language you use. Had we not done that and done it effectively, we would not be here today. It was fundamental social and cultural changes that brought us here . . . We decide what is right, never mind what the people think . . . we know what we have to do which is necessary for the people's survival. Then we set out to persuade the people to accept it. (National Day Rally 1986)

Although some Singaporean government policies were decidedly authoritarian, much of these public campaigns were incentivized but not mandated,[4] attempts to shape Singaporeans' behaviors and identity. In short, they were practices that fall within the definition of nudges. Examining how Singapore's government employed nudges as a tool of nation-building at both individual and group levels is illustrative of how nudges can be used to forge group identity. This analysis also demonstrates how behavioral economic insights can help explain political, social, and historical phenomena.

KEEP SINGAPORE CLEAN

In 1968, Prime Minister Lee Kuan Yew introduced the first "Keep Singapore Clean" campaign, telling the young country: "We have built. We have progressed. But there is no hallmark of success more distinctive and more meaningful than achieving our position as the cleanest and greenest city in South Asia" (1968). The campaign first and foremost aimed to change individual behavior to help address serious public health problems. In 1968, Singapore had a population of about one million and lacked modern sewers. The city's slums did not have running water and waste collection or disposal was inadequate. In addition, litter was openly left in the street and street vendors often indiscriminately dumped waste, leading to poor sanitation and the spread of infectious diseases (Teo 2004, 7). But the campaign also sought to change social beliefs and norms for cleanliness and to create a sense of shared ownership and identity of the territorial space that constituted the nation-state (Teo 2004; Ong 2016).

The Singapore government kicked off its efforts for a clean city with a month-long publicity campaign, with advertisements aimed not only at keeping the city clean but also at encouraging active participation by citizens in the campaign itself. In addition to getting the message out with televised pro-motions, posters, songs, and stickers, the government launched a cleanliness competition and organized "sweeping brigades" to clean streets and other common areas (Keep Singapore Clean Campaign, National Library Board). The success of the campaign was evident in widespread participation as well as events organized independently of those sponsored by the national govern-ment (Tan et al. 2015, 54–55).

In the context of cultural change and nation-building, these early efforts are clearly individual-oriented nudges. And, in changing individual behavior, they were successful. Participation was widespread: individuals joined the move-ment and took action to clean up the city. Using the idea of institutional sticki-ness (Boettke et al. 2008) as an indicator of likely success, this makes sense. Although this was by far the most ambitious cleanliness campaign undertaken by the government, it was not the first time that Singapore's leaders had encouraged inhabitants to keep the city clean (Lim 2015, 313). It also aligned with the interests of residents to address a real public health need while operat-ing well within the cultural limits of the population. In short, asking people to "bin litter" did not violate existing beliefs or sociocultural norms.

But Keep Singapore Clean was about more than simply addressing "incon-siderate littering" and public health concerns, and instead aimed, as the prime minister explained his speech, to change social beliefs. As he put it, "[t] his campaign marks the raising of our social targets. Not only our young in schools, but also our adults must learn new habits" (Lee 1968). He contin-ues, "[a]s standards of social behaviour rise, so social pressures will increase against anti-social behaviour of the unthinking or the incorrigible" (Lee 1968). Indeed, in addition to the positive reinforcements of friendly radio jingles and encouragement, the government recognized that a lasting shift in behavior would have to be paired with consequences. Thus, after the initial month-long warm-up period which included only warnings of potential future consequences for behavior like littering, the government enacted fines and other penalties (Keep Singapore Clean Campaign, National Library Board). Here, the campaign functions as a group-oriented nudge. The prime minister has laid out clear ideas about citizenship and appropriate behavior with the objective to socialize environmentally aware behaviors and inculcate them into the national identity.

As a group-oriented nudge, the Keep Singapore Clean campaign also visually unifies the state through the physical alteration of space, mani-fested not only in clean streets but also the state-wide project of creating a "Garden City." Those changes, including moving street vendors to central-ized locations, removing old housing stock, and cleaning up Singapore's rivers, removed historical and ethnic reminders and replaced them with uniform spatial landscapes. That imposition of order also replaced existing communities and historic markers with common references to Singapore's modern identity. As Harvey explains, such aspirations for a physical environment are really "proposals for social change" (1996, 119). Nations, after all, are defined in part by their territory and the relationship of the nation to that land. Thus, spatial unification can be considered a nudge because it seeks to induce the desired behavior (identification with the nation) through specific cues (here, the physical landscape).

These group-oriented nudges toward both social beliefs about cleanliness and (implicitly) national identity were successful. Although not all projects initially enjoyed full popular support as they disrupted lifestyles, eventually they saw widespread buy-in, as citizens felt the benefits and understood themselves to be the beneficiaries. That meant that, as Ong puts it:

> "Molding the idea of 'cleaning' and 'greening' into people's attitudes through education has formed a vital part of building a cohesive national mindset" (2016, 7). Teo echoes a similar position, explaining that these efforts were an effective way to "'socialize' the general public into what the government deemed to be 'socially correct' behavior." (2004, 10)

Likewise, the creation of a unified landscape as an element of national identity was successful in creating shared spaces as a tool of nation-building. As Ong explains,

> The formation of this "clean and green" national identity has encouraged social integration and distracted people from issues of racial, cultural and demographic differences. Hence, the apparent negativity if the loss of heritage and cultural diversity could perhaps be considered a positive in that it helped develop a sense of unity among the multiracial society of Singapore. (2016, 4–33)

These group-oriented nudges of the campaign successfully molded how Singaporeans saw themselves and how outsiders saw the city-state. Indeed, a broader aim of the campaign was to instill both ownership and "a sense of pride among Singaporeans in their newly independent country" (Teo 2004, 26). Acceptance of those values and participation in this national identity, of course, remained optional and avoidable; those who did not wish to take the values as their own or see themselves within this national identity did not have to do so. These ambitious group-oriented nudges that aimed to change culture and identity worked because they were within the existing social and cultural framework, aligned with the interests of the population and built on existing institutions and behaviors.

Institutional change, even when guided by skilled choice architects, however, remains susceptible to new influences. Although Singapore internalized its reputation as a clean city, the work of cleaning changed as Singapore became wealthier. Instead of relying on citizens, inexpensive foreign labor could now be hired to do the work. Recent reporting indicates that despite the emphasis on keeping the city clean, Singapore is not so much a clean city, but a "cleaned city" where the cleanliness is the result of employing clearers to meet now-accepted social standards. In 2018, the chairman of the Public Hygiene Council explained that this cleaning cost 87 million USD a year, an expenditure that could largely be avoided (and redirected to other priorities) if individuals did more cleaning themselves (McDonald 2018). While norms and expectations changed, individual habits have diverged. This suggests that cultural changes in expectations (the result of group-oriented nudges) may be more "sticky" than individual action (the result of nudges aimed at individuals). In short, people will continue to expect their country to live up to the values they have embraced long after they themselves stop acting on those values.

SPEAK MANDARIN

Language is a key component of identity and particularly important for fostering a shared national and cultural understanding (Hill and Lian 1995, 79). This is both practical, for instance, a group must be able to communicate with other members, and abstract, since individuals are more likely to see as "other" those who do not share a common tongue (Hobsbawm 1996). In newly formed Singapore, the prevalence of dialects spoken by the Chinese population was of particular concern to the People's Action Party who viewed the linguistic diversity as a barrier to establishing the nation-state (Kuo and Jernudd 1994). To address this, the government launched the Speak Mandarin campaign in 1979 to promote the use of standardized Chinese as a "mother tongue" (the primary language spoken at home). In his 1986 National Day address, Prime Minister Lee reflected on the campaign:

> We intervene with Mandarin, promoted it and asked people to drop dialects. Big uproar. It was the right decision. If we had not done that then the teaching of Mandarin in school must fail. It was interference in a personal preserve. Intervention. But it was necessary intervention. 1980 we stopped all television broadcasts in dialects. Grave unhappiness . . . 1986, all the old folk now can understand Mandarin. They may not speak it, but they watch the programs and understand what is going on. So, it has succeeded. (National Day Rally 1986)

The "Speak Mandarin" campaign included actions that can clearly be considered individual nudges meant to shape the behavior of citizens: distribution of pamphlets with Mandarin Chinese expressions, free dial-in Mandarin lessons, daily vocabulary printed in newspapers, and posters bearing phrases such as "Start with Mandarin not Dialect" and "Mandarin is Chinese" (Teo 2005; Newman 2010, 446). As Lee's remarks make clear, it also included more heavy-handed measures meant to normalize beliefs about language and identity, a type of group-oriented nudge.

As the prime minister acknowledged, individual-oriented nudges were not as successful as the government had hoped—especially among older generations. As he notes, even cutting television shows broadcast in dialects (which is decidedly not a nudge, but instead a ban) did not push people to speak Mandarin. Lacking other options, they watched Mandarin television and continued speaking dialects at home. This result is not surprising; the older generation had little need for Mandarin and learning it was not within their interest.

The campaign, however, was much more successful among the children of Singapore's Chinese population as demonstrated by overall shifts in language use. In 1980, one year after the program began, 59.5 percent of all Singaporeans spoke a Chinese dialect as their primary language with only 10.2 percent speaking Mandarin. By 2000, the number of Singaporeans speaking a Chinese dialect as their primary language had dropped to 23.8 percent, with speakers of Mandarin at 35 percent (Cavallaro and Ng 2014, 34). By 2015, just 12.2 percent of Singaporeans reported speaking Chinese dialects at home while 34.9 percent reported speaking Mandarin (General Household Survey 2015, 10).

Those results are intuitive. Speaking Mandarin at home had clear benefits in terms of education and professional opportunities for younger Singaporeans, while for parents, speaking Mandarin with their children likewise had clear social and economic benefits. As previous literature suggests, the success of a nudge is dependent on its alignment with the interest of the population.

As a group-oriented nudge meant to normalize Mandarin and foster a bilingual (Mandarin/English-speaking) society, the Speak Mandarin campaign's results were mixed. Government promotion of Chinese was seen as marginalizing other ethnic and linguistic groups (e.g., Malay-speakers and speakers of Chinese dialects and Indian languages) within Singapore. Even within the Chinese population, the campaign met with criticism as "it created a tension between Mandarin as the officially sanctioned means of cultural transmission and the dialects with which most Chinese had emotional affiliations" (Teo 2005, 31).

Moreover, the nation-building effects of the Speak Mandarin campaign were largely superseded by another language campaign meant to promote English. Indeed, far from creating a shared, bilingual identity among Singaporeans, these dueling efforts divided the nascent nation between often better educated and better paid English speakers and those primarily speaking Chinese (Tan 2003, 758–762). Although a degree of social cohesion emerged among Mandarin speakers and, separately English speakers, this alone did not achieve the desired outcome of a shared, bilingual Singaporean identity.

The Speak Mandarin campaign and subsequent campaigns promoting English developed national unity and individual linguistic skills. These campaigns, however, like other attempts to privilege some linguistic expressions and silence others, exacted a social cost. On an individual level, the children of Chinese immigrants who did not grow up learning the dialects spoken by their grandparents are unable to share that linguistic bond or, on a practical level, communicate with their own families (Gupta and Siew 1995). Socially, dialect-speaking communities suffered a loss of vibrancy and identity through what Rappa and Wee have termed "linguistic sacrifice"; social ties to family and community in China were diminished (2007).

Despite the success of the campaign at changing individual behaviors among younger Singaporeans, attempts to foster national identity through creating new language norms were far less successful. This suggests that (despite language's importance in self-identity) developing real communal or national bonds requires more than just encouraging a new language. For nation-building choice architects, this suggests that to realize goals of identity formation, successfully nudging individual behavior is not sufficient.

TWO IS ENOUGH

The most famous family-planning program in the world is China's now-discontinued one-child policy. But Singapore also experimented with encouraging small families and limited childbearing. Singapore, unlike China, never mandated limits on family size but did encourage small families with posters, slogans, advertisements, and, eventually, incentives (Kanagaratnam 1968).

Faced with a postwar baby boom, Singapore faced real challenges in providing food, housing, and other basic needs for its citizens. The government saw limiting family size as a way to better distribute scarce resources among its citizens and curtail overcrowding (Swee-Hock 1980, 348–349). Among the programs undertaken under the National Family Planning Programme was a publicity campaign to encourage women to accept government-provided family-planning services. This was clearly an individual-oriented nudge to encourage women to take the necessary steps to have smaller families. The government started radio shows, offered free family-planning services, and distributed posters and pamphlets to the public. These outreach campaigns were successful within the first year: the goal of providing family-planning services to 25,000 women in 1966 had been exceeded, with more than 30,000 women accepting these services that year (*The Straits Times* 1966, 16). Since the postwar era meant shortages for not just the government but also families, that women would respond well to government marketing of family planning is unsurprising. The nudge aligned with individual interest.

In 1970, the government launched the "Two is Enough" campaign, as the name implies, to encourage parents to have only two children (Quah 1981, 39). This effort, in addition to changing individual behavior, was aimed at social perceptions about the "right" number of children to have. As Quah (1981, 39) puts it, the campaign focused on "the suggestion of an 'appropriate' behavior" and sought to instill among Singaporeans that having two or fewer children was a social responsibility (Wan and Loh 1979, 103).

This normalization is evident in slogans like "Small Family: Brighter Future" (Seng and Cheong 2013, 2) and posters that played into familial obligations and national responsibility. One poster, for example, stated that "small families enjoy better health" with fine print adding "Singapore wants all married couples to have no more than two children so that there will be food, work, a home and security for everyone" (Small families enjoy better health, Singapore Family Planning and Population Board). In addition, beginning in 1972 the government introduced significant disincentives—heavy-handed nudges—for those with more than two children, including loss of maternity leave, no priority for public housing, and lower priority for education. Having more than two children, however, was never banned (Yap and Gee 2015, 10). By 1975, the birth rate had dropped to the natural replacement rate, indicating that government efforts had successfully changed individual behavior (Yap and Gee 2015, 4). To be sure, it is likely that as more women entered the workforce and Singapore rapidly developed, birth rates would have fallen even without a nudge from the government (Wong and Yeoh 2003, 8). This likelihood reinforces that the success of nudges is determined by what the nudged population already wants or has a propensity to do.

On a group level, the campaign was also successful in changing cultural norms about an appropriate family size. When, starting in 1987, the government tried to nudge both individuals and broader social beliefs in the other direction with a new campaign emphasizing, "Have Three or More, if You Can Afford It," those efforts were far less successful despite heavy incentives (Wong and Yeoh 2003, 12). As other research has demonstrated, this is likely because there were no significant reasons for families to change their existing views on family and have more children, especially in light of Singapore's increasingly high cost of living and work-related pressures for mothers and fathers.

In sum, both individual-oriented nudges toward smaller family sizes and the group-oriented nudges aimed at normalizing small families fit within the needs and inclinations of Singaporeans, making them successful. Conversely, efforts to shift cultural norms of family size without changing other underlying factors proved much less successful, as it is more difficult to change individual behavior or remake cultural understandings of "ideal" family size in the absence of a preexisting need or inclination to do so.

ANALYSIS AND CONCLUSION

This chapter has attempted to fill a gap in the existing literature by examining nudges as a tool of institutional and cultural change within the context of nations. As the case studies drawn from Singapore's nation-building demonstrate, nudges are a useful lens through which to understand attempts to shift individual and group behavior. The framework of individual-oriented nudges and group-oriented nudges highlights how government efforts to promote social shifts must be understood both in terms of the relationship between the government and individual citizens and between the government and the general population of citizens.

As the case studies demonstrate, changes in individual behavior are not necessarily linked to changes in identity. The Singaporean government was able to successfully promote individuals speaking Mandarin without fostering a shared identity through a common language. Likewise, the Singaporean government was able to foster a persistent sense of collective ownership over the city without creating similar long-term shifts in individual cleanliness. With the family-planning campaign, however, the government was able to institute successful individual- and group-oriented nudges in tandem resulting in persistent ("sticky") changes to both individual behavior and social norms.

These results are consistent with the expected limitations suggested by the literature on institutional change, nation-building, and ideological entrepreneurship. The success of nudges, even from powerful state actors acting as choice architects, is limited by existing conditions. Nudges require a social buy-in. Attempts at national or institutional culture change—or even more narrowly defined social change—cannot simply be top-down projects of elites or ideological entrepreneurs acting as "choice architects." Rather, nudges' success is determined by complex interactions between those doing the nudging and the nudged. In the context of a nation, this interaction is between the government and the governed, the power of any given nudge limited by what its recipients are willing to accept. In other words, nudges must have some measure of support from the nudged.

For critics of nudge theory who worry that behavioral economics could be used to enact sweeping change without the consent of the nudged population, this should be a relief. If the nudge reflects existing norms and institutions that are already accepted, at least to some degree, by the nudged population at the individual and group levels, then the nudge is more likely to be successful. Conversely, if an attempted nudge reflects a radical departure from the nudged population's preexisting values (or social and economic needs and incentives), a choice architect is much more likely to meet more resistance and achieve less success.

Nudges clearly have powerful explanatory power for modeling how nation-building and identity formation occurs. This model, especially as applied within Austrian models of understanding culture and entrepreneurship, can help us understand what nation-building efforts (and other institutional changes) are likely to succeed and which are likely to fail.

Finally, this chapter leaves open several possibilities for future research on the nature of nudges and their limits. For example, are group-oriented nudges really nudges? Can nudges create incremental change on the path to radical social transformation? Can group-oriented nudges also model radicalization? What other examples of government or institutional applications of nudges might challenge the conclusions here? Are there instances where nudges are more or less subject to these limits? Additionally, several concepts touched on here deserve further treatment. Among them are the role of the ideological entrepreneur in the context of nation-building and state-making, the process of cultural investment, and differences between commercial and ideological markets.

NOTES

1. Although Durkheim's (2012) work on social integration applied to the development of class, similar ways to understand cohesion are applicable to nations. In the process of nation-building, what Durkheim termed *mechanical* solidarity (shared beliefs and perceived commonality) and *organic* solidarity (interdependence) are both fostered by the state-builders.

2. To understand how this necessary identity formation works in practice, it is helpful to see how internal and external identities are used in the private sector. Private firms, like nations, need to foster both internal and external identities. Internally, firms seek to develop a shared sense of purpose, trustworthiness, and camaraderie among employees, so that they can effectively work together and, ultimately, benefit the firm. Put another way, firms seek to create a sense of belonging among employees that leads them to consider the firm as part of their identity. Externally, firms also seek to develop a unique brand identity that allows outsiders to distinguish them from their competition and thus better appeal to potential consumers. Firms clearly view developing these forms of identity as worthwhile investments. This is demonstrated

by company expenditures on parties, retreats, team-building workshops, and similar efforts to encourage employees to identify with coworkers and the company. External identity is likewise developed through brand identity campaigns, logos, marketing campaigns, and public relations efforts.

3. To offer a somewhat contrived example of investment in culture, consider video games (such as the *Civilization* series) where investing in cultural institutions offers added bonuses when it comes to physical defense (Cook 2014). Stronger cultural bonds not only make for more efficient communication but also form thicker bonds of community less likely to break when threatened by outside forces, which fits with the existing political theory literature.

4. Among the other policies mentioned in the prime minister's speech was the National Courtesy Campaign. With songs, posters, and other advertisements, the government encouraged people to be kind to each other and visitors to the country. There was no legal penalty for being mean and no reward for practicing everyday kindness, thus qualifying these efforts as a nudge. For a critical look at details of the campaign and how it has changed over time, see Lazar's article, "Semiosis, social change and governance: a critical semiotic analysis of a national campaign" (2003).

REFERENCES

Afif, Zeina. 2017. "'Nudge Units'—Where They Came From and What They Can Do." *World Bank Blogs.* https://blogs.worldbank.org/developmenttalk/nudge-units -where-they-came-and-what-they-can-do.

Akerlof, George and Robert Shiller. 2015. *Phishing for Phools: The Economics of Manipulation and Deception.* Princeton: Princeton University Press.

Alesina, Alberto, and Nicola Fuchs-Schündeln. 2007. "Goodbye Lenin (or Not?): The Effect of Communism on People." *American Economic Review* 97, no. 4: 1507–1528.

Alesina, Alberto, and Paola Giuliano. 2015. "Culture and Institutions." *Journal of Economic Literature* 53, no. 4: 898–944.

Anderson, Benedict. 1983. *Imagined Communities: Reflections on the Origins and Spread of Nationalism.* London: Verso.

Anholt, Simon. 2006. "Why Brand? Some Practical Consideration for Nation Branding." *Place Branding* 2: 97–107.

Austin, J., H. Stevenson, and J. Wei-Skillern. 2006. "Social and Commercial Entrepreneurship: Same, Different, or Both?" *Entrepreneurship Theory and Practice* 30, no. 1: 1–22.

Beng, Ooi Kee. 2011. "GOH KENG SWEE: Thinker and Institution Builder." *Southeast Asian Affairs*: 271–283.

Bernays, Edward L. 1928. *Propaganda.* New York: H. Liveright.

Bilz, Kenworthey and Nadler, Janice. 2014. "Law, Moral Attitudes, and Behavioral Change." In *Oxford Handbook of Behavioral Economics & the Law*, edited by Eyal Zamir and Doron Teichman, 241–267. Oxford: Oxford University Press.

Boettke, P. J., C. J. Coyne, and P. T. Leeson. 2008. "Institutional Stickiness and the New Development Economics." *American Journal of Economics and Sociology* 67: 331–358.

Cavallaro, Francesco and Bee Chin Ng. 2014. "Language in Singapore: From Multilingualism to English Plus." In *Challenging the Monolingual Mindset,* edited by John Hajek and Yvette Slaughter, 33–48. Bristol: Multilingual Matters.

Chaiken, S., and M. W. Baldwin. 1981. "Affective-Cognitive Consistency and the Effect of Salient Behavioral Information on the Self-Perception of Attitudes." *Journal of Personality and Social Psychology* 41, no. 1: 1–12.

Chamlee-Wright, Emily, and Justus A. Myers. 2008. "Discovery and social learning in non-priced environments: An Austrian view of social network theory." *The Review of Austrian Economics* 21: 151–166.

Chamlee-Wright, Emily, and Virgil Henry Storr. 2010. "The Role of Social Entrepreneurship in Post-Katrina Community Recovery." *International Journal of Innovation and Regional Development* 2: 149–164.

Clendinnen, Inga. 2002. *Reading the Holocaust.* Cambridge: Cambridge University Press.

Cook, Karen. 2014. "Music, History, and Progress in Sid Meier's Civilization IV." In *Music in Video games; Studying Play,* edited by K.J. Donnelly, William Gibbons and Neil Lerner. New York and London: Routledge.

Department of Statistics Singapore. 2015. General Household Survey. Department of Statistics Singapore. https://www.singstat.gov.sg/media/files/publications/ghs/ghs2015/ghs2015.pdf.

Diggs-Brown, Barbara. 2011. *Strategic Public Relations: Audience Focused Practice.* Boston: Wadsworth Cengage Learning.

Durkheim, Emile. 2012. *The Division of Labour in Society.* Translated by George Simpson. Mansfield: Martino Publishing.

Gellner, Ernest. 1983. *Nations and Nationalism.* New York: Cornell University Press.

Goldstein, N. J., and R. B. Cialdini. 2007. "The Spyglass Self: A Model of Vicarious Self-Perception." *Journal of Personality and Social Psychology* 92, no. 3: 402–417.

Guiso, Luigi, Paola Sapienza and Luigi Zingales. 2016. "Long-Term Persistence." *Journal of the European Economic Association* 14, no. 6: 1401–1436.

Güntner, Anna and Julia Sperling. 2017. "How to Nudge Your Way to Better Performance." *Leadership & Organization Blog.* McKinsey & Company. https://www.mckinsey.com/business-functions/organization/our-insights/the-organization-blog/how-to-nudge-your-way-to-better-performance.

Gupta, A and Siew, P.K. 1995. "Language Shift in a Singapore Family." *Journal of Multilingual and Multicultural Development* 16, no. 4: 301–313.

Halonen, Elina. 2013. "In the Wild: Rory Sutherland." *In Decision: Inside Decision Making Science.* https://indecisionblog.com/2013/03/18/in-the-wild-rory-sutherland/.

Harrison, Henrietta. 2001. *China: Inventing the Nation.* London: Arnold.

Harvey, David. 1996. *Justice, Nature and the Geography of Difference.* Cambridge: Blackwell.

Hill, Michael and Lian Kwen Fee. 1995. *The Politics of Nation Building and Citizenship in Singapore.* London: Routledge.

Hirschman, Elizabeth C. 1983. "Aesthetics, Ideologies and the Limits of the Marketing Concept." *Journal of Marketing* 47, no. 3: 45–55.

Hobsbawm, Eric. 1983. "Introduction: Inventing Traditions." In *The Invention of Tradition,* edited by Eric Hobsbawm and Terence Ranger, 1–14. Cambridge: Cambridge University Press.

———. 1996. "Language, Culture, and National Identity." *Social Research* 63, no. 4 (Winter): 1065–80.

Hroch, Miroslav. 1996. "From National Movement to the Fully-formed Nation: The Nation-building Process in Europe." In *Mapping the Nation*, edited by Gopal Balakrishnan. New York and London: Verso.

John, Arielle. 2015. "Culture as a Constitution." In *Culture and Economic Action*, edited by Laura E. Grube and Virgil Henry Storr, 225–242. Cheltenham and Northampton: Edward Elgar Publishing.

Kanagaratnam, K. 1968. "Singapore: The National Family Planning Program." *Studies in Family Planning* 1, no. 28: 1–11.

Kathirithamby-Wells, J. 1969. "Early Singapore and the Inception of a British Administrative Tradition In the Straits Settlements (1819—1832)." *Journal of the Malaysian Branch of the Royal Asiatic Society* 42: 48–73.

Keating, Sarah. 2018. "The Nation that Thrived by 'Nudging' its Population." *BBC*. 20 February. https://www.bbc.com/future/article/20180220-the-nation-that-thrived -by-nudging-its-population.

Keep Singapore Clean Campaign, National Library Board. National Government of Singapore. http://eresources.nlb.gov.sg/infopedia/articles/SIP_1160_2008-12-05 .html.

Kirzner, Israel M. 1973. *Competition and Entrepreneurship.* Chicago: University of Chicago Press.

Kuo, C.Y. and Jernudd, B.H. 1994. "Balancing Macro and Micro-Sociolinguistic Perspectives in Language Management: The Case of Singapore." In *English and Language Planning: A Southeast Asian contribution,* edited by T. Kandiah & J. Kwan-Terry. Singapore: Times Academic Press.

Kwok J. 2015. "Memories of the Japanese Occupation: Singapore's First Official Second World War Memorial and the Politics of Commemoration." In *Japan as the Occupier and the Occupied*, edited by C. de Matos and M. E. Caprio. London: Palgrave Macmillan.

Lavoie, Don and Emily Chamlee-Wright. 2000. *Culture and Enterprise.* New York: Routledge.

Lazar, Michelle M. 2003. "Semiosis, Social Change and Governance: A Critical Semiotic Analysis of a National Campaign." *Social Semiotics* 13, no. 2: 201–221.

Lee Kuan Yew. 1968. Speech by the Prime Minister Inaugurating the "Keep Singapore Clean" Campaign on Tuesday, October 1, 1968. National Archives of Singapore Online. http://www.nas.gov.sg/archivesonline/data/pdfdoc/lky19681001.pdf.

Lee Kuan Yew. 1986. Singapore National Day Rally. August 9, 1986. Video Recording. National Archives of Singapore Online. https://www.nas.gov.sg/ar chivesonline/audiovisual_records/record-details/48aabfb1-1164-11e3-83d5-005 0568939ad.

Leifer, Michael. 1964. "Communal Violence in Singapore. *Asian Survey* 4, no. 10: 1115–1121.

———. 1972. *Dilemmas of statehood in Southeast Asia.* Vancouver: University of British Columbia Press.

Lemay-Hébert, Nicolas. 2009. "Statebuilding without Nation-building? Legitimacy, State Failure and the Limits of the Institutionalist Approach." *Journal of Intervention and Statebuilding* 3: 21–45.

Lepenies, Robert and Magdalena Malecka. 2015. "The Institutional Consequences of Nudging—Nudges, Politics, and the Law." *Review of Philosophy and Psychology* 6, no. 3: 427–437.

Lim, Linda Y.C. 2015. *Singapore's Economic Development: Retrospection and Reflections.* New Jersey: World Scientific.

Marsden, William E. 2000. "'Poisoned History': A Comparative Study of Nationalism, Propaganda and the Treatment of War and Peace in the Late Nineteenth and Early Twentieth Century School Curriculum." *History of Education* 29, no. 1: 29–47.

McDonald, Tim. 2018. "The Cost of Keeping Singapore Squeaky Clean: What did it Take for this Sovereign-City State to Become Asia's Cleanest, Greenest Metropolis?" *BBC.* 28 October 2018. https://www.bbc.com/worklife/article/20181025-the-cost-of -keeping-singapore-squeaky-clean.

Mitchell, Gregory. 2005. "Libertarian Paternalism is an Oxymoron." *Northwestern University Law Review* 99, no. 3: 1245–1277.

Newman, John. 1988. "Singapore's Speak Mandarin Campaign." *Journal of Multilingual and Multicultural Development* 9, no. 5: 437–448.

North, Douglass C. 1981. *Structure and Change in Economic History.* New York: W. W. Norton.

———.1990. *Institutions, Institutional Change, and Economic Performance.* Cambridge: Cambridge University Press.

———.1994. "Economic Performance Through Time." *The American Economic Review* 84, no. 3: 359–368.

Ong, Jun Yi. 2016. *Building the Garden City: The Clean and Green Movement in Singapore, 1965-2010.* University of Sydney: Faculty of Architecture, Design & Planning. http://hdl.handle.net/2123/14710.

Ortmann, Stephan. 2009. "Singapore: The Politics of Inventing National Identity." *Journal of Current Southeast Asian Affairs* 28: 23–46.

Putnam, Robert D. 1993. *Making Democracy Work: Civic Traditions in Modern Italy.* Princeton: Princeton University Press.

Quah, S. R. 1981. "Impact of Policy on the Family: Can the Family Be Strengthened by Legislation?" *Southeast Asian Journal of Social Science* 9, no. 1–2: 33–53.

Raftopoulou, Effi and Margaret K. Hogg. 2010. "The Political Role of Government-Sponsored Social Marketing Campaigns." *European Journal of Marketing* 44, no. 7/8: 1206–1227.

Rappa, A., and L. Wee. 2007. *Language Policy and Modernity in Southeast Asia.* New York: Springer.

Schumpeter, Joseph Alois. 1943. *Capitalism, Socialism and Democracy.* New York and London: Routledge.

Scull, N. C., C. D. Mbonyingabo, and M. Kotb. 2016. "Transforming Ordinary People into Killers: A Psychosocial Examination of Hutu Participation in the Tutsi Genocide." *Peace and Conflict: Journal of Peace Psychology* 22, no. 4: 334–344.

Seng, Lim Tin and Kha Kit Cheong. 2013. "Singapore: A City of Campaigns." *IFLA WLIC Singapore*. http://library.ifla.org/137/1/161-seng-en.pdf.

"Small families enjoy better health." 1967–1969. Singapore Family Planning and Population Board. Poster. National Archives of Singapore Online. https://www.nas.gov.sg/archivesonline/posters/record-details/307dcb92-115c-11e3-83d5-0050568939ad.

Smith, Anthony D. 1986. "State-Making and Nation-Building." In *States in History*, edited by John Hall, 228–263. Oxford: Basil Blackwell.

———.1988. "The Myth of the 'Modern Nation' and the Myths of Nations." *Ethnic and Racial Studies* 11, no. 1: 1–25.

———. 1996. "The Origins of Nations." In *Becoming National: A Reader,* edited by Geoff Eley and Ronald Grigor Suny, 106–131. New York: Oxford University Press.

Spector, Stanley. 1956. "Students and Politics in Singapore." *Far Eastern Survey* 25, no. 5: 65–73.

Storr, Virgil Henry. 2011. "North's Underdeveloped Ideological Entrepreneur." *The Annual Proceedings of the Wealth and Well-Being of Nations*, edited by Emily Chamlee-Wright: 99–115. Beloit: Beloit College Press.

———. 2013. *Understanding the Culture of Markets.* New York: Routledge.

———. 2015. "A critical appraisal of the concept of cultural capital." In *Culture and Economic Action,* edited by Laura E. Grube and Virgil Henry Storr, 204–244. Cheltenham and Northampton: Edward Elgar Publishing.

Sunstein, Cass. 2015. "The Ethics of Nudging." *Yale Journal on Regulation* 32: 413–449. https://digitalcommons.law.yale.edu/cgi/viewcontent.cgi?article=1415&context=yjreg.

Swedberg, R. 2006. "Social Entrepreneurship: The View of the Young Schumpeter." In *Entrepreneurship and Social Change,* edited by Daniels Hjorth and Chris Steyaert, 21–34. Cheltenham and Northampton: Edward Elgar Publishing.

Swee-Hock, Saw. 1980. "The Development of Population Control in Singapore." *Contemporary Southeast Asia* 1, no. 4: 348–366.

Tan, Eugene K. B. 2003. "Re-Engaging Chineseness: Political, Economic and Cultural Imperatives of Nation-Building in Singapore." *The China Quarterly* 175: 751–774.

Tan, Soon Yong, Tung Jean Lee and Karen Tan. 2015. *Clean, Green and Blue: Singapore's Journey Towards Environmental and Water Sustainability.* Singapore: ISEAS–Yusof Ishak Institute.

Teo, P. 2004. " 'Clean and Green—That's the Way We Like It': Greening a Country, Building a Nation." *Journal of Language and Politics, 3*, no. 3: 485–505.

———. 2005. "Mandarinising Singapore: A Critical Analysis of Slogans in Singapore's 'Speak Mandarin' campaign." *Critical Discourse Studies* 2, no. 2: 121–142.

Thaler, Richard and Cass Sunstein. 2009. *Nudge: Improving Decisions about Health, Wealth, and Happiness*. New York: The Penguin Group.

Tham, K. W. 1986. "National Campaigns." In *Singapore Taking Stock: Readings in General Paper*, edited by C. W. Ng, 41–57. Singapore: Federal Publications.

The Straits Times. 1966. "Birth Control Success." October 25, 1966: 16. National Library Board Singapore. https://eresources.nlb.gov.sg/newspapers/Digitised/Article/straitstimes19661025-1.2.30.

Turnbull, C. M. 1989. *A History of Singapore 1819—1988*, 2d edition. Singapore: Oxford University Press.

Tye, Larry. 2002. *The Father of Spin: Edward L. Bernays and the Birth of Public Relations*. New York: Henry Holt.

van Ham, Peter. 2001. "The Rise of the Brand State." *Foreign Affairs* (September/ October). https://www.foreignaffairs.com/articles/2001-09-01/rise-brand-state.

Wan, F. K. and M. T. F. Loh. 1979. "Fertility policies and the National Family Planning and Population Programme." In *Public Policy and Population change in Singapore*, edited by P. S. J. Chen and J. T. Fawcett, 97–108. New York: Population Council.

Wang Gungwu. 2005. *Contemporary and National History: A Double Challenge*. In *Nation-Building: Five Southeast Asian Histories*, edited by Wang Gungwu, 1–20. Singapore: ISEAS–Yusof Ishak Institute.

Weber, Eugen. 1976. *Peasants into Frenchmen: The Modernization of Rural France 1870–1914*. Stanford: Stanford University Press.

Wong, Theresa, and Brenda S. A. Yeoh. 2003. "Fertility and the Family: An Overview of Pro-natalist Population Policies in Singapore." *Asian MetaCentre Research Paper Series* 12: 1–25.

Yap, Mui Teng, and Christopher Gee. 2015. "Singapore's Demographic Transition, the Labor Force and Government Policies: The Last Fifty Years." *The Singapore Economic Review* 60, no. 3: 1–22.

Yeoh, Brenda S. A. 1993. "Urban Sanitation, Health and Water Supply in Late Nineteenth and Early Twentieth Century Colonial Singapore." *South East Asia Research* 1, no. 2: 143–172.

Yeung, Karen. 2012. "Nudge as Fudge." *The Modern Law Review* 75, no. 1: 122–148.

Chapter 6

Nudging Lobbyists to Register with Online Registration and Grace Periods

James M. Strickland

Lobbyists are people who try to influence government policy by meeting with lawmakers or testifying before legislative hearings. Their influence on law-makers raises concerns over democratic accountability. Successful lobbyists might play a part in diverting policies away from the preferences of voters and toward their own desired ends. In response to these concerns and politi-cal scandals involving lobbyists, officials in the United States have enacted a variety of laws that attempt to disclose and regulate the activities of lobbyists. Many lobbyists, however, fail to register, thereby avoiding some disclosure requirements and regulations. Better lobbying laws might nudge more of these "shadow" agents into registering and disclosing their activities.

A challenge facing policymakers and political reformers today is the increasing presence of unregistered or "shadow" lobbyists. When lobbyists fail to register, members of the public lack information about who all are try-ing to influence their policymakers. Moreover, lobbyists who do not register are not required to report the details of their activities to ethics agencies and are not subject to special regulations that apply only to registered agents. There is increasing evidence that lobbyists choose whether to register in response to such regulations, and that policymakers face a trade-off between increasing registration rates and regulating the activities of registered agents. Thus, there is a trade-off between lobby transparency and regulation.

Transparency may play a role in ensuring greater alignment between public opinion, policies, and subverting the efforts of lobbyists seeking particularis-tic benefits or rents (see Tullock 1967; Krueger 1974). Most interest groups active within government consist of private interests seeking particularistic benefits such as subsidies and tax or regulatory exemptions (see Olson 1965; Gray and Lowery 2001). As opposed to collective benefits such as clean air or national defense, particularistic benefits affect specific economic sectors or individuals more than others. Transparency of lobbying activities ensures that voters, reporters, and public-interest advocates (e.g., Common Cause[1]) have information regarding rent-seeking activities. Voters, reporters, and public-interest advocates cannot counter rent-seeking activities without reliable information about lobbying. Rent-seeking lobbyists (and rent-granting lawmakers) have incentives to hide their activities from the public, but greater transparency may limit the degree to which these actors form mutualistic relationships. With successful rent-seeking, the provision of particularistic goods undermines economic growth and threatens the state provision of public goods or state preservation of common goods (see Tullock 1988).

This chapter explores one aspect of transparency: whether "nudges" can induce more lobbyists to register with government authorities. In general, nudges consist of small adjustments to the contexts and presentation of decisions. Changing how options are arranged and presented, or even changing default options, is an example of nudges. Nudges are a part of choice architecture and they are employed often by policymakers and employers to encourage citizens and consumers to make better, or more informed, decisions (see Thaler and Sunstein 2008). In the case of lobbyist registration, nudges consist of small adjustments to the costs and benefits of registering. If lobbyists can register and report their activities online, for example, then they can forgo the inconvenience of registering in person. If lobbyists can register days after first contacting lawmakers, including those who were unable or forgot to register prior to lobbying, then fewer will refuse to register late for fear of accruing fees and penalties. In this chapter, I present tests for whether online registration and grace periods are correlated with totals of registered interest groups and lobbyists. Whereas interest groups are organizations such as businesses and associations that hire lobbyists, lobbyists are the individuals who represent groups and communicate with lawmakers.

The remainder of this chapter begins with a normative discussion of the role of lobbyists in democratic governance, and how transparency can help deter lobbyists from skewing policy outcomes away from voter preferences. I then present a dilemma facing policymakers wherein they must choose between disclosing the activities of more lobbyists and regulating their activities directly. I outline several contemporary examples of the transparency-regulation trade-off. I then argue that nudges might be effective means for getting more lobbyists to register, thereby addressing the trade-off between transparency and regulation. Before testing these ideas empirically, I use a case study to show that one type of nudge—non-expiring registration—harms transparency. I find limited results that nudges (in the forms of online registration and longer grace periods) improve registration rates for lobbyists. Considering these findings, I suggest ultimately that getting more interest groups and lobbyists to register requires amending regulations of lobbying.

Rent-seeking lobbyists have incentives that are at odds with those of transparency advocates. Improved regulations remain the only effective means for improving registration rates.

LOBBYING AND DEMOCRATIC GOVERNANCE

In a democratic regime, policy outcomes ideally represent the preferences of the electorate. Otherwise, there is a misalignment between public opinion and policies. In deliberative settings such as legislative assemblies, there is potential for lobbyists or special-interest groups to influence elected lawmakers by meeting with them personally and persuading or pressuring them to shift policies away from the preferences of the public and toward those of the special interests. Thus, lobbyists, or special interests, can play a role in misaligning public policies and opinion and undermining representation. Special interests seek benefits from the government that benefit themselves or similar firms. Their interests in government pertain only to their insular activities. It is for this reason that such interests are referred to as "special." Indeed, lobbyists tend to represent businesses or special interests seeking particularistic benefits (e.g., subsidies, tax breaks, regulatory exemptions, or occupational protections; see Mitchell 2014). Whereas public-interest groups that consist of dues-paying members and that seek public goods (e.g., environmental protections, justice system reform) tend more often to rely on outside tactics such as letter-writing campaigns and protests (Kollman 1998; Strickland 2020). Hence, laws intended to limit the influence of lobbyists mostly affect the efforts of businesses or special interests rather than public-interest groups. Such laws can help balance the influence of competing interests and attempt to realign public opinion and policy.

For decades, political reformers have expressed concerns over and have attempted to limit the influence of lobbyists and special interests on elected policymakers. Particularly in the Gilded Age, reformist governors such as Robert La Follette of Wisconsin and Theodore Roosevelt of New York regularly denounced the influence of special-interest groups on legislators. Some of these governors were successful in encouraging legislators to adopt lobby transparency, but reform often came because of political scandal. Massachusetts was the first U.S. state to enact lobby transparency (Opheim 1991). In 1890, after a Boston street railway company flooded the legislature with paid lobbyists, public outcry led to lobby transparency (Quincy 1891). Later in New York, investigations revealed a variety of unethical business practices occurring within the Equitable Life Insurance Company. In response, Governor Frank Higgins encouraged legislators to adopt lobby transparency. New York enacted its first lobby law in 1906 (Zeller 1937,

251–53). Throughout the following decades, more states began to require lobbyists to register. By 1975, all U.S. states required registration.[2]

Social scientists have also criticized special interests for being unrepresentative of society at large. Schattschneider (1960) argued that interest groups active in Congress do not reflect every class of American society. Instead, such groups tend to reflect economic (i.e., business) and upper-class interests, and advocate for economically regressive policies. Olson (1965) later argued that interest groups active in government consist mostly of private interests (i.e., businesses and institutions) seeking particularistic benefits because it is otherwise difficult to mobilize individuals into joining groups that advocate for public goods. Schlozman, Verba, and Brady (2012) further confirmed that groups active in government hardly represent all the groups latent in American society.

Lobbyists can achieve influence more easily under two conditions. They need access to policymakers and staff to convey the interests of their clients. Lobbyists who have personal relationships with legislators and staff tend to get access more often (Crain 2018). As a result, lobbyists with insider connections deliver results for their clients more often (see Bertrand et al. 2014). Former members of U.S. Congress have personal relationships with their prior colleagues in Congress, and often become high-paid lobbyists (LaPira and Thomas 2017). Such "revolving-door" lobbyists have been found to represent mostly business interests in Congress and before regulatory agencies, and they deliver results (Makse 2017; Gormley 1979). There are also other ways to gain access than by serving in the legislature. Legislators tend to grant access based on campaign donations (Hall and Wayman 1990). It is common for lobbyists to make such donations (Drutman 2015, 93–96). Second, lobbyists can be influential when they lack any credible competition. Lobbyists operating in competitive political environments in which different interests compete for policy wins face greater incentives to temper their positions or attempt to form coalitions (Holyoke 2009). Without such competition, however, lobbyists are freer to seek benefits that their clients desire. Indeed, when examining a large sample of bills presented in the U.S. Congress and the kinds of interests actively lobbying on those bills, Baumgartner et al. (2009) found that groups spending the most on lobbyists won victories most often on bills where there was little or no opposition. Ultimately, even though rents may benefit special interests, it is costly to engage in effective lobbying. Revolving-door lobbyists are the highest-paid lobbyists in Congress, and campaign costs are increasing over time. Once rents are granted, companies have incentives to continue lobbying and donating to campaigns. Not doing so threatens profitability (as in Tullock 1975).

There are two different approaches to limiting the influence of lobbyists on policymakers. The first approach consists of making lobbying more transparent. This idea rests on the assumption that, in a democracy, the public interest is best served when political information is shared with voters (Lane 1964, 15). Disclosing lobby activities often involves requiring lobbyists to register and indicate which interests they represent. Some U.S. states also require lobbyists to report whom they meet with and the topics of their conversations. Ideally, these activities are disclosed and monitored by members of the public, including the press and organizations advocating for good government practices. Disclosure laws otherwise do not limit the efforts of lobbyists.

Transparency has the potential to stymie rent-seeking activities and improve the provision of public goods, and preservation of common goods. The provision of rents or particularistic benefits undermines the provision of public goods (non-rivalrous and non-excludable) or the preservation of common goods (non-excludable but rivalrous). Examples of public goods include protections of due process and civil liberties, and ethical standards in government. Given the potential for free-riding, public goods are most often provided by governments. Depending on the public good, governments need to levy taxes or impose regulations to ensure provision. Rent-seeking institutions desire exemptions from these costs. Examples of common goods include aquafers, and wild fish and game. Given the potential for overuse by various organizations or individuals, common resources are often protected by governments. Rent-seeking institutions may seek special access to such common resources, particularly the sole rights to extract natural resources. Transparency about rent-seeking activities allows members of the public and advocacy groups to identify policies in which rent-seeking is occurring, and to organize opposition movements. Various advocacy groups may mobilize in response. Examples include the American Civil Liberties Union, Common Cause, and the Sierra Club. Many of these groups can rally dues-paying members to pressure legislators.[3] Initial successes by these groups may also discourage legislators from awarding rents during later sessions, particularly by preventing the development of relationships with special-interest lobbyists. However, while transparency might limit the success of rent-seeking interests, it does not guarantee the provision of public goods or preservation of the commons, per se.

The second approach to limiting lobbyists' political influence consists of direct regulation of lobbying. Regulations limit or ban specific activities. Some U.S. states prevent lobbyists from making campaign contributions during legislative sessions. Other examples of regulation include limits on the value of meals or gifts that interests may purchase for lawmakers, limits on honoraria for speeches by lawmakers, and laws that prevent former lawmakers from lobbying immediately after retiring from office. Such regulations define ethical standards or conflicts of interest explicitly and hinder the development of politically mutualistic relationships between lobbyists and lawmakers. Agencies and committees responsible for implementing lobby regulations conduct audits, subpoena witnesses, and sometimes forward to attorneys general the names of offending lobbyists.

THE TRANSPARENCY-REGULATION TRADE-OFF

Governments around the world are increasingly turning to mandatory registration as a means to reveal the identities and activities of lobbyists (see Chari et al. 2010). Registration is the first step toward transparency. When lobbyists register, they provide state authorities with their names and the identities of clients. Registration is typically a simple task for lobbyists. Despite the simplicity of registration, however, new studies raise concerns over lobbyists failing to register. Lobbyists in Congress, U.S. state legislatures, and international legislatures have all been shown to skirt registration because of additional legal constraints or burdens that apply only to registered lobbyists. Studies show that lobby regulations that apply only to registered agents affect registration rates among lobbyists and interest groups (Thomas and LaPira 2017; Strickland 2019).

Policymakers face a trade-off between disclosing more lobby activities and regulating them. While many governments try both approaches, the trade-off between transparency and regulation occurs when regulations apply only to registered lobbyists. When the activities of registered persons are limited, some lobbyists fail to register. Unregistered lobbyists are not required to report their activities to the government and public and can give campaign donations more freely (even if they disobey registration requirements). Such lobbyists are known as "shadow" agents (LaPira 2016). When lobbyists fail to register, transparency suffers because the public is not informed about the individuals and interests attempting to exercise influence. As outlined earlier, rent-seeking efforts may be more successful when watchdog groups, members of the public, and the media cannot retrieve information about organized lobbying.

The numbers of missing lobbyists can be identified by comparing registration data from both before and after the implementation of a new regulation, or by comparing data across political systems such as nations or states. After collecting biographical information on nearly 32,000 advocates listed on *Lobbyists.info*, and then using a variety of other sources to verify the nature and intensity of advocacy activities, Thomas and LaPira (2017) estimate that there are likely as many unregistered lobbyists active in Congress as registered ones. Former legislators are particularly adept at skirting lobbyist registration (LaPira 2016). Totals of registered lobbyists active in Congress began to decline after the enactment of the Honest Leadership and Open Government Act (HLOGA) of 2007 (Auble 2013). The act increased reporting requirements and placed new restrictions on former Congressional members and staff seeking to lobby. In addition, the Obama administration banned registered lobbyists from serving on federal advisory committees in 2009. As a result, some lobbyists promptly canceled their registrations (Bogardus and Leven 2012). These changes in registration totals reflect the transparency-regulation trade-off. When registered lobbyists become subject to additional regulations or restrictions, some of them choose not to register (LaPira and Thomas 2017, 191–201).

The gap between reported and actual lobbying also varies across U.S. states. The states differ in the kinds of regulations they impose on lobbyists. In some states, for example, registered lobbyists cannot make campaign donations during legislative sessions. In other states, former legislators must wait one or two years after leaving office before registering to lobby.[4] Upon examining totals of registered interest groups (not lobbyists) in all 50 states between 1988 and 2013, Strickland (2019) finds that totals are suppressed in states with heavier reporting burdens. His statistical analysis indicates that, after controlling for state size and other factors, there are at least some non-registered (shadow) interest groups in every state, and hundreds of such groups in large states. If one adds all the interest groups registered to lobby in the states from 2013, the total is approximately 58,000. When one also considers non-registered groups, Strickland's analysis implies that there are approximately 72,000 total groups actively lobbying: a nearly 25-percent difference. In other words, nearly one in every five interest groups active in state legislatures is not registered to lobby.

Lobby transparency is relatively new in countries beyond the United States. As of 2017, 16 countries have lobby registration processes of some kind (Crepaz 2017). Most of these laws were adopted after 2001. Registration is voluntary in some other countries (including the United Kingdom). Many member states of the European Union refuse to regulate lobbying despite the EU having published model laws. Since international standards for lobby registration vary significantly, comparing cross-country data proves difficult for statistical inference.

Given the simplicity of registering, why would some lobbyists fail to register? Many lobbyists prefer not to reveal their identities to the public or to competing interest groups. This is particularly true for those seeking rents or particularistic goods from the government. Lobbyists may also not register because the statutory definition of lobbying does not apply to their activities. The U.S. Lobbying Disclosure Act (LDA) of 1995, for example, requires only those who are paid to contact multiple officials and who spend more than 20 percent of their time lobbying to register. The third reason for non-registration is that registration might cause inconvenience. Registering might require paying a fee or, alternatively, trigger reporting requirements that would not otherwise apply. Importantly, registering may limit the abilities of lobbyists to make campaign donations (particularly during sessions) or give personal gifts to lawmakers. Thomas and LaPira (2017) and Strickland (2019) propose that laws or regulations that apply only to registered persons discourage some lobbyists from registering. Hence, while registering is the first step toward lobby transparency and might be a simple task, related regulations might prove too burdensome or inconvenient for some lobbyists.

USING NUDGES TO IMPROVE TRANSPARENCY

Nudges consist of "any aspect of choice architecture that alters people's behavior in a predictable way without forbidding any options or significantly changing their economic incentives" (Thaler and Sunstein 2008, 6). For Thaler and Sunstein, examples of nudges include rearranging the order of items on grocery store shelves or at buffets, or changing the default insurance or pension options for new or continuing employees. These changes must be made with the goal of improving the decision maker's well-being in mind, such as encouraging healthier eating or more responsible financial planning. Thaler and Sunstein consider nudges to be part of a larger movement that they call "libertarian paternalism." They argue that individual people tend not to make wise decisions that ensure long-term health, wealth, or happiness, and that policymakers simply cannot avoid having to make decisions over how options are presented to consumers. They also argue that paternalistic nudges do not include forms of coercion.

Nudges often involve marginal decisions. These decisions involve little upfront cost or benefit and are typically made quickly. For example, choosing items from a lunch buffet is often a simple, straightforward task that is (ideally!) performed quickly. Yet, the cumulative effects of healthy or unhealthy eating come slowly. Thaler and Sunstein (2008, 40–74) emphasize that individuals often suffer from short time horizons whenever considering tangible, immediate options. For this reason, people are inclined to choose unhealthy food options. Nevertheless, the items on lunch buffets can be rearranged to encourage healthier eating. In general, then, nudges involve encouraging people to consider the cumulative, long-term effects of short-term decisions, and thereby "nudging" them to consider options they otherwise would ignore.

Nudging lobbyists into registering may help improve registration rates. For lobbyists, choosing to register is typically a marginal decision that involves slight short-term costs or inconvenience. Registration does not directly affect lobbyists' activities, but it might be too difficult or inconvenient for some lobbyists. Nudges can change the context of, or costs related to, registering. The accessibility of registration might explain differences in rates. Procedures are more convenient for registrants if they can register online or after they have begun to engage in lobbying. Online registration allows lobbyists to register from a home or office computer. If lobbyists cannot register online, then they must travel to a state agency and register during business hours. This might prove too inconvenient for lobbyists to consider. Moreover, if lobbyists can register without penalty *after* they started lobbying, then this grants lobbyists more flexibility over when to register. With grace periods, negligent lobbyists who initially forget to register prior to lobbying might also be more likely to register later. As nudges, online registration and grace periods for lobbyists might therefore improve registration rates.

CASE STUDY: A NUDGE THAT HURTS TRANSPARENCY

While some nudges might help transparency, at least one kind of nudge undermines it. Nudges sometimes include changing default options. Each year at the University of Chicago, for example, employees can make new selections regarding their insurance and pension contribution amounts. These decisions are made online. For those who neglect to confirm their current choices for the next calendar year, contribution amounts revert to nearly zero. Thaler and Sunstein (2008, 11) argue that the default option should instead be "same as last year." Making this adjustment would lead to fewer employees inadvertently making irresponsible financial decisions. In the context of lobbyist registration, such a nudge would allow lobbyists to remain registered from year to year without having to reregister. This is currently the practice of the U.S. Congress and state of Michigan. Lobbyists are not required to resubmit registration forms each year, but they are required to submit lobby disclosure reports while registered (even if they did not engage in lobbying). All other U.S. states currently require lobbyists to renew their registrations during each legislative session.

   While not requiring lobbyists to reregister each year might increase the numbers of registered lobbyists, this practice undermines transparency. When lobbyists are no longer required to reregister, it becomes more difficult for members of the public to identify the lobbyists and interest groups that are active during each legislative session, including current sessions. Excess or inactive lobbyist registrations accrue. While lobbyists are required to submit quarterly reports while registered, the transparency law is enforced by the House Clerk and Senate secretary. These offices lack resources to monitor reporting by all lobbyists. Instead, random audits are conducted by the

Government Accountability Office. As a result, federal lobby records contain hundreds of inactive registrations. It is likely that the bulk of lobbyists who decertified their registrations after 2007 were inactive lobbyists who no longer wanted to report their activities or who wanted instead to serve on federal advisory committees (LaPira and Thomas 2017, 191–201). In this regard, the new reporting requirements of the HLOGA and bans imposed on lobbyists by the Obama administration might have improved transparency by purging the registration rosters of inactive lobbyists. Nevertheless, not all inactive lobbyists might have de-registered, and more inactive registrations likely will accrue over time as new lobbyists and groups mobilize and old ones demobilize (Gray and Lowery 1996, 111–36).

In Michigan, lobbyists historically preferred not to reregister each year. Michigan enacted its first registration law in 1947. The provisions of the act were sparse by the standards of the time (Lane 1964, 54). The law did not regulate the activities of lobbyists much but instead required them only to register. Throughout the 1950s, multiple attempts were made to amend the law. One successful amendment, approved on April 18, 1958, required lobbyists to register during each legislative session instead of every two years (Zeller 1954, 231). There were other attempts to strengthen the law, but no changes were approved until the 1970s. On October 19, 1978, Governor William Milliken signed a stronger transparency law. Among other provisions, the act included more registration criteria for lobbyists and numerous bans on gifts. Despite being signed by the governor, the bill could not become effective until the secretary of state drafted rules for implementation (*Lansing State Journal* 1980). Even though new rules were approved in November 1980, the Michigan Chamber of Commerce spearheaded a fundraiser for litigation and a coalition of more than 100 interest groups filed a lawsuit to stop the act from going into effect (*Gongwer News Service Report* 1981). The coalition branded itself the Committee to Protect the First Amendment Right to Lobby. The lobby law was deemed an infringement on free speech by an Ingham County circuit judge in October 1981. In the absence of a new law, the old statute from 1947 went back into effect.

Within a year of the decision, a higher court (the Michigan Court of Appeals) reversed this ruling in *Pletz v. Secretary of State*. In September 1983, the Michigan Supreme Court refused to hear an appeal, and the revised law went into effect on January 1, 1984 (see McDiarmid 1983; Moskal 1983). Once implemented, the new law did not require lobbyists to reregister during each legislative session. Figure 6.1 illustrates the increase in lobbyists and interest groups over time in Michigan.

Figure 6.1 illustrates the changing numbers of registered lobbyists and interest groups in Michigan ranging 1951–2018. For observations from before 1984, totals of lobbyists and interest groups are generated using

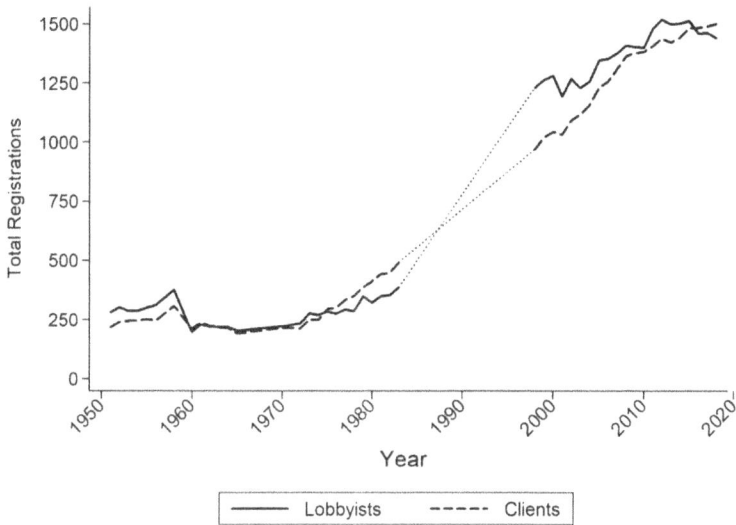

Figure 6.1   Lobbyist and Client Registration Totals in Michigan. *Source*: Author's creation based on registration rosters and statistics provided by Michigan secretary of state.

registration lists maintained in Michigan's state library, in Lansing. When Michigan first required lobbyists to register during each legislative session in 1958, total registration figures dropped slightly. This may be due to nonactive registrations being dropped from the rolls. Registration total began to increase in the 1970s as the legislature considered campaign finance and lobby reforms. With Michigan's current lobby law going into effect in 1984, lobbyists are no longer required to reregister during each legislative session. Observations from between 1984 and 1997 are missing because the state's lobbyist records include numerous inactive lobbyists (causing records to be thousands of pages long, requiring hours of processing). Figures from after 1997 are based on annual statistics provided by the secretary of state. These newer figures include inactive registrations. Declines occur as some lobbyists decertify registrations.

MEASURING LOBBY TRANSPARENCY

Statistical analysis can be used to detect if nudges improve registration rates of interest groups and lobbyists. In separate regression models, I predict interest group and lobbyist totals from the U.S. states. Interest groups consist of organizations in society that choose to lobby. Examples include individual business firms, associations of businesses (such as chambers of commerce), trade associations (such as bar associations), and membership-based groups such as the American Civil Liberties Union, Sierra Club, and labor unions. Using regression, I can parse the separate effects of nudges from those of other factors on registration rates. While nudges might explain why some states have more registered groups or lobbyists, other factors include state size, registration criteria, and lobby regulations. It is possible for all factors to influence registration rates concurrently.

MODELS PREDICTING INTEREST GROUP TOTALS

Gray and Lowery (1996) developed the Energy-Stability-Area model to predict how many interest groups register in each state every year. Energy refers to political factors occurring within state government that spur more groups into lobbying. For example, a prominent budget battle within a state may energize more interest groups into registering lobbyists to convey their messages to legislators (see Brasher et al. 1999). Whereas some groups, like businesses, hospitals, or churches, may normally not lobby, more political activity encourages more latent groups to lobby. If a state's legislature is more evenly divided between the major parties and the policy outcomes are less predictable, then more groups will register as well (Strickland 2019). After controlling for energizing factors, numbers of interest groups display stability over time if there are no major existential threats to a political system's institutions or customs (see Olson 1982). Lastly, area describes the size or carrying capacities of political systems for interest groups. There are substantially more groups in large political systems with more businesses and constituents. For example, there are more than 2,000 registered interest groups in California on a yearly basis, but only a few hundred groups in small-population states like North and South Dakota. Importantly, while larger states contain more interest groups, increases in registrations experience diminishing marginal returns as states increase in size. This is due to more and more groups crowding each other out for constituents.

The components of the Energy-Stability-Area model should explain most of the differences between states in terms of totals of interest groups. Indeed, in Gray and Lowery's (1996) analyses, area explains most of the interstate variation in group counts. In statistical analyses that predict group totals, I incorporate the size of each state's economic output or gross state product (GSP). These statistics are provided by the Bureau of Economic Analysis in real 1997 U.S. dollars. To reduce the number of insignificant digits within my statistical results, I measure each state's economic output in terms of trillions of U.S. dollars. Following Gray and Lowery (1996), I incorporate this variable into my models in a polynomial form. As a result, there are two coefficients that capture the diminishing marginal returns of economic growth on group registrations. The first coefficient for real GSP is expected to have a positive value while the second is expected to have a negative value. Total economic output is preferred to population count or per capita statistics given that most interest groups are economic in nature (i.e., are business firms or associations) and not membership-based groups. Regarding stability, there were no existential threats to the political institutions of the United States during the period 1989–2011 that I examine, so I exclude that measure from my statistical regressions.

As for energizing factors, I include three variables in my analyses: measures for legislative professionalism and one-party dominance, and a dichotomous indicator for whether a state allows direct democracy. Legislative professionalism refers to how similar a state legislature is to the U.S. Congress in terms of staff support, member income, and session length (Squire 2007). Professionalism has been found to depress group registrations since staff substitute out for the informational functions of groups and lobbyists (Berkman 2001). Squire's (2007) measure of professionalism ranges from zero to one, with more professional legislatures receiving higher scores. One-party domination is correlated with depressed group registrations. I incorporate a folded Ranney (1976) index into my models. The index is based on legislative election returns for the preceding six years and can assume values between 0.5 and 1. States with more one-party dominance receive higher scores. I also include a dichotomous (0, 1) indicator within my models for whether direct-democracy techniques (e.g., initiatives and referenda) can occur within a state. Boehmke (2002) found that direct-democracy states house more interest groups and that most of the additional groups consist of membership-based citizens' interests. Taken together, the five variables associated with the Energy-Stability-Area model should explain most variation in group figures, but I expect nudges, registration criteria, and regulations to provide some additional explanatory power.

I incorporate several measures of nudges into models that predict registered interest groups. I first include a dichotomous indicator for the state of Michigan. Since lobbyist registrations in that state do not expire from year to year, there are likely inactive registrations (and Michigan's client and lobbyist counts are therefore inflated). The second nudge I measure is whether a U.S. state allowed lobbyists to register online. I use the 2012 edition of the *Lobbying, PACs, and Campaign Finance 50 State Handbook* to identify whether lobbyists could register online (Poliakoff and Dyer 2012). Twenty-one states allowed lobbyists to register online in 2011.[5] The third nudge consists of the grace period afforded to lobbyists. Lobbyists do not always have to register prior to lobbying but instead can register after making initial contact with state officials. In 2011, three states allowed lobbyists to register up to 15 days after initially engaging in lobbying.[6] Information on grace periods was also located in Poliakoff and Dyer (2012). I expect that online registration and longer grace periods will increase registration rates. I also include in my models a measure for registration fees. Fees do not count as nudges since they change economic incentives directly (Thaler and Sunstein 2008, 6). Nevertheless, high fees might discourage some lobbyists from registering, and therefore push down overall registration rates.[7]

For registration criteria (which are not nudges), I incorporate into my models Newmark's (2005) index. His index consists of a count of seven common registration criteria found in the U.S. states. These include whether an interest group or lobbyist is targeting legislative officials, executive officials, whether state agencies and officials may register as lobbyists while serving, whether public employees must register when lobbying; and whether registration criteria include compensation, expenditure, and time thresholds. The index ranges from zero to seven. For lobby regulations (which apply only to registered groups and lobbyists), I use Newmark's index of commonly prohibited activities in my models as well. For this scale, a state received an additional point for each of the following actions it limited or banned: lobbyists making contributions at any time, lobbyists making contributions only during legislative sessions, lobbyists being limited in the dollar amounts they could expend on officials each year, and whether officials were banned from soliciting lobbyists for gifts. This index ranges in value from zero to four. Reporting requirements might also be a burden to lobbyists, and I use Newmark's index of seven common requirements for this measure. Just as with criteria and prohibitions, states receive an additional point for each requirement: whether reporting is semiannual or more frequent, and whether lobbyists must disclose the subject matter of their lobbying, expenditures benefiting public officials, compensation received broken down by employer, total compensation received, categories of expenditures made, or just totals of expenditures.[8]

MODELS PREDICTING LOBBYIST TOTALS

To get a better sense of whether nudges, registration criteria, and lobby regulations affect registration rates among lobbyists, I analyze totals of lobbyist-group pairings. Whenever lobbyists (individual persons) register with state officials, they indicate the interest groups they represent. Lists of registered lobbyists consist of lobbyist names and the names of interest groups each lobbyist represents. From these lists, individual pairings of lobbyists and groups can be counted, and the average number of lobbyists hired by groups can be calculated. For example, if a list includes 100 unique interest groups with 150 unique lobbyist-group pairings, then each group is represented by an average 1.5 lobbyists. Some lobbyists represent multiple groups, so dividing client totals by the total numbers of lobbyists does not yield accurate measures of how many lobbyists the groups hire on average. Lobbyist-group pairings can also be considered individual contracts (Hunter et al. 1991).

To determine if nudges, registration criteria, and regulations get interest groups to register more lobbyists, I estimate a second set of models that predict totals of lobbyist-group pairings. Just as economic output is a leading predictor of (i.e., is quite correlated with) group totals, group totals should be a leading predictor of lobbyist-group totals. After all, lobbyists cannot lobby without some interest groups to represent.[9] Once one controls for group totals, the remaining variance in lobbyist totals might be explained in part by nudges, criteria, or lobby regulations. Just as in my models of group populations, I suspect that similar Energy-Stability-Area factors induce interest groups into hiring more or fewer lobbyists.

DATA, METHODOLOGY, AND RESULTS

Using lists of interest groups with registered lobbyists published by state agencies, I calculate totals of unique interest groups, lobbyists, and lobbyist-group pairings registered in all U.S. states for 1989 and 2011. Lists from 1989 are collected mostly from Wilson (1990), although original lists published by state authorities were located for several states. Lists from 2011 are provided by the National Institute on Money in State Politics, a nonpartisan organization dedicated to improving transparency.[10] For some states, lists provided by the National Institute on Money in State Politics are filtered of duplicate lobbyist-group pairings. Altogether, my data set consists of 100 observations. There are two observations for each state, providing for two national cross-sections. Having repeated observations for each state allows me to measure change over time in each of my variables. The appendix includes a discussion of my regression specifications.

In the appendix, table 6.1 presents results for regression models that predict totals of registered interest groups in the U.S. states for 1989 and 2011. As expected, the size of a state's economic output is positively correlated with total groups, but with diminishing marginal returns. In models with fixed effects, legislative professionalism is negatively correlated with totals of registered groups. Changes over time in legislative professionalism are not correlated with changes in group totals. Partisan dominance depresses group registration numbers while the potential for direct democracy energizes more groups into registering. Nudges, including the non-expiration of registrations in Michigan, online registration, and longer grace periods, appear not to be correlated with totals of interest groups with registered lobbyists. Fees also are not correlated with group totals. Instead, registration criteria and lobby

Table 6.1   Models Predicting Registered Interest Groups

Explanatory Variable	Model 1 Clustered Errors	Model 2 Clustered Errors	Model 3 Fixed Effects	Model 4 Fixed Effects
Real GSP	5.874***	5.708***	2.231***	2.080***
	(0.644)	(0.600)	(0.795)	(0.797)
(Real GSP)^2	−2.788***	−2.707***	−0.957***	−0.937***
	(0.377)	(0.355)	(0.341)	(0.347)
Professionalism	−1.518***	−1.338***	−0.691	−0.730
	(0.416)	(0.398)	(0.610)	(0.628)
One-Party Dominance	−0.914**	–	−0.670**	–
	(0.385)		(0.305)	
Initiative State	0.248***	0.261***	0.696*	0.944***
	(0.0789)	(0.0816)	(0.362)	(0.356)
Registration Criteria	0.0559	0.0948	−0.0160	0.0154
	(0.0896)	(0.0869)	(0.0371)	(0.0355)
Prohibitions	0.420***	0.408***	0.102	0.0782
	(0.130)	(0.132)	(0.0868)	(0.0858)
Reporting Burden	−0.0351	−0.0088	−0.0396	−0.0280
	(0.0368)	(0.0317)	(0.0308)	(0.0299)
Criteria*Prohibitions	−0.0883***	−0.0846***	−0.0344*	−0.0261
	(0.0266)	(0.0269)	(0.0191)	(0.0187)
Criteria*Reporting	0.0117	0.0030	0.0262***	0.0201**
	(0.0170)	(0.0159)	(0.0088)	(0.0081)
Michigan	0.243	0.295*	–	–
	(0.167)	(0.155)		
Online	0.131	0.175*	−0.0052	0.0644
	(0.111)	(0.105)	(0.0765)	(0.0730)
Grace Period Length	−0.0053	−0.0075	0.0058	0.0067
	(0.0080)	(0.0080)	(0.0173)	(0.0178)
Registration Fee	−0.440	−0.322	0.176	0.234
	(0.483)	(0.479)	(0.277)	(0.277)
Constant	5.694***	5.442***	5.726***	5.578***
	(0.198)	(0.143)	(0.196)	(0.193)
Log(alpha)	−2.215***	−2.180***	−3.954***	−3.890***
	(0.149)	(0.165)	(0.156)	(0.154)
Observations	98	100	98	100
No. of States	49	50	49	50
AIC	1351.514	1379.432	1284.066	1312.982

Notes: Standard errors in parentheses. Models 2 and 4 do not include a measure for partisan dominance since Nebraska's unicameral legislature is officially nonpartisan. The dichotomous indicator for Michigan is included among the state fixed effects in Models 3 and 4, and therefore not reported. *** $p<0.01$, ** $p<0.05$, * $p<0.1$.
Source: Author created.

regulations are correlated with group totals. As shown in table 6.1, there is evidence that lobby regulations (e.g., campaign finance and gift limits) suppress the ability of registration criteria to capture more groups. In models with fixed effects, there is also some evidence (based on an interactive effect) that reporting requirements contribute to this effect. In other words, requiring registered lobbyists to report more information does not prevent broader registration criteria from capturing more registrations but may, in fact, have the opposite effect. In general, nudges do not affect the totals of registered interest groups.

In a second set of models, I estimate a series of similar regressions that predict how many lobbyist-group pairings registered within a state. Instead of holding constant the size of each state's economy, I hold constant the number of unique interest groups (in thousands) with lobbyists represented, which should explain most of the variation in pairing totals. Any residual variation in pairings may be explained by energizing factors, nudges, registration criteria, or lobby regulations.[11]

The results presented in table 6.2 in the appendix provide limited insight into the numbers of lobbyist-group pairings in the U.S. states. As expected, the number of interest groups within a state is the leading predictor for how many lobbyist-group pairings there are. However, none of the variables that might energize groups into hiring more lobbyists are correlated with lobbyist-group pairings.

Interestingly, Michigan does have more pairings registered than in other states, and states with online lobbyist registration also have more registered pairings. This is the strongest evidence so far that nudges might play a role in helping more lobbyists to register. Since all my observations of online registration occurred in 2011, I reestimated my models with data from only that year. Among all U.S. states observed in 2011, those with online registration had approximately 31 percent more registered lobbyist-group pairings than states without online registration.[12] This relationship is not found, however, when one compares changes in registration rates across time. In models with state and year fixed effects, the implementation of online registration is not correlated with more lobbyists registering. This suggests that the finding could be due to omitted variable bias and that further investigation is needed. States with online registration may also, after all, have better monitoring and enforcement, stricter penalties, or both. Also, my findings present no evidence that grace periods increase registration rates among lobbyists, or that registration fees depress lobbyist totals. I describe additional results in the appendix.

DISCUSSION

This chapter presented an exploration of whether nudges can improve registration rates among interest groups and lobbyists. I estimated a series of statistical models that test whether non-expiring registration, online registration,

Table 6.2   Models Predicting Registered Lobbyist-Group Pairings

Explanatory Variable	Model 1 Clustered Errors	Model 2 Clustered Errors	Model 3 Fixed Effects	Model 4 Fixed Effects
Interest Groups	1.14***	1.14***	0.711***	0.709***
	(0.194)	(0.204)	(0.134)	(0.133)
Professionalism	0.756*	0.882*	−1.306	−1.362
	(0.409)	(0.474)	(1.024)	(1.023)
One-Party Dominance	−0.789	–	−0.710	–
	(0.535)		(0.470)	
Initiative State	0.0946	0.0860	0.895	1.174**
	(0.102)	(0.104)	(0.561)	(0.532)
Registration Criteria	−0.0152	0.0090	0.0091	0.0390
	(0.0451)	(0.0458)	(0.0575)	(0.0541)
Prohibitions	0.162	0.151	0.159	0.130
	(0.119)	(0.121)	(0.130)	(0.127)
Reporting Burden	−0.0347	−0.0230	0.0223	0.0372
	(0.0362)	(0.0326)	(0.0482)	(0.0463)
Criteria*Prohibitions	−0.0296	−0.0249	−0.0299	−0.0208
	(0.0273)	(0.0279)	(0.0288)	(0.0281)
Criteria*Reporting	0.0080	0.0029	0.0091	0.0023
	(0.0100)	(0.0104)	(0.0133)	(0.0123)
Michigan	0.815***	0.856***	–	–
	(0.232)	(0.227)		
Online	0.265**	0.285**	0.0864	0.141
	(0.117)	(0.113)	(0.109)	(0.103)
Grace Period Length	−0.0069	−0.0067	0.0224	0.0236
	(0.0101)	(0.0104)	(0.0277)	(0.0277)
Registration Fee	−0.156	−0.178	−0.161	−0.086
	(0.681)	(0.675)	(0.449)	(0.443)
Constant	6.199***	6.007***	5.864***	5.692***
	(0.244)	(0.180)	(0.300)	(0.281)
Log(alpha)	−1.814***	−1.797***	−2.992***	−2.988***
	(0.233)	(0.247)	(0.144)	(0.142)
Observations	98	100	98	100
No. of States	49	50	49	50
AIC	1536.259	1564.435	1515.866	1542.353

Notes: Standard errors in parentheses. Models 2 and 4 do not include a measure for partisan dominance since Nebraska's unicameral legislature is officially nonpartisan. The dichotomous indicator for Michigan is included among the state fixed effects in Models 3 and 4, and therefore not reported. *** $p<0.01$, ** $p<0.05$, * $p<0.1$.
Source: Author created.

and grace period length are correlated with totals of interest groups and lobbyist-group pairings. Non-expiring registrations and online registration might play a role in getting more lobbyists to register.

These results do not suggest that other kinds of nudges would not help improve transparency. Secretaries of state or ethics agencies may send reminders to lobbyists about registering or host training or educational sessions on a regular basis. Several states already host such tutorials (National Conference of State Legislatures 2002, 23–33), but required attendance might place an unconstitutional burden on lobbyists' freedom of speech. State officials also might send reminders or host training sessions, but these nudges likely occur informally and at the will of agency heads. It is difficult to determine in retrospect when informal nudges might have occurred.

Why might nudges prove ineffective at getting more interest groups and lobbyists to register? Lobbyists, particularly those who seek particularistic benefits from the government for their clients, have incentives to hide their activities from the public and opposing interests. Choi and Storr (2019) argue that rent-seeking is more common in some countries than in others due to local cultures. Whereas formal, state institutions might affect the success of those seeking rents, cultural norms or expectations will affect the likelihood that individuals and businesses seek rents at all. In the context of U.S. states, Elazar (1966) argues that Southern states generally have a traditionalistic political subculture in which residents are less willing to engage in activism and view political processes as appropriate domains for elite interests. Gray and Lowery (1999) indeed find that Southern states have discernibly fewer groups than other states. It might be the case that southern states have a stronger culture of rent-seeking in which elite interests have more influence over local legislators. With such a culture, fewer residents may be interested in transparency, or more lobbyists may disregard nudges and registration criteria to preserve established particularistic benefits.

In addition, getting interest groups and lobbyists to register likely requires going beyond nudges and instead changing substantially the incentives that lobbyists face when choosing whether to register. A different approach to encouraging groups and lobbyists to register is to adopt a version of registration procedures found in Congress and Michigan. Lobbyists register once they achieve spending and time thresholds that trigger required registration. They are then obligated to submit disclosure reports regularly, and their registrations do not expire from one year to the next. While this procedure might obscure who is lobbying since only a small number of lobbyists in Washington and Lansing terminate their registrations each year, allowing registrations not to expire might improve transparency if inactive lobbyists have strong enough incentives to de-register on a timely basis. This is currently not the case in Congress or Michigan's legislature. As an example, when the Obama administration imposed a ban on lobbyists serving on federal advisory committees, more inactive lobbyists de-registered than in previous years. Two ways to incentivize inactive lobbyists to de-register would be to require more frequent reporting or to monitor how well registered lobbyists are complying with reporting requirements (and penalize late filers). Such an approach could help to ensure better transparency in Congress, Michigan, and elsewhere.

While nudges may have limited potential for addressing the transparency-regulation trade-off, better sets of registration criteria and lobby laws might be more effective. Nations and states can adopt broad criteria that cover multiple facets of lobbying, including expense, compensation, and time thresholds. Moreover, those thresholds should be reasonably low so that paid and part-time lobbyists have no room to hide. Other regulations, such as limits on campaign donations or gifts, should apply to both registered and non-registered groups and individuals. This would decrease the incentive for lobbyists not to register.

With the adoption of better lobby laws, whether in the United States or elsewhere, members of the public and advocacy groups are made better-informed of who is trying to influence policymakers. This can improve democratic representation. Policymakers in the U.S. and elsewhere can learn from inefficiencies in existing laws and work to improve transparency.

APPENDIX

Regression Specifications

Since both my dependent variables of interest consist of counts (integers) that cannot assume negative values, and because both variables are overdispersed (right-skewed), I employ the negative binomial variance function. This variance function includes an additional parameter for capturing the overdispersion of my dependent variables (see Long 1997). Moreover, since I have multiple observations for each state, I adjust for state-level clustering. Since states are observed twice (in 1989 and 2011), observations for each state are likely affected by state-specific contextual factors. In other words, the group and lobbyist totals from 2011 are likely influenced in large part by totals from 1989 for each state. To adjust for this, I estimate two sets of regressions. The first set clusters my standard errors by state. This step helps to control for state-level confounders but allows my models to utilize variation that occurs between states when estimating effect sizes (Primo et al. 2007). In my second set of models, I utilize state- and year-level dummy variables or fixed effects (not reported). Using these effects forces my models to utilize only within-state variation within estimating effect sizes (Allison 2009). In other words, estimated, overall effect sizes of each of my independent variables are based only on changes in the values of those independent variables that occurred within each state, between 1989 and 2011. As a result, the estimates for these models are more conservative. Of course, these models cannot be used to measure the effects of factors that *do not* change over time within states (hence, I estimate models with clustered errors as well). I expect both sets of models to produce substantively similar results, although they measure different types of variation among the states.

Tests for Interactive Effects

Nudges might affect registration rates among only some lobbyists. Whereas contract lobbyists might work on a full-time basis and be unable to avoid registering regardless of how few criteria a state has on the books, part-time and citizen lobbyists who are unsure about whether they should register might be more likely to do so if nudged. If this is the case, then we can expect nudges to have their greatest positive effects on registration rates in states with the fewest definitions. In other words, the effects of nudges might be contingent on how many criteria there are within a state, which might in turn influence group and lobbyist registration rates. To test these hypotheses, I estimated a series of regression models, resembling those in tables 6.1 and 6.2, that included interactive terms between criteria and online registration, and criteria and grace period length. Interactive terms are used to test for whether the effects of one variable on an outcome of interest are magnified or reduced by the presence of another variable (see Kam and Franzese 2007). Those model results, not reported here, did not indicate that the effects of nudges are contingent on registration criteria. None of the interactive coefficients achieved statistical significance.

NOTES

1. The website for Common Cause is https://www.commoncause.org/.

2. The U.S. Congress did not pass its first lobbyist law until 1946, but this law was gutted by the Supreme Court in *United States vs. Harriss* (1954). The Court struck down as unconstitutional several provisions of the law. As a result, only paid lobbyists who spoke directly with members of Congress were then required to register. It was not until 1995 that Congress reenacted a more comprehensive lobby statute.

3. It should come as no surprise that interest groups have been found to exercise more influence during the opaquer steps of the legislative process in Congress. These steps include committee markup (see Hall and Wayman 1990; Baumgartner and Jones 1993; Kingdon 1995).

4. In Florida, voters recently approved a constitutional amendment that includes a six-year waiting period for former legislators, which will be the longest waiting period in the United States. The new law goes into effect in 2022.

5. For observations from 1989, all states were assumed to require lobbyists to register by mail or in person.

6. As of 2011, lobbyists active in Congress had 45 days to register from the time they achieved spending or time thresholds that triggered required registration (Buck 2011).

7. In my models, fees are calculated in thousands of real 2011 U.S. dollars.

8. If a U.S. state required lobbyists to report compensation by employer or categories of expenditures, then it was also classified as requiring the reporting of compensation or expenditure total, as well.

9. On occasion, lobbyists register for personal interests and do not list interest groups. Lobbyists who do not list client names are assumed to be representing themselves.

10. New Jersey's list is from 2013.

11. Moreover, I incorporate a dichotomous indicator (not reported) for whether firms could register directly in the U.S. state. In those few states—California, New Jersey, and New York—lobbyists could register as members of firms, and clients could authorize firms to represent them. This prevented the Institute from discerning which individual lobbyists were authorized to represent which clients. In producing lists of lobbyist-group pairs for these states, the Institute appears to have assumed that all lobbyist members of firms were authorized to represent all clients associated with the firm. As a result, the Institute's lists of lobbyist-group pairings for these states were unusually long and might contain spurious pairings. Table 6.2 includes a series of regression models predicting total lobbyist-group pairings registered in a state.

12. This relationship is robust to the exclusion of California, New Jersey, and New York. Once those states are excluded, states with online registration have an average of 33 percent more lobbyists.

REFERENCES

Allison, Paul D. 2009. *Fixed Effects Regression Models.* Thousand Oaks, CA: SAGE.
Baumgartner, Frank R., Jeffrey M. Berry, Marie Hojnacki, David C. Kimball, and Beth L. Leech. 2009. *Lobbying and Policy Change: Who Wins, Who Loses, and Why.* Chicago: University of Chicago Press.
Berkman, Michael B. 2001. "Legislative Professionalism and the Demand for Groups: The Institutional Context of Interest Population Density." *Legislative Studies Quarterly* 26: 661–79.
Berry, Jeffrey M. 1999. *The New Liberalism: The Rising Power of Citizen Groups.* Washington, DC: Brookings Institution Press.
Bertrand, Marianne, Matilde Bombardini, and Francesco Trebbi. 2014. "Is It Whom You Know or What You Know? An Empirical Assessment of the Lobbying Process." *American Economic Review* 104 (12): 3885–920.
Boehmke, Frederick J. 2002. "The Effect of Direct Democracy on the Size and Diversity of State Interest Group Populations." *Journal of Politics* 64 (3): 827–44.
Brasher, Holly, David Lowery, and Virginia Gray. 1999. "State Lobby Registration Data: The Anomalous Case of Florida (and Minnesota too!)." *Legislative Studies Quarterly* 24 (2): 303–14.

Buck, Melanie. 2011. "Did I Miss the Deadline? And So What if I Did?" *Sunlight Foundations,* June 23, 2011. https://sunlightfoundation.com/2011/06/23/did-i-miss-the-deadline-and-so-what-if-i-did/ (accessed February 19, 2019).

Chari, Raj, John Hogan, and Gary Murphy. 2010. *Regulating Lobbying: A Global Comparison.* Manchester: Manchester University Press.

Choi, Seung Ginny and Virgil Henry Storr. 2019. "A Culture of Rent Seeking." *Public Choice* 181: 101–26.

Crain, Joshua. 2018. "Revolving-Door Lobbyists and the Value of Congressional Staff Connections." *Journal of Politics* 80 (4): 1369–83.

Drutman, Lee. 2015. *The Business of America is Lobbying: How Corporations Became Politicized and Politics Became More Corporate.* Oxford: Oxford University Press.

Elazar, Daniel. 1966. *American Federalism: A View from the States.* New York: Thomas Crowell.

Hamm, Keith E., Andrew R. Weber, and R. Bruce Anderson. 1994. "The Impact of Lobbying Laws and Their Enforcement: A Contrasting View." *Social Science Quarterly* 75: 378–81.

Hunter, Kennith G., Laura A.Wilson, and Gregory G. Brunk. 1991. "Societal Complexity and Interest-Group Lobbying in the American States." *Journal of Politics* 53: 488–503.

Gongwer News Service Report. 1981. "Suit Challenging Lobbyist Registration Act Expected by May 1." *Gongwer News Service Report* 20 (73), April 17, 1981.

Gormley, William T., Jr. 1979. "A Test of the Revolving Door Hypothesis at the FCC." *American Journal of Political Science* 23 (4): 665–83.

Gray, Virginia and David Lowery. 1996. *The Population Ecology of Interest Representation: Lobbying Communities in the American States.* Ann Arbor, MI: University of Michigan Press.

———. 1999. "The Underpopulated Interest Communities of the South: Partially Decomposing a Dummy Variable." *Southeastern Political Review* 27 (4): 747–62.

———. 2001. "The Institutionalization of State Communities of Organized Interests." *Political Research Quarterly* 54 (2): 265–84.

Kam, Cindy and Robert Franzese. 2007. *Modeling and Interpreting Interactive Hypotheses in Regression Analysis.* Ann Arbor, MI: University of Michigan Press.

Kollman, Ken. 1998. *Outside Lobbying: Public Opinion and Interest Group Strategies.* Princeton, NJ: Princeton University Press.

Krueger, Anne O. 1974. "The Political Economy of the Rent-Seeking Society." *The American Economic Review* 64: 291–303.

Lane, Edgar. 1964. *Lobbying and the Law.* Berkeley, CA: University of California Press.

Lansing State Journal. 1980. "State's Lobbyist Control Bill Remains in Limbo." April 8, 1980.

LaPira, Timothy M. 2016. "Lobbying in the Shadows: How Private Interests Hide from Public Scrutiny and Why That Matters." In A. J. Cigler, B. A. Loomis, and A. J. Nownes (eds.), *Interest Group Politics,* pp. 224–48. Washington, DC: CQ Press.

Long, Scott. 1997. *Regression Models for Categorical and Limited Dependent Variables.* Thousand Oaks, CA: SAGE.

McDiarmid, Hugh. 1983. *Lobbyists' Whine Has a Bitter Taste.* Detroit Free Press.

Mitchell, Matthew. 2014. *The Pathology of Privilege: The Economic Consequences of Government Favoritism.* Arlington, VA: Mercatus Center at George Mason University.

Moskal, Jerry. 1983. "State Lobbyists Searching for Loopholes in New Law." *Lansing State Journal* pp. A1, 2B.

National Conference of State Legislatures. 2002. *The State of State Legislative Ethics.* Denver: National Conference of State Legislatures.

Newmark, Adam. 2005. "Measuring State Legislative Lobby Regulation, 1990—2003." *State Politics and Policy Quarterly* 5: 182–91.

Olson, Mancur. 1965. *The Logic of Collective Action: Public Goods and the Theory of Groups.* Cambridge: Harvard University Press.

———. 1982. *The Rise and Decline of Nations: Economic Growth, Stagflation, and Social Rigidities.* New Haven, CT: Yale University Press.

Opheim, Cynthia. 1991. "Explaining the Differences in State Lobby Regulation." *Western Political Quarterly* 44: 405–421.

Poliakoff, Edward, and Jocelyn Y. Dyer. 2012. *Lobbying, PACs, and Campaign Finance: 50 State Handbook.* Eagan, MN: Thomson Reuters.

Primo, David M., Matthew L. Jacobsmeier, and Jeffrey Milyo. 2007. "Estimating the Impact of State Policies and Institutions with Mixed-Level Data." *State Politics and Policy Quarterly* 7 (4): 446–59.

Quincy, Josiah. 1891. "Regulation of the Lobby in Massachusetts." *Forum* 12: 346.

Ranney, Austin J. 1976. "Parties in State Politics." In H. Jacob and K. Vines (Eds.), *Politics in the American states* (3rd ed. pp. 51–94). Boston, MA: Little, Brown.

Schattschneider, Elmer E. 1960. *The Semisovereign People: A Realist's View of Democracy in America.* New York: Holt, Rinehart and Winston.

Schlozman, Kay Lehman, Sidney Verba, and Henry E. Brady. 2012. *The Unheavenly Chorus: Unequal Political Voice and the Broken Promise of American Democracy.* Princeton, NJ: Princeton University Press.

Squire, Peveril. 2007. "Measuring Legislative Professionalism: The Squire Index Revisited." *State Politics and Policy Quarterly* 7: 211–27.

Strickland, James. 2019. "A Paradox of Political Reform: Shadow Interests in the U.S. States." *American Politics Research* 47 (4): 887–914.

———. 2020. "Bifurcated Lobbying in America: Group Benefits and Lobbyist Selection." *Interest Groups and Advocacy* 9: 131–58.

Thaler, Richard H. and Cass R. Sunstein. 2008. *Nudge: Improving Decisions about Health, Wealth, and Happiness.* New York: Penguin Books.

Thomas III, Herschel F. and Timothy M. LaPira. 2017. "How Many Lobbyists Are in Washington?: Shadow Lobbying and the Gray Market for Policy Advocacy." *Interest Groups and Advocacy* 6 (3): 199–214.

Tullock, Gordon. 1967. "The Welfare Costs of Tariffs, Monopolies, and Theft." *Western Economic Journal* 5: 224–32.

———. 1975. "The Transitional Gains Trap." *Bell Journal of Economics* 6 (2): 671–78.

———. 1988. "Rent Seeking and Tax Reform." *Contemporary Policy Issues* 6: 37–47.

Wilson, Robert (ed.). 1990. *American Lobbyists Directory: A Guide to the More Than 65,000 Registered Federal and State Lobbyists and the Businesses, Organizations, and Other Concerns they Represent.* Detroit: Gale Research.

Zeller, Belle. 1937. *Pressure Politics in New York: A Study of Group Representation Before the Legislature.* New York: Prentice-Hall.

Chapter 7

Nudging Choices in Education Policy

Shannon Lee

As a young student, I was fairly tech-savvy and, more accurately, a bit of a geek. I was actively creating websites and the only "experimenting" I did was with coding languages like HTML and PHP. I was also interested in politics and spent much of my time blogging about President Bush's response to September 11, 2001, and the subsequent U.S. involvement in the Iraq war. At 11 years old, you can probably imagine that these journal entries lacked quite a bit of substance.

In 2008, I headed off to college in the midst of a global financial crisis with a college fund that had been devastated by the stock market crash. When I expressed interest in studying computer science, I was told by my parents and other mentors that information technology was a dying industry and that there were no jobs in that field due to outsourcing to other countries and automation. Instead, they recommended political science. I was told that government jobs were immune to the tumultuous nature of the economy, and that there just *had* to be a job opening for me somewhere within the city, county, state, and federal levels of government.

At the time, I was heavily influenced by people that I believed had my best interests in mind when giving me advice. Fear-mongering headlines portraying mass unemployment, layoffs, and downsizing also played a significant role. It never occurred to me to do independent research on what the employment outcomes were of certain degree majors, or what the average salary or employment rates of graduates from my university were. These data did not exist for my university and still does not in a practical, informative, or usable format. What I had at my disposal was anecdotal evidence of what career would be best suited for me. Reflecting on this, I have to wonder:

- Would knowing what the employment prospects of a political science major versus a computer science major have made a difference?
- Would knowing the comparative first-, five-, or ten-year earnings have changed my mind?
- Would seeing the outcomes of other majors or other universities have better informed my decision?

My story is not unique. Instead, it is demonstrative of the life-changing effects resulting from the information and incentives that influence decisions. The process of deciding on a career path after high school is often difficult and overwhelming. Much of this decision relies on information presented to the student and their family before they graduate and the preparatory work that they engage in to be a competitive college candidate. This decision can also be influenced by the availability of options for postsecondary or vocational education, the cost of those options, and the biases or knowledge regarding the outcomes of those programs.

Every year, millions of students are enrolled in America's colleges and universities. From 2000 to 2016, the United States saw a 28 percent increase in the number of students annually enrolled in postsecondary education, from 13.2 million to 16.9 million (NCES 2018a). The majority of these are traditional students pursuing further education following K-12 enrollment. According to the U.S. Federal Reserve, more than half of these students incur debt for their education, and those who did not complete their degree program were more likely to struggle to pay back their loans on time (Board of Governors of the Federal Reserve System 2018). With an increasingly globalized and interconnected economy and more than $1.5 trillion national student loan debt, it has become imperative for young adults to make smart decisions about their future that will enable them to pay for the cost of their education and simultaneously succeed in the workforce.

"In a republic, the mission of higher education is to empower individuals to live fully in their time free from economic or public dependency" (Carnevale and Cheah 2018, 3). In the United States, providing opportunities for students to pursue a quality education has become a societal commitment (Thaler and Sunstein 2008). This obligation has encouraged the public funding of higher education institutions, taxpayer subsidies for private or nonprofit colleges or universities, student financial aid programs, and federally backed student loans. In 2017, nearly $95 billion in state and local appropriations were earmarked for public colleges and universities (SHEEOA 2017). As such, governments at all levels have a vested interest in the positive individual and societal returns to education.

In their landmark book, *Nudge*, Thaler and Sunstein (2008) briefly discuss the development of choice architecture systems in Texas, Florida, and California high schools that influence students to enroll in college. These systems involve completing an application for college as a condition of graduating. As a result, creative and nonintrusive solutions that maximize choices have been advocated as methods to solve complex problems in education policy.

This chapter is an endeavor to expand on the discussion of educational nudges by understanding how the involvement in and consequences of postsecondary educational or training activities are influenced using signaling theory and human capital theory. It is structured to understand the importance of various types of education for a productive workforce, and the public policies and incentives in place for investments made in those types of education.[1] This chapter also explores the influence of the availability of employment and earnings data for education programs, if they exist, and how they are used to influence education planning.

HUMAN CAPITAL THEORY

Adam Smith (1776) first articulated the concept of investing in talents or abilities, commonly referred to now as human capital, in his magnum opus, *An Inquiry into the Nature and Causes of the Wealth of Nations*. As the father of modern economics, Smith had quite a bit to say about capital creation resulting from labor and education. Smith (1776) wrote that a person that invests in their own education can, and should, expect a wage that is higher than that of common labor to compensate for the costs of their education.[2] He goes on to say that the diversity of liberal arts education, from "painters and sculptors, of lawyers and physicians," allows for a wider, more liberal, wage differentiation between those educated disciplines as opposed to the earnings gap between educated and uneducated laborers (Smith 1776, 119). Of particular interest is his discussion on the societal effect and positive spillovers of human capital, within the context of the division of stock. He wrote the following:

> Fourthly, of the acquired and useful abilities of all the inhabitants or members of the society. The acquisition of such talents, by the maintenance of the acquirer during his education, study, or apprenticeship, always costs a real expence, which is a capital fixed and realized, as it were, in his person. Those talents, as they make a part of his fortune, so do they likewise of that of the society to which he belongs. (Smith 1776, 282)

In this discussion, Smith (1776) emphasizes the opportunity costs associated with educational investments, namely the costs borne on the apprentice and their family while learning their trade. To that end, there remains an ongoing debate regarding the value of education when reflecting on the costs of loans and other maintenance and opportunity costs incurred while pursuing education. This debate focuses on the costs as well as both the real or perceived benefits of making these investments, and the incentives in place that encourage individuals to do so.

It is these assertions by Smith that serve as the foundation for human capital theory, developed and articulated two centuries later by economists Gary Becker and Theodore Schultz. Becker's work on human capital theory essentially develops on Smith's concept of what talent investment means for economies and arrives at a similar conclusion that education is a valuable input, and when people invest in education, their ability to produce increases and there are positive spillover effects that boost society overall (Becker 1962). Becker determined that human capital is a subject of economics that links both macro and microeconomics. This link is observed at the individual, micro, level between parents and their children, and at the macro level when understanding how much of economic growth is determined by increasing human capital. Schultz's research emphasized human capital theory in the context of agricultural economics, or, as the title of his 1979 Nobel Prize Lecture aptly put it, the economics of the poor. In that speech, Schultz asserts that most of the people in the world are poor and that most of the world's poor earn their living from agriculture. He goes on to say that differing levels of farmland productivity are not sufficient to explain why people are poor in long-settled areas of the world, such as India and Africa. Rather, Schultz makes the argument, in the context of farmland, that most important variables in understanding why people are poor are the incentives and associated opportunities that people have to augment the effective supply of land by means of investments that include the contributions of agricultural research and the improvements of human skills. To that end, Schultz suggested a reframing of the importance of farmland and an increased emphasis on skills and knowledge is necessary for the modernization of low-income countries (Schultz 1979).

Explicit in human capital theory is the belief that investments made into the stock of human capital benefit not only those specific individuals but society as well. Society, therefore, has a stake in influencing its members to invest in their human capital to boost productivity. These positive spillovers benefit society in the form of higher taxes paid through earning more income, social efficacy, economic productivity, innovation, technology advancement, and good citizenship. As a result, there exist additional incentives to promote education as a means of independence from social safety nets or as a deterrent to incarceration.

SIGNALING THEORY

The job market signaling model, developed by economist Michael Spence, captures the method by which employers can observe potential employees and make judgments regarding their skills and abilities. Signals are defined as "observable characteristics attached to the individual that are subject to manipulation by him" (Spence 1973, 357). As such, investing in education is a signal. The alteration of these signals can be expensive, and in this case, educational signals require time and financial investment. Individuals seeking to modify these signals are influenced to select signals that "maximize the difference between offered wages and signaling costs" (Spence 1973, 358). F. A. Hayek (1945) articulated that people face a knowledge problem that makes planning the optimal allocation of resources difficult. Signals help to mitigate some of this problem by increasing the efficiency of allocating the right people to the right jobs. Spence (1973) goes on to say that an equilibrium is created through an information feedback loop where employers offer wages at differing levels scaling with education and thus rational individuals are encouraged to invest in education. After employers hire individuals using these signals, their information regarding productivity and output becomes known and new data influences future hiring and promotion practices.

In *The Case against Education*, Bryan Caplan's (2018) core argument is that education has a low social return due to the fact that it is almost entirely signaling. He argues that education signals three traits, conformity, conscientiousness, and intelligence, as those traits are honed through persistence and credential attainment. Employers seek out this trifecta because

> [t]he road to academic success and the road to job success are paved with the same materials. An intelligent worker learns quickly and deeply. A conscientious worker labors until the job's done right. A conformist worker obeys superiors and cooperates with teammates. (Caplan 2018, 18)

Thus, education acts as a signal (one of several) that influences hiring decisions made by employers in lieu of being able to directly observe the productivity of the individual. This is important in a choice architecture framework because nudges can be particularly effective when individuals are motivated to send specific signals to prospective employers. However, information regarding the signaling costs and the wages associated with those investments is lacking due to the limited availability and localization of data on earnings. As is elaborated later in this chapter, data systems that provide data directly to students can inform their decision-making and allow them to adjust their signals to provide the largest difference between costs and earnings. Signals are particularly important in behavioral economics because, "when faced with a decision that requires complex calculations and predictions about the future, many people rely on signals embedded in the choice, such as default options and framing" (Boatman, Evans, and Soliz 2014, 5).

The problem with education as a signal in contemporary society is that it tends to be the *only* or *most important* signal for many jobs. With a large supply of over-qualified candidates in the labor market, employers will fill the "highest jobs with those who have the highest qualifications" (Van de Werfhorst and Andersen 2005, 322). This process then repeats for mid and lower tier jobs and qualified employees. The oversaturation of overeducated individuals in the labor market can lead to degree or credential inflation, which is the concept that a certain level of education just *isn't enough*. In a survey of 600 business owners, two driving factors of credential inflation emerge: the environment of quickly changing middle-skills jobs and "employers' misperceptions of the economics of investing in quality talent at the non-graduate level" (Fuller and Raman 2017, 2). Today, there is an increasing number of postgraduate enrollment and mandatory bachelor's degree or postgraduate degree requirements on job postings where such education is not always necessary. In a 2017 analysis of 26 million job postings, the "discrepancy between the demand for a college degree in job postings and the employees who are currently in that job who have a college degree is significant" (Fuller and Raman 2017, 2). One example from the study illustrates where 67 percent of job postings for a production supervisor required a bachelor's degree, yet only 16 percent of persons with that job had one (Fuller and Raman 2017). The need to present the right signals to employers and be a competitive candidate for the "best" jobs and "highest" salaries is the most significant influence that encourages the pursuit of postsecondary education today. In the United States, postsecondary education is not mandatory, unlike compulsory K-12 education. It follows that this need to compete for the "best" jobs is exacerbated when there are downturns in the economy because the "best" jobs become scarce and employers that are still hiring seek the most qualified candidates. Underlying credential inflation is a concept that more qualifications can provide insulation against downturns in the economy. Motivated by positive correlations between education and earnings and the desire to transmit signals of intelligence and persistence to employers, individuals seek the assurance that they can "recession-proof" themselves by acquiring more qualifications. This influence, when combined with social and financial pressures, can nudge individuals to make a choice to pursue additional education.

THE PARENTAL INFLUENCE ON EDUCATION CHOICES

The role of familial and societal influences on education and career choices, or lack thereof, has been an active discussion in education policy for several decades. For most students, their families and social circles are their primary influence on college plans (Hossler et al. 1999). Research studying African-American students, in particular, has found that the key influences shaping their college prospects appear to stem from parents, teachers, counselors, and their overall interest in school (Howard 2003). Parents also influence their children's occupational aspirations innately through their socioeconomic status and the financial and educational resources they are able to provide to their children (Schnabel et al. 2002). Research by Peter Davies et al. (2014) found strong correlations between the intentions of high-school students to engage in higher education and the education levels of their parents, the student's cultural capital, and the expectation of return on investment in education. Other research suggests that nearly one-half of the relationship between a parent's education and their child's education is causal (Holmlund et al. 2011). In a choice architecture framework, Thaler and Sunstein (2008) ascribe the role of choice architect, the nudger, to parents that describe possible educational options to their children. But while they highlight the importance of the parent's involvement in the school choice process, Thaler and Sunstein (2008) stop short of discussing the role that nudges have in influencing discipline decisions and that what affects those decisions have on a microeconomic and macroeconomic level with regard to the school-to-work pipeline.

Interviews with school guidance counselors in research conducted by Rosenbaum et al. (1996) reveal that counselors do not want the responsibility or authority to influence who applies to college, a stark contrast from the role of this position in earlier times. As these authors note, the "counselors' unwillingness to act as gatekeepers can prevent students from getting the information and advice they need to prepare for their futures" (Rosenbaum et al. 1996, 257).

This conversation becomes more complicated when discussing the educational equity of students from diverse family backgrounds and income levels. Of the millions of students pursuing postsecondary education every year, many are the first in their families to attend college. These first-generation students and their families are exposed to the processes of selecting and applying to colleges, applying for financial aid or other funding sources for their education, and course selection for the first time. As a result, they often have difficulty navigating the steps. First-generation college students and their parents can especially be influenced by anecdotal evidence of success offered by certain disciplines, as they may not be as familiar with alternatives. To that end, these students rely on the recommendations of teachers and other nonfamily members when planning their postsecondary education (Roderick et al. 2011). Non-first-generation students are thus more likely to have an easier time preparing for college and engaging in the process and see college as a place they are entitled to attend (McDonough 1997).

Parents can become desperate for their children to have the best educational opportunities available, and can even go to extreme and sometimes *illegal* methods to make that happen. Often is the case where wealthy donors can contribute hefty sums to a university in exchange for a second look at their child's application. But, as that method is not guaranteed, parents may seek alternatives. As illustrated in the Operation Varsity Blues college bribery scandal, parents of children that were not qualified to attend elite schools engaged in bribery (upward of millions of dollars) to ensure their children would be admitted to the school of their choosing. What exactly is it about the pursuit of higher education that would encourage individuals to commit illegal acts on behalf of their children, who would otherwise be financially stable for life? Commentary from the *Los Angeles Times* indicates that social signaling is to blame as these wealthy parents are under intense pressure to demonstrate their excellent parenting skills as it relates to their own public perception and branding (Roy 2019). Other commentary in the *Huff Post* and *Newsweek* suggests that the status of certain American universities as gatekeepers to the upper-echelons of society and certain industries, coupled with the legitimization of social position granted by attending these institutions, is what motivated parents to go to such lengths on behalf of their children (Kingkade 2019; Goodkind 2019).

WHO ELSE NUDGES IN HIGHER
EDUCATION, AND HOW?

Is it legitimate for public and private institutions to affect enrollment behavior in higher education? According to Thaler and Sunstein (2008), such behavior is demonstrative of libertarian paternalism. This is the notion that the behavior can be affected while simultaneously respecting the freedom of choice. Libertarian paternalism tries to influence choices "that will make the choosers better off, as judged by themselves" (Thaler and Sunstein, 2008, 5). Higher education has many stakeholders that exist outside of the typical family unit described in the previous section. Government agencies, legislators, businesses, communities, and educational institutions all have an interest in maintaining a well-educated workforce and act in different ways to influence higher education. The methods used by stakeholders vary in scope and effectiveness. Writing for the Brookings Institute, Castleman (2015) denotes three guiding principles for how nudges should be applied in educational settings and poses important questions regarding the role and appropriateness of nudges. This set of principles encourages nudges to promote active and informed decision-making for parents as well as students. Castleman also emphasizes not overstating the value of nudges; rather they should be seen as supplemental to existing educational opportunities and investments.

Governments have initiated programs to reward college enrollment and studying disciplines that are seen as beneficial to society. In the United States, at the federal level, broad scholarship and research initiatives sponsored by organizations like the National Science Foundation (NSF) fund thousands of students pursuing education, research, or training in STEM (science, technology, engineering, and mathematics) fields every year (NSF N.d.), with 2,000 graduate research fellowships awarded in 2018 (NSF 2018). In other countries, most notably those in Europe, heavily subsidized or free college tuition even further incentivizes postsecondary enrollment.

At the state level, subsidies for public institutions can serve as a nudge to encourage enrollment. State governments also encourage students to pursue specific careers to meet their local workforce needs. In Maryland, the Workforce Shortage Student Assistance Grant program provides financial assistance to high-school seniors and college students that plan on having a career in certain fields, including childcare, human services, teaching, nursing, physical and occupational therapy, social work, and public service (Maryland Higher Education Commission N.d.). In Arkansas, the ArFuture grant covers tuition and fees for students that pursue STEM or areas of study that are in high demand in their region. A stipulation of this program is that it requires that a recipient of this program reside in Arkansas for three years *after* completing a degree or certificate program (Arkansas Department of Higher Education 2014). Programs like these have the capacity to nudge students into these fields, and away from others, by providing assistance *only* for certain types of education. State governments also provide subsidized tuition and merit-aid to students with residency in that state, with the intention to encourage those students to remain and work within the state postgraduation. Research shows that the state where a student attends college is likely to be the same state where they are working 15 years after graduation (Groen 2004).

Across the United States, legislators at the state level allocate billions of state funds to public institutions of higher education. Universities are increasingly demonstrating the return on investment of these funds by producing economic impact studies. Recent economic impact studies from the University System of Maryland (Clinch 2011) and the Pennsylvania State University (Swenson 2019) have found positive returns for every dollar spent, with their respective states receiving $2.70 and $1.24 in revenue per dollar allocated. These findings can be used by higher education lobbyists to inform legislators of the positive contributions related to government investment, which can justify or encourage legislators to maintain or increase funding for public colleges and universities.

Thaler and Sunstein (2008) discuss a legal requirement of the No Child Left Behind Act that required secondary schools to disclose student and/or parent directory information (name, phone number, address) to local recruitment branches of the U.S. military. This requirement bypassed the consent of those whose information was shared by mandating their participation with a cumbersome opt-out process. The outreach offered to these students by the military adds options to their career choice, although the mandatory method to which their personal information was acquired to enable this solicitation seems inappropriate. The influence military recruitment offices have, coupled with the targeted advertising demographic, makes nudging individuals that may or may not have been predisposed to military service more convenient. There is debate regarding the nature of military recruitment efforts, with the term "poverty draft" being used by activists and scholars to allege targeted military recruitment of the poor due to their limited alternative options. During the Vietnam War, the ability to defer draft enlistment for students who could attend college (students wealthy enough to afford college and educated enough to gain admission) lead to a disproportionate draft pool of Hispanic and African-Americans, which subsequently lead to higher casualty rates for those groups (Talbot 2003). As the United States has not implemented a draft since 1973, the military relies entirely on voluntary enlistment and persuades enlistees, primarily high-school-aged students, with the promise of job/skills training and higher education opportunities after completion. However, questions regarding the recruitment and enlistment of the poor remain. In 2007, The Associated Press reported that nearly 75 percent of U.S. soldiers killed in the Iraq war came from towns where the per-capita income was below the national average and over 50 percent came from towns where the percentage of people living in poverty was higher than the national average (The Associated Press 2007). On the other hand, a Heritage Foundation analysis disputes the notion of the U.S. military exploiting the poor, young, and ignorant as a "caricature" (Kane 2005). Rather, it is argued the "high-skill human capital" (Kane 2005) of the U.S. military makes it the most efficient and productive combat force in history.

In 2011, the Pew Research Center found that black women were enlisting in the military at a disproportionately high rate relative to the overall female civilian population, comprising 31 percent of enlisted military women (Patten and Parker 2011). This represents more than double the proportion of the civilian population. Among their male peers, black men represented 16 percent of the male enlisted population, which was equal to their proportion of the civilian population (Patten and Parker 2011). Research suggests that such high enlistment among black women is the result of various factors including welfare reform, the dramatic rise in female-headed households, and the economic crisis of 2008 (Melin 2016). These factors provide the necessary pressure for those seeking the stability, job training, and postsecondary education opportunities provided by the military.

The U.S. military nudges postsecondary education enrollment through a number of its programs. The Reserve Officers' Training Corps (ROTC) program encourages a career in military service by providing military training and scholarships to college students in exchange for mandatory service after degree completion (U.S. Army 2018). Other initiatives, such as the GI Bill, nudge postsecondary education enrollment by providing funding after service in the military. The U.S. Department of Veteran's Affairs provides aptitude testing to influence the career path decision of GI Bill beneficiaries. This tool, called CareerScope, gauges interests and ability and gives recommendations about what careers or courses would be best suited for the individual (VBA 2017). However, the GI Bill only covers three years, or 36 months, of full-time enrollment support (VBA 2018). Veterans may receive additional funding through the Edith Nourse Rogers STEM Scholarship program, of up to $30,000, but *only* for students pursuing education in STEM fields (VBA 2019). Since a typical bachelor's degree takes approximately four years to complete, the additional scholarship changes the choice architecture by providing additional incentives to pursue a fully funded bachelor's degree in STEM as opposed to a three-fourths funded degree in any other field. Programs like this demonstrate the perceived value of certain types of education over others and encourage enrollment in those programs through financial incentives. This type of encouragement is not unique to veterans and can often be found in other types of higher education programming as well. One such program is the Pennsylvania State University's Millennium Scholars program, which provides a generous financial support package over four years contingent on the student's academic success in a STEM program of study (Penn State Millennium Scholars 2019). It can be implied that, through the support of these programs, the sponsoring organization is clearly supportive of certain educational choices over others. It is reasonable then to assume that these financial incentives and inherent influences have an effect on how students chose to enroll and what academics they pursue while enrolled. It is also possible that the value of their degree becomes distorted, as not all STEM degrees are treated equally in the labor market and, further, not all

STEM degrees lead to employment in an area where the student may choose to reside. For example, an aerospace engineering student may wish to live in the same state as their family or community, but if that region does not have a thriving aerospace sector, it becomes difficult to determine if their skills are still valuable in the regional labor market. Not only that, but as STEM fields develop, skills may become outdated over time and require additional skills training. Technology fields are notorious for this as the development of the Internet over the last decade has caused a significant retooling of the skillset necessary to become a web designer or web developer.

Nudge interventions in education generally stem from a desire to improve existing systems by making choices more available and easier to engage. Personal assistance nudging has shown to have a positive effect on college enrollment. In one example, applications for federal financial aid (FAFSA) were facilitated by a tax preparation company for low-income high-school seniors. To simplify the process, the tax company was able to use the tax information that was provided by the family and the student to complete their taxes to fill out the required FAFSA forms electronically. Tax preparers were also able to provide guidance throughout the process. This assistance alleviated much of the anxiety, procrastination, confusion, and error in completing the FAFSA application. It also improved the likelihood of students enrolling in college the following year by more than 28 percent over a control group of students that did not participate in the program (Bettinger et al. 2012). Thaler and Sunstein (2008) also suggest simplifying the FAFSA application process, noting that the complexity often "can discourage students from applying for financial aid and cause them to seek pricey direct-to-consumer loans instead" (Thaler and Sunstein 2008, 141). Other interventions in the form of tax breaks, stipends, and in-state subsidies have not necessarily had as significant an effect on college enrollment (Benartzi et al. 2017).

In Louisiana, completion of the FAFSA application has recently become a requirement to graduate from high school. This requirement has led to an increase in FAFSA applications from 44 percent in the 2012–2013 student-aid year/FAFSA cycle (Camera 2015) to 82.6 percent in 2019–2020 (Form Your Future 2019), making it the state with the most students completing the application. Louisiana's effort to increase FAFSA applications is largely due to the Louisiana Department of Education's recognition that the success in the current and future labor market requires employees to have postsecondary degrees. A report by the Louisiana Department of Education (2014) estimated that students not completing the FAFSA application "forego roughly $54 million each year in federal grants, state opportunities, and other funding for postsecondary education" (Louisiana Department of Education 2014, 1). Students and parents are provided one-on-one assistance to encourage participation and application completion. Beginning in the 2020–2021 academic year, Texas will follow suit by making FAFSA or Texas Application for State Financial Aid mandatory for high-school graduation (Krieghbaum 2019). Both Louisiana and Texas have waivers and opt-out protocols that allow parents and students over 18 to not participate, and school counselors have the ability to waive the FAFSA requirement with "good cause." In the 2019–2020 academic year, Texas ranked 31 with a FAFSA completion rate of 55.2 percent. Administrators are hoping that Texas will experience some of the same success that Louisiana has seen by adopting this mandatory measure, because even a fraction of that success still means that thousands of students could complete applications that would not have otherwise (Krieghbaum 2019). It is important to understand that while programs like this encourage students to complete a FAFSA application and eliminate a significant barrier to college enrollment, another choice architecture emerges that can influence what financial aid or loans students end up receiving. For example, a student with limited financial literacy could be offered a $10,000 loan for college, enroll in a class, and then drop out of the course. That student is still responsible for the loan, even if they do not complete the coursework. The nudge that financial loans and aid provide can encourage enrollment in coursework, but because the consequences are separated from the choices made, and the fact that students are young and often lack financial literacy or stability, issues with self-control (loan-size) and decision-making (school choice) arise.

Providers of academic aptitude testing have a vested interest in the college selection process, as most universities require submission of test scores for admission or merit scholarships, and therefore the default college choice architecture requires prospective college applicants to engage with these organizations. In 2018, over 2.1 million students took the SAT, 1.9 million students took the ACT, 138,597 took the LSAT, over 500,000 took the GRE, and over 200,000 took the GMAT.[3] Recent studies have provided conflicting evidence on whether education nudges in the form of test score waivers and engagement with application materials provided by testing administrators have had an impact. One nudge included changing the number of free ACT score reports sent to colleges from three to four. Prior to fall 1997, sending three score reports was free and each subsequent report cost six dollars. After 1997, the default changed to four free score reports, with the fee for sending subsequent reports remaining the same. Pallais (2015) found that changing the default of three free report submissions to four substantially increased the amount of score reports and college applications among both high- and low-income students, with low-income students attending more selective colleges. However, because it is the new default, it can be interpreted as ACT recommending that three or four applications are enough, while the College Board (2019) recommends five to eight. The College Board recently conducted research inspired by Hoxby and Turner's (2013) work but did not quite come to the same conclusions. Hoxby and Turner (2013) found that sending college information and application fee waivers to low-income, high-achieving students encouraged them to enroll at more selective colleges. When the College Board (Gurantz et al. 2019) tried a similar approach, they found no changes in college enrollment patterns among 785,000 low- and middle-income students in the top 50 percent of PSAT and SAT distributions. The authors attribute the failure of this program to the level of trust and confidence students have in the College Board, given the various roles and interactions it has with these students, relative to other organizations providing similar information and waivers (Gurantz et al. 2019).

Because college enrollment is competitive and admission relies heavily on aptitude test scores, organizations have made a business of selling test preparation services. These services operate on the belief that practice, specialized test-taking knowledge, and strategy can improve test scores (MacGowen 1999). High socioeconomic status high-school students view these programs as a method to gain a competitive edge in the applications process (McDonough 1997). Promises of significant score increases and winning strategies by these companies are countered by research by the Educational Testing Service, the company behind the GRE (Powers and Rock 1999). Companies are so confident in their strategies that they will often offer guarantees, refunds, or additional courses to students who do not see significant increases in their standardized test scores after enrolling in their programs. Regardless, their existence encourages enrollment among college-bound students that seek the most desired test score outcomes. The encouragement of students to spend money and participate in these test preparation courses serve as another influence due to the escalation of commitment to college enrollment.

Other nudges in the form of text message alerts and reminders such as those described by Thaler and Sunstein (2008) are now being used in education to gently remind students and their families of deadlines for applications. Research shows that these simple, cost-effective, nonintrusive methods have had an effect on the rate of students completing these tasks and engaging in postsecondary education, particularly on students with less-developed plans for college and among students with limited college planning support (see Castleman and Page 2015, 2016, 2017). Among college students without a college plan at graduation, text message outreach increased their on-time college enrollment by 7 percent (Castleman and Page 2015). In Dallas, the text message intervention increased the likelihood of students to enroll at two-year institutions by nearly 5 percent and by 8 percent when adjusting for a functioning cell phone number for either the student or the parent (Castleman and Page 2015).

Educational institutions have a significant influence in the process and leverage that influence in many different ways. In one arena, they can manipulate their targeted messaging and advertising to influence a type of student to enroll. Pamphlets and brochures showing a diverse student body are common, and they can influence a student's decision to consider an institution. But the reality is that the institutions present exaggerated representations of campus diversity as part of their recruitment efforts. A recent study revealed that the majority of 165 four-year higher education institutions studied in the United States "provided images of diversity to prospective students in 2011 that were significantly different than the actual student body" (Pippert et al. 2013, 258). The study also found that institutions portrayed higher rates of African-American students in these materials in an effort to symbolize diversity, rather than a more representative student body (Pippert et al. 2013). Now consider the influence this type of messaging has on a first-generation ethnic or racial minority. Such a student has a limited knowledge of college and campus environments, and may be looking for a campus where they fit in and feel included. When considering the influence of this messaging on lower income families, students may suffer from a lack of resources to visit prospective universities and come to their own determination about the demographic composition of campuses. In both cases, deceptive images of diversity can contribute to college mismatch if a student's expectations are misled by advertising a certain environment. The case here is that colleges can and do leverage their messaging to nudge or encourage the enrollment of certain students.

Colleges can also leverage their advertising in a predatory manner to encourage enrollment. ITT Technical Institute is one such institution. ITT was a for-profit higher education institution that provided associate, bachelor's and master's degrees geared toward people who perceive themselves as not having other options but who want to improve their life and the lives of their family members. ITT offered "some of the most expensive programs of any for-profit college, forcing many students to borrow the maximum available Federal aid and to take on additional private debt" (U.S. Senate Report 112–37, 2012). It charged approximately $45,000 for an associate's degree and over $90,000 for a bachelor's degree, and in 2008 the default rate of ITT's students was over 26 percent (Senate Report 112–37, 2012). It was characterized by its predatory student recruiting practices and was sued by the Consumer Financial Protection Bureau in 2014 for predatory lending related to its targeting of low-income students and promising better career prospects. The organization declared bankruptcy in 2016 after the U.S. Department of Education took action to prevent students from using federal loans for ITT education. ITT and similar institutions that capitalize on students wanting to make a change in their lives utilize marketing that promises a career and a better future. These institutions are financially incentivized to nudge students to make poor educational decisions and benefit immensely from their aggressive marketing and recruitment strategies. According to a U.S. Senate report on for-profit higher education, ITT trained its recruiters to respond to prospective student's questions about tuition costs with responses like: "Do you want a discount education, or a valuable one that will give you a return in the future?" and "Education is an investment in you and an investment in yourself is never a bad investment" (U.S. Senate Report 112-37, 2012, 558). Such tactics can influence students with limited financial literacy to make poor decisions about their education. The desire and pressure to acquire and leverage education signals can nudge poor decision-making by discarding the quality of the degree just for the sake of having a degree at all.

Universities can also influence people to make better, or smarter, decisions about their educational investment. In addition to marketing, universities also provide academic advising to help students select courses and pursue their interests. Artificial intelligence and machine learning are currently being used in higher education to assist with advising. Essentially, information about a student that is enrolled in Sociology 301 for the upcoming semester is fed into a machine that contains data on all students that have ever taken that course, their academic profiles, when they took that course, what professor taught that course, and so on. The algorithm is able to predict how a student will perform based on their academic history as well as the rigor of other classes they are enrolled in. Such information can be used by academic advisors to encourage or discourage enrollment in certain coursework or schedules due to the predicted high risk of withdrawal or failure. Students are generally not aware of this algorithm, but because advisors are, it can manipulate how information is transmitted and how decisions are made.

Through traditional general education requirements, universities encourage exposure to various academic fields. These general education requirements allow some degree of freedom in the courses that the student must choose. Professors can nudge or recommend enrollment in their courses by sending out email bulletins, placing posters on common wall space, or discussing that course in other courses. Universities provide students a chance to complete and submit feedback about the professor at the end of a course, encouraging honest review of instructors and the coursework. Higher education institutions also provide online education options, but this also can have nudge educational choices. Not all course options are available in an online format, yet the convenience of being able to work on schoolwork or participate in a course from home at any time, day or night, can influence how a student chooses to enroll.[4]

Universities have a long-term stake in producing high-earning alumni that can become donors, which then produce potential students that tend to be predisposed to enrolling in an institution their family members attended. These potential students, known as legacies, can have an advantage in the admissions process because universities often include legacy status in the admissions decision. This can sometimes influence an admissions decision for a university for a few reasons: (1) to keep the donors, the legacy's family members, happy; (2) encourage family enrollment to discourage competition; and (3) increased retention. A potential legacy student is influenced by their family's experience in a way that a first-generation student is not, and it is this familial nudge, coupled with beneficial nudges on behalf of the university's Office of Admissions, that makes enrolling in a familiar school easier.

Organizations that provide college ranking information can significantly nudge college enrollment decisions. In 1995, more than 40 percent of college freshmen indicated that national college rankings had a significant role in their college choice (McDonough et al. 1998). In the United States, the *U.S. News and World Report* maintains the most recognized college rankings publication. They calculate a college's ranking based on several factors, among them peer assessment, guidance counselor assessment, retention, faculty resources, student selectivity, financial resources per student, graduation rate, and alumni giving rate (*U.S. News and World Report* 2019). Research on the significance of the *U.S. News and World Report* on college decisions has found that a one-rank increase leads to nearly a 1 percent increase in the number of applicants (Luca and Smith 2013). Universities that are able to move into the top 50, or the front page of the rankings list, can expect an increase of 3.9 percent in the overall applications and 2.3 percent increase in the number of incoming students that graduated in the upper 10 percent of their high-school class (Bowman and Bastedo 2009). Research has also found that school choice decisions are responsive to rank changes, with sensitivity declining at lower rankings (Griffith and Rask 2005). Universities that drop out of the top 50 experience fewer applications, between 2 and 6 percent, depending on how far out of the top 50 a university falls (Meyer et al. 2017).

Students and their parents may view the *U.S. News and World Report* and organizations that provide similar services as experts, leading them to trust their ability to define the quality of an institution (McDonough et al. 1998). This is particularly important when considering the limited experience and knowledge of first-generation students. The choice architect, *U.S. News and World Report*, can manipulate how information about colleges is presented to affect engagement rates among potential students. When the *U.S. News and World Report* rankings are sorted alphabetically, college rankings have no effect on applications (Luca and Smith 2013). This demonstrates that the nudge for college sorting is strongest when related to how the information is shown to prospective students. One of the most significant criticisms of the *U.S. News and World Report* surrounds its rankings methodology and the institutional reputation surveys issued to academics outside of the college being surveyed. Critics argue that the methodology is catered toward Ivy League schools, like Princeton, Harvard, and Yale, due to the methodology's emphasis on perceived reputation, alumni donations, and financial resources. Regardless of its questionable formulas, it still maintains its position as the most popular ranking tool in the United States.

Rankings lists exist and are advertised by universities to transmit desired education signals to prospective students. Education signals are often related to the quality of the education and the cost incurred to acquire that education. A bachelor's degree in the same major from a local hometown university and Stanford University transmits different signals. The Stanford degree is more prestigious, harder to acquire, more expensive, and implies access to a wealthy and expansive alumni network. Students and their families rely on these lists in the ranked format to efficiently access and digest information on institutions.

THE SCHOOL-TO-WORK PIPELINE

The concept of a school-to-work pipeline is fairly self-evident. It is essentially the pathway that connects all educational investments in an individual, from preschool to higher education, and results in employment. This pipeline is essentially a creative articulation of the process of human capital theory and returns to education. However, there are many barriers that can limit the effectiveness of transitioning students from school to the workforce.

As discussed previously, there are many costs associated with educational investment. Most of these occur in the present. Some of these costs can be tangibly quantified: housing expenses, student tuition and fees, school materials. Other expenses present themselves as less quantifiable, particularly when discussing the costs associated with psychological or mental exertion, morale, and opportunities foregone by enrollment in an educational program. In the United States, the annual average cost of college attendance exceeds $20,000 (National Center for Education Statistics 2018b). With an undergraduate education generally requiring four years of schooling, it is no surprise that students pursuing higher education may turn to student loans to defer these costs.

Thaler and Sunstein (2008) acknowledge that issues with self-control generally result when choices and consequences are separated in time. In the context of education, the choice presents itself as an option to pursue additional schooling and even more choices regarding the specialization. These choices are separated from the outcomes (availability and expectations of employment and earnings) and consequences (e.g., student loan debt repayment, limited practical experience), which occur sometime after the choice has been made. Those choices can be made in an environment that is, at least temporarily, insulated from the reality of those consequences. There exists a plethora of research exposing the inconsistent preferences of college students and other individuals that choose to invest in education (Boatman et al. 2014).

Student loan repayment generally occurs months after earning a degree; however, it can also occur when a student falls below a certain threshold of course enrollment or drops out from schooling. Approximately 20 percent of the students that incurred student loan debt to pursue higher education were behind on their payments in 2017 (Board of Governors of the Federal Reserve System 2018). Debt burden can influence a student's specialization by inadvertently discouraging certain professions that may not pay enough to cover the cost of the loans. Programs like the Public Sector Loan Forgiveness (PSLF) provide assistance for those that are willing to engage in qualifying nonprofit or government-sponsored work for a period of 10 years. This program in particular creates an incentive to pursue costly education that may not return significant financial benefits, at least not immediately. Teacher Loan Forgiveness provides up to $17,500 of student loan forgiveness for five consecutive years of full-time teaching in certain schools or agencies serving low-income families. This type of program can nudge a career path, but it also encourages education choices by serving as something a student believes they can rely on before they graduate as a means to repay their loan. Loan forgiveness almost sounds too good to be true, and as it turns out, it seems that can be the case. As of September 30, 2020, there were 5,069 eligible PSLF applications out of 210,813, representing a rejection rate of 97.5 percent of all completed applications (Federal Student Aid 2020). Imagine a scenario in which you are an aspiring law student and are led to believe you might qualify for PSLF following graduation. You might consider a more costly or prestigious law school over your local hometown university. You might also tailor your education to specialize in law that might benefit you in the public or nonprofit industries so that you will succeed in upholding your end of the deal to work in those industries for ten years. You might eschew other opportunities, such as internships or networking events, as a result. At the end of your legal education, you graduate with six figures of student loan debt and have been successfully nudged into a career you may not have otherwise chosen. Then, if you're unlucky enough to be in the 97.5 percent of rejected PSLF applications, your loan debt is not forgiven. This is a reality for those who made life-altering educational choices contingent on the promise and their reliance on loan forgiveness. Now consider the plight of those who pursue higher education and end up not completing their degree.

Between 2014 and 2016, 3.9 million undergraduate students with federal student loan debt dropped out of college (Barshay 2017). Because these students left college and did not complete their degrees, it follows that their education signals and qualifications are not enough to compete in the labor market with those who did finish college. They therefore often struggle to find good jobs to pay back the loans for the education they *did* receive. According to the U.S. Department of Education (2015), non-completers are three times more likely to default than borrowers who earn their degrees. There is no doubt that the existing choice architecture and societal expectations of college being the only pathway to success has had an effect on these student's choices. Could better decisions have been made, factoring in whether students should have taken on loans in the first place, how much they should have been taken on, and whether they were stable or persistent enough to complete a degree?

A recent Gallup (2017) survey found that students currently enrolled in college nationwide did not feel prepared to enter the workforce. Nearly two-thirds of respondents felt they would not graduate with the skills necessary to succeed in the workforce or job market, and only half of the respondents felt their major would lead to a good job. These metrics do not bode well for maintaining a stable and sustainable pipeline of qualified candidates into the workforce. It also suggests significant disconnects between institutions and the needs of their students.

DATA AND STEPS TO IMPROVE DATA AVAILABILITY

Across the nation, data on employment and earnings outcomes for postsecondary education and training programs are uneven, limited in scope, and generally not localized for local or regional labor markets. Often, these data are not available in a manner that can be easily accessed and understood by a student or their family. As noted by Thaler and Sunstein (2008), when it is costly to acquire and process information, individuals will logically create methods that eliminate options for consideration. This process, particularly in the context of low-income, middle-income, or first-generation students, can worsen the problem of inequality and mismatches in education. In the aforementioned Gallup (2017) survey, the majority of respondents (51 percent) responded that they would change their major, institution, or degree type if they could re-do their college experience. One of the influencers of this sentiment in the poll was the lack of information regarding degrees and the associated career paths. Universities have engaged in their own metrics, but the uneven nature of these measures and inconsistent definitions make it difficult to compare across institutions. Legal restrictions, such as FERPA and federal bans prohibiting the tracking of college alumni, have limited the accessibility and availability of outcomes data to inform students and their families.

The College Scorecard (2019) tool provides limited information on median earnings for college and university alumni. This tool attempts to increase transparency in the college comparison process, allowing students and their families to see costs and outcomes. However, there are some significant drawbacks to this tool. Not only are the data not comprehensive, but they are not longitudinal, and they do not differentiate the outcomes of branch campuses from main campuses of a university. Because the outcomes-related data are based on a specific subset of students,[5] they are inherently biased and are not adequate for decision-making.

At the university level, institutions have been implementing an outreach survey with the goal of compiling data to better inform prospective students about employment outcomes is the National Association of Colleges and Employers' (NACE) First Destination Survey. In 2016, 350 schools and their career centers submitted bachelor's graduates survey responses to NACE, representing 516,000 bachelor's degree recipients. Factoring in associate's degree and master's degree recipients, the total number of graduates from these reporting institutions increase to 650,000. NACE asserts that their survey offers "[t]o our knowledge, this represents the most comprehensive view of graduate outcomes currently available" (NACE 2017, 6). However, they also recognize that there are challenges with data collection. Because this instrument is a survey, it suffers from input validation issues and response bias. However, universities have been able to use it as a marketing tool in addition to informing decision-making about effective programming.

Other measures that are currently being explored are partnerships with state and federal agencies to provide administrative data matching. However, due to the Higher Education Opportunity Act of 2008, the federal government is prohibited from creating or maintaining any database containing student-level educational records and employment data. As a result, most employment data that are available are on a state-level basis. The exception being data recently acquired through higher education partnerships with the U.S. Census Bureau's Post-Secondary Employment Outcomes (PSEO) project. This is a massive step forward in acquiring national employment and earnings information as well as making these data generally accessible to the public. This partnership between the higher education institutions and the U.S. Census Bureau has mutual benefits. Because the federal tracking ban extends to the U.S. Census Bureau, the data that the federal government has on employment and earnings related to a college degree is limited. Using data submitted by the participating higher education institutions, the U.S. Census Bureau can improve their research while providing informative data for use in education planning. Universities have begun to display these data in a

public-facing and interactive format to maximize the utility of this information. Universities have taken further steps to associate these data with median
student loan debt at graduation and publicly displaying loan debt to income
ratios in an effort to be transparent about both the cost of a college education
and the ability of alumni to pay back their student loan debt following graduation. As of September 2021, over 330 institutions are participating in the
PSEO project, including all public postsecondary institutions in the states of
Colorado and Texas, the campuses of the City University of New York and
the State University of New York system, the Pennsylvania State University,
the University of Michigan, and the University of Wisconsin-Madison have
matched national outcomes data with the PSEO project. Additionally, the
Ohio Department of Higher Education, representing public postsecondary
institutions in Ohio, has engaged the U.S. Census Bureau regarding this project and is soon to receive matched data.

Recent proposals by Senator Elizabeth Warren (D-MA) and the Trump
administration's Department of Education have sought to mitigate or over-
turn the federal tracking ban that prohibits the collection of these data for
outcomes metrics. Thus, it remains to be seen how new information provided
in new ways will influence the decisions of individuals.

CONCLUSION

The policy implications for this research are manifold and have been articulated throughout the chapter. First, a skilled workforce is critical for a glob-
ally competitive economy, and the demand for education and training has
been increasing for years. Recognizing the influences that exist when individuals seek to invest in human capital is crucial to understanding how those
influences can be manipulated. This becomes especially important when
considering the negative effects of skills shortages in the workforce and the
premium that professions can earn as a result of those shortages.

Second, billions of dollars in government spending are allocated to
higher education pursuits every year. There are a multitude of federal and
state programs designed to help students pursue postsecondary education.
The effectiveness of these programs, comparatively, is varied. Researchers
sought to determine the cost-effectiveness nudge interventions compared to
three traditional financial incentives to subsidize the cost of enrollment. The
three traditional interventions consisted of a Social Security Student Benefit
program that supplied monthly student stipend for students with parents that
were eligible for benefits, states providing education subsidies for students
to enroll in-state public university enrollment, and the effectiveness of the
Hope Scholarship, Lifetime Learning, and American Opportunity tax credits.

Compared to the nudge to complete FAFSA with when preparing taxes, researchers have found the nudge intervention to be significantly more cost-effective, with an approximate cost of the nudge at $53 per participant and the traditional interventions costing between $4,400 and $5,200 per participant (Benartzi et al. 2017). Demonstrating the return on investment of these programs is important to maintain their funding and prove that interventions are working. Nudges have been successfully implemented in public schools and have made significant differences relative to their cost of implementation.

With the increased prevalence of federally backed student loans and a nationwide student loan debt skyrocketing toward $2 trillion, the public has even more of an incentive to monitor how these loans are administered. Simultaneously, individuals seeking education need to make smart decisions that will enable them to pay back their debts while working and living comfortably using the knowledge and skills developed from pursuing higher education. However, if students are to make smart decisions about their education, they need to have quality data available to them. Due to federal policies and disconnected systems, this has been difficult to accomplish in the past. But the necessity of these data demonstrates why it is a pressing public policy issue.

Throughout this chapter, the emphasis has been on the freedom to choose: choices regarding institution, specialization, level of degree, cost, and so on; how those choices are delivered through influencers; and how decisions are made based on available information. The notion of libertarian paternalism, articulated by Thaler and Sunstein (2008), becomes relevant when we recognize that barriers to making these choices should be easier to overcome. In making them so, institutions, both private and public, can have a legitimate role in influencing behavior. It is through the lens of libertarian paternalism that we must regard actions taken by the various entities involved in education policy to implement or improve systems that promote freedom of choice.

NOTES

1. Much of this chapter is predicated on the notion that postsecondary education itself provides economic returns and that these returns are a large motivating factor for enrollment. However, education serves a variety of purposes and can also be seen as a consumption good. The consumer benefits of higher education are plentiful, including the desire and satisfaction to learn, engage in social networking, obtain status or prestige, and so on.

2. In his observation, Smith (1776) indicated that earnings gains of journeymen who have completed apprenticeship education are "very little more than the day

wages of common labourers" (Smith 1776, 119), and that while their earnings may be slighter higher, they are no more than "what is sufficient to compensate the superior expense of their education" (Smith 1776, 119). While the fundamental principle remains the same, today we can see disparities between educated and uneducated laborers, particularly in the skilled trades or fields like construction. Smith (1776, 119) seems to indicate the difference between the wages between the two is just enough to recover the costs of investing in education; however, the context for "very little more" is lacking.

3. Aptitude test participation numbers retrieved from:

SAT: https://reports.collegeboard.org/pdf/2018-total-group-sat-suite-assessments-annual-report.pdf

ACT: http://www.act.org/content/dam/act/unsecured/documents/cccr2018/P_99_999999_N_S_N00_ACT-GCPR_National.pdf

LSAT: https://www.lsac.org/data-research/data/lsat-trends-total-lsats-administered-admin-year

GRE: https://www.ets.org/s/gre/pdf/snapshot_test_taker_data_2018.pdf

GMAT: https://www.gmac.com/gmat-other-assessments/about-the-gmat-exam/the-gmat-advantage

4. The COVID-19 pandemic caused a significant shift in utility and acceptance of online education formats by the general public and institutions. Institutions that previously only offered in-person education for certain courses were forced to transition to fully remote education. But online education is not without its challenges, as students grappled with technological difficulties and unstable home environments due to large-scale unemployment. Enrollment declines rose in 2020 as students chose to defer enrollment until they could fully enjoy the college experience or justify the tuition and fees cost what was effectively an online education, with a 3.6 percent decline (National Student Clearinghouse 2020) in enrollment among undergraduate students. In addition, international students enrolling in the United States struggled to obtain visas to enter the country. Historically, the ministries of education in students home territories will not recognize or sponsor online education, leading to difficulty among students who are forced to enroll online due to the cancellation of in-person courses. Grades for online coursework during this time have also changed to Pass/Fail or Satisfactory/Unsatisfactory at many universities, allowing students to adopt a binary set of grades over the traditional scale. It remains to be seen how these grades will send signals to graduate school admissions officers reviewing transcripts.

5. College Scorecard only reports data on students that have received federal grants and loans in the pursuit of their education. Thus, there is implicit bias in the student outcomes being reported, as not all students fund their education this way.

REFERENCES

Arkansas Department of Higher Education. 2014. *Arkansas Future Grant (ArFuture)*. Little Rock, AR. Retrieved from https://scholarships.adhe.edu/scholarships/detail/arfutures

Barshay, Jill. 2017. "Federal data shows 3.9 million students dropped out of college with debt in 2015 and 2016." *The Hechinger Report*, November 6. https://heching erreport.org/federal-data-shows-3-9-million-students-dropped-college-debt-2015 -2016/

Becker, Gary S. 1962. "Investment in human capital: A theoretical analysis." *Journal of Political Economy* 70, no. 5: 9–49.

Benartzi, Shlomo, John Beshears, Katherine L. Milkman, Cass R. Sunstein, Richard H. Thaler, Maya Shankar, Will Tucker-Ray, William J. Congdon, and Steven Galing. 2017. "Should governments invest more in nudging?" *Psychological Science,* 28, no. 8: 1041–55.

Bettinger, Eric. P., Bridget T, Long, Philip Oreopoulos, and Lisa Sanbonmatsu. 2012. "The role of application assistance and information in college decisions: Results from the H&R Block FAFSA experiment." *Quarterly Journal of Economics* 127: 1205–42.

Board of Governors of the Federal Reserve System. 2018. *Report on the economic well-being of U.S. households in 2017.* Washington, DC: United States Government. https://www.federalreserve.gov/publications/2018-economic-well-be ing-of-us-households-in-2017-description-of-the-survey.htm

Boatman, Angela, Brent Evans, and Adela Soliz. 2014. *Applying the lessons of behavioral economics to improve the federal student loan programs: Six policy recommendations.* Indianapolis, IN: Lumina Foundation. https://www .luminafoundation.org/files/publications/ideas_summit/Applying_the_Lessons _of_Behavioral_Economics_to_improve_the_Federal_Policy_Loan_Programs .pdf

Bowman, Nicholas A. and Michael N. Bastedo. 2009. "Getting on the front page: Organizational reputation status signals, and the impact of U.S. News and World Report on student decisions." *Research in Higher Education* 50, no. 5: 415–36.

Camera, Lauren. 2015. "No FAFSA, no diploma in Louisiana." *U.S. News and World Report*, December 22. https://www.usnews.com/news/articles/2015-12-22/louisia na-to-require-students-to-fill-out-fafsa

Caplan, Bryan. 2018. *The case against education: Why the education system is a waste of time and money.* Princeton, NJ: Princeton University Press.

Carnevale, Andrew P., and Ban Cheah. 2018. *Five rules of the college and career game.* Washington, DC: Georgetown University Center on Education and the Workforce. https://cew.georgetown.edu/cew-reports/5rules/

Castleman, Benjamin L. 2015. *Knowing when to nudge in education.* Washington, DC: Brookings Institution. https://www.brookings.edu/blog/brown-center-chalkb oard/2015/08/06/knowing-when-to-nudge-in-education/

Castleman, Benjamin L., and Lindsay C. Page. 2015. "Summer nudging: Can personalized text messages and peer mentor outreach increase college going among low-income high school graduates." *Journal of Economic Behavior and Organization* 115, 144–60.

Castleman, Benjamin L., and Lindsay C. Page. 2016. "Freshman year financial aid nudges: An experiment to increase FAFSA renewal and college persistence." *Journal of Human Resources* 51, no. 2: 389–415.

Castleman, Benjamin L., and Lindsay C. Page. 2017. "Parental influences on postsecondary decision making: Evidence from a text messaging experiment." *Educational Evaluation and Policy Analysis* 39, no. 2: 361–77.

Clinch, Richard. 2011. *The economic impact of the University System of Maryland. A fiscal perspective.* Baltimore, MD: University of Baltimore, Jacob France Institute. http://www.usmd.edu/newsroom/docs/USMEconomicImpact_final-1.pdf

College Scorecard. 2019. *Data documentation for college scorecard.* Washington, DC: U.S. Department of Education. https://collegescorecard.ed.gov/assets/FullData taDocumentation.pdf

Davies, Peter, Tian Qiu, and Neil M. Davies. 2014. "Cultural and human capital, information and higher education choices." *Journal of Education Policy* 29, no. 6: 804–25.

Federal Student Aid. 2020. *Public service loan forgiveness data.* Washington, DC: U.S. Department of Education. https://studentaid.gov/data-center/student/loan-fo rgiveness/pslf-data

Form Your Future. 2019. *Form your future FAFSA tracker.* Washington, DC: National College Assessment Network. https://formyourfuture.org/fafsa-tracker/

Fuller, Joseph, B., and Manjari Raman. 2017. *Dismissed by degrees: How degree inflation is undermining U.S. competitiveness and hurting America's middle class.* Cambridge, MA: Harvard Business School, Accenture, Grads of Life. https://www .hbs.edu/managing-the-future-of-work/Documents/dismissed-by-degrees.pdf

Hayek, Friedrich A. 1945. "The use of knowledge in society." *The American Economic Review* 35, no. 4: 519–30.

Holmlund, Helena, Mikael Lindahl, and Erik Plug. 2011. "The causal effect of parents' schooling on children' schooling: A comparison of estimation methods." *Journal of Economic Literature* 49, no. 3: 615–51.

Hossler, Don, Jack Schmidt, and Nick Vesper. 1999. *Going to college: How social, economic, and educational factors influence the decisions students make.* Baltimore, MD: Johns Hopkins University Press.

Howard, Tyrone C. 2003. "A tug of war for our minds: African American high school students' perceptions of their academic identities and college aspirations." *The High School Journal* 87, no. 1: 4–17.

Hoxby, Caroline and Sarah Turner. 2013. "Expanding college opportunities for high-achieving, low-income students." *Stanford University Institute for Economic Policy Research Working Paper,* No. 12-014. https://siepr.stanford.edu/research/publicati ons/expanding-college-opportunities-high-achieving-low-income-students

Gallup. 2017. *College student survey.* Washington, DC. https://stradaeducation.gallup .com/reports/225161/2017-strada-gallup-college-student-survey.aspx

Goodkind, Nicole. 2019. "An end to affirmative action? Why the college-admissions scandal could fulfill critics' wish to scrap race-based program." *Newsweek*, March 22. https://www.newsweek.com/2019/04/12/affirmative-action-college-admissions -statistics-scandal-1372652.html

Griffith, Amanda, and Kevin Rask. 2005. "The influence of the U.S. News and World Report collegiate rankings on the matriculation decision of high-ability students: 1995–2004." *Economics of Education Review* 26, no. 2: 244–55.

Groen, Jeffrey A. 2004. "The effect of college location on migration of college-educated labor." *Journal of Econometrics* 121, no. 1–2: 125–42.

Gurantz, Oded, Jessica Howell, Mike Hurwitz, Cassandra Larson, Matea Pender, and Brooke White. 2019. "Realizing your college potential? Impacts of College Board's RYCP campaign on postsecondary enrollment." *Annenberg Institute at Brown University Ed Working Paper*, No. 19-40. http://edworkingpapers.com/ai19-40

Kane, Tim. 2005. *Who bears the burden? Demographic characteristics of U.S. military recruitment before and after 9/11.* Washington, DC: The Heritage Foundation. https://www.heritage.org/defense/report/who-bears-the-burden-demographic-ch aracteristics-us-military-recruits-and-after-911

Kingkade, Tyler. 2019. "This is why Canadian universities don't have college admissions scandals." *HuffPost*, April 26. https://www.huffpost.com/entry/ college-admissions-scam-inequality-university-canada_n_5cc16918e4b0ad77ff7 fd4e8

Krieghbaum, Andrew. 2019. "Making the FAFSA Mandatory." *Inside Higher Ed*, July 10. https://www.insidehighered.com/news/2019/07/10/texas-becomes-second -state-require-fafsa-completion

Louisiana Department of Education. 2014. *Louisiana FAFSA completion report.* Baton Rouge, LA. https://www.louisianabelieves.com/docs/default-source/links- for-newsletters/fafsa-12-14-bese-bor.pdf

Luca, Michael, and Jonathan Smith. 2013. "Salience in quality disclosure: Evidence from the U.S. News college rankings." *Journal of Economics and Management Strategy* 22, no. 1: 58–77.

MacGowen, Bradford. 1999. "Toward chaos or clarity: Examining college admission for the next millennium." *Journal of College Admission* 165: 6–13.

Maryland Higher Education Commission. n.d. *Workforce shortage student assistance grant program.* Baltimore, MD. https://mhec.maryland.gov/preparing/Pages/Fin ancialAid/ProgramDescriptions/prog_WSSAG.aspx

McDonough, Patricia M. 1997. *Choosing colleges: How social class and schools structure opportunity.* Albany, NY: State University of New York Press.

McDonough, Patricia M., Anthony Lising, Antonio M. Walpole, and Leonor X. Perez. 1998. "College rankings: Democratized college knowledge for whom?" *Research in Higher Education* 39, no. 5: 513–37.

Melin, Julia. 2016. "Desperate choices: Why black women join the U.S. military at higher rates than men and all other racial and ethnic groups," *New England Journal of Public Policy* 28, no. 2: 1–14.

Meyer, Andrew G., Andrew R. Hanson, and Daniel C. Hickman. 2017. "Perceptions of institutional quality: Evidence of limited attention to higher education rankings." *Journal of Economic Behavior and Organization* 142: 241–58.

National Association of Colleges and Employers. 2017. *First destinations for the college class of 2016.* Bethlehem, PA: National Association of Colleges and Employers. http://www.naceweb.org/uploadedfiles/files/2017/publication/report/ first-destinations-for-the-college-class-of-2016.pdf

National Center for Education Statistics. 2018a. *Enrollment in elementary, sec- ondary, and degree-granting postsecondary institutions, by level and control of institution: Selected years, 1869-70 through fall 2027.* Washington, DC: U.S. Department of Education. https://nces.ed.gov/programs/digest/d17/tables/dt17 _105.30.asp

National Center for Education Statistics. 2018b. *Tuition costs of colleges and universities.* Washington, DC: U.S. Department of Education. https://nces.ed.gov/fastf acts/display.asp?id=76

National Science Foundation. n.d. *About funding.* Alexandria, VA: United States Government. https://www.nsf.gov/funding/aboutfunding.jsp

National Science Foundation. 2018. *NSF announces graduate research fellowships for 2018.* Alexandria, VA: United States Government. https://www.nsf.gov/news/ news_summ.jsp?cntn_id=245024&org=NSF

Pallais, Amanda. 2015. "Small differences that matter: Mistakes in applying to college." *Journal of Labor Economics* 33, no. 2: 493–520.

Patten, Eileen, and Kim Parker. 2011. *Women in the U.S. military: Growing share, distinctive profile.* Washington, DC: Pew Research Center. https://www.pewsocia ltrends.org/wp-content/uploads/sites/3/2011/12/women-in-the-military.pdf

Pippert, Timothy D., Laura J. Essenburg, and Edward J. Matchett. 2013. "We've got minorities, yes we do: Visual representations of racial and ethnic diversity in college recruitment materials." *Journal of Marketing for Higher Education* 23, no. 2: 258–82.

Powers, Donald E., and Donald A. Rock. 1999. "Effects of coaching on SAT I: Reasoning test scores." *Journal of Educational Measurement* 36, no. 2: 93–118.

Roderick, Melissa, Vanessa Coca, and Jenny Nagaoka. 2011. "Potholes on the road to college." *Sociology of Education* 84, no. 3: 178–211.

Rosenbaum, James E., Shazia R. Miller, and Melinda S. Krei. 1996. "Gatekeeping in the era of more open gates: High school counselors' views of their influence on students' college plans." *American Journal of Education* 104, no. 4: 257–79.

Roy, Jessica. 2019. "A lingering question in the college admissions scandal: Why?" *Los Angeles Times,* March 14. https://www.latimes.com/local/lanow/la-me-col lege-admissions-scandal-psychology-why-20190314-story.html

Schnabel, Kai U., Corinne Alfeld, Jacquelynne S. Eccles, Olaf Köller, and Jürgen Baumert. 2002. "Parental influence on students' educational choices in the United States and Germany: Different ramifications—same effect?" *Journal of Vocational Behavior* 60, no. 2: 178–98.

Schultz, Theodore. 1979. *The economics of being poor. Lecture.* The Nobel Foundation, Stockholm, Sweden. December 8, 1979. https://www.nobelprize.org/ prizes/economic-sciences/1979/schultz/lecture/

Smith, Adam. 1776. *An inquiry into the nature and causes of the wealth of nations.* Eds. R. H. Campbell and A. S. Skinner. Indianapolis, IN: Liberty Fund.

Spence, Michael. 1973. "Job market signaling." *Quarterly Journal of Economics* 87, no. 3: 355–74.

State Higher Education Executive Officers Association. 2017. *State higher education finance: FY 2017.* Boulder, CO. http://www.sheeo.org/news/sheeo-releases-state -higher-education-finance-fy-2017

Swenson, David. 2019. *The economic contribution of Pennsylvania State University.* University Park, PA: The Pennsylvania State University. https://opair.psu.edu/files/2019/04/Penn-State-Study-2-13-19.pdf

Talbot, Richard P. 2003. *White, black and Hispanic casualty rates during the Vietnam conflict: Any differences?* In *meeting of the American Sociological Association.*

Thaler, Richard H., and Cass R. Sunstein. 2008. *Nudge: Improving decisions about health, wealth, and happiness.* New York: Penguin Group.

The College Board. 2019. *How many applications are enough?* https://professionals.collegeboard.org/guidance/applications/how-many

U.S. Army. 2018. *Army ROTC scholarships.* Washington, DC: U.S. Department of Defense. https://www.goarmy.com/rotc/college-students/four-year-scholarships.html

U.S. Congress. Senate. Committee on Health, Education, Labor and Pensions. *For profit higher education: The failure to safeguard the federal investment and ensure student success.* 112th Cong. 2d sess., 2012. S. Rep. 112-37, 558–91.

U.S. Department of Education. 2015. *Fact sheet: Focusing higher education on student success.* Washington, DC. https://www.ed.gov/news/press-releases/fact-sheet-focusing-higher-education-student-success

U.S. News and World Report. 2019. *How U.S. News calculated the 2019 best colleges rankings.* https://www.usnews.com/education/best-colleges/articles/how-us-news-calculated-the-rankings

Van de Werfhorst, Herman. G., and Robert Andersen. 2005. "Social background, credential inflation and educational strategies." *Acta Sociologica* 48, no. 4: 321–40.

Veterans Benefits Administration. 2017. *Education and training: CareerScope.* Washington, DC: United States Department of Veteran's Affairs. https://www.benefits.va.gov/gibill/careerscope.asp

Veterans Benefits Administration. 2018. *Comparison chart/payment rates.* Washington, DC: United States Department of Veteran's Affairs. https://www.benefits.va.gov/GIBILL/comparison_chart.asp

Veterans Benefits Administration. 2019. *Edith Nourse Rogers science technology engineering math (STEM) scholarship.* Washington, DC: United States Department of Veteran's Affairs. https://benefits.va.gov/gibill/fgib/stem.asp

Chapter 8

Public Policy, the Environment, and the Use of Green Nudges

Cynthia Boruchowicz

As part of my recent Black Friday shopping spree, I ended up buying clothes online from stores I had never heard of before. After waiting for days, the items I had purchased arrived and I noticed a tag I had never seen before: "WARNING: This product contains chemicals, including lead, known to the State of California to cause cancer and birth defects or other reproductive harm. Wash hands after handling." That warning label ultimately encouraged me to return the items I had bought. It made me change my behavior—even after reading about it online and learning that the actual risk of getting cancer or reproductive problems from wearing the items is actually quite low.

While my individual risk is low, the fashion industries' impact on the climate is not. It is estimated that around 5 percent of total global CO_2 equivalent emission is caused by the fashion industry—that is, more than what the international flights industry produces (Nature Climate Change 2018). Would I have also been incentivized to return the items if I had seen a label stating, "WARNING. This product is contributing to global warming," instead of the Proposition 65 warning label?

There is a difference between nudges that are aimed at increasing well-being at the individual level and those that are aimed at incentivizing people to contribute voluntarily to a broader public good (Nagatsu 2015; Schubert 2017). The latter are called social nudges (Nagatsu 2015) and the exploration of the possible effectiveness and limitations of their use as a tool in environmental policy will be discussed in this chapter.

Schubert (2017) recognizes that environmental economics traditionally uses pollution permits, government regulation on industry production (including bans or production caps), international environmental agreements, market-based incentives in the form of Pigouvian taxes (a tax on an activity that generates negative externalities), and information-based instruments to provide policy recommendations. Nudging in environmental policy—commonly known as green nudging—on the other hand, uses the insights of behavioral economics to encourage eco-friendly behavior and as such contributes to mitigating the consequences of climate change. But is it the appropriate public policy instrument for combating climate change?

This chapter shows that green nudges can be an extra tool in the portfolio of policies that can promote environmentally conscious behavior (List et al. 2017). The first part of the chapter presents the concept of green nudging, describes the characteristics of different types of green nudges, and provides a review of some that have been applied so far. The second and third parts of the chapter then discuss public policy and green nudging. In particular, the mechanisms through which green nudging works are explored in the second part, and the third part discusses the practical limitations to their implementation as well as the broader concerns that might arise when using it as a policy tool. These include the level of intervention of a nudge, the potential biases of policymakers as well as their potential corrupt or rent-seeking behavior, and the risks of applying a "one-size fits all" solution without taking into consideration the cultural context. The different aspects of good governance necessary for the application of green nudges are also described. The fourth part concludes.

SOCIAL NUDGES AND THE ENVIRONMENT

In the book that gave rise to the idea of nudges and their implication for policy, Thaler and Sunstein (2009, 6) define nudges as a mechanism that "alters people's behavior in a predictable way, without forbidding any options or significantly changing their economic incentives. To count as a mere nudge, the intervention must be easy and cheap to avoid."

Hagman et al. (2015) characterize this definition as individual since these types of nudges involve a choice architecture that is intended to help individuals sort possible behavior biases that decrease their well-being in the long run. Examples of individual nudges are those that prevent people from smoking, save for retirement, or eat healthier food (like the cafeteria redesign example at the beginning of Thaler and Sunstein 2009).

Social nudges, on top of the aforementioned characteristics, attempt to serve society at large by encouraging the voluntary provision of public goods (Nagatsu 2015; Hagman et al. 2015). Public goods are defined by two terms: non-rivalry (one's consumption does not affect the opportunity of others to consume it as well) and non-excludability (the impossibility of excluding people who do not contribute from benefiting from the good, also known as "free-riders"). Usually, public goods are underprovided, as individuals do not internalize their costs and benefits. An example of a public good is a clean and hospitable environment, where millions of people affect the global atmosphere and it is not possible to exclude anyone from the benefit of cleaner air nor does one person's use reduces the supply of clean air for others (Ostrom 2009).

Social nudges emerge, then, as a middle ground solution between government interventions and a purely private approach to the collective action problem that the under-provision of public goods represents. Government interventions in the form of public provision financed through taxation, or regulations like mandates and permits, can be expensive and distortive. On the other hand, private solutions that involve market negotiations depend on an initial set of conditions hard to achieve.[1] Social nudges are targeted at incentivizing the voluntary provision of public goods directly through individuals by encouraging them to behave in a pro-social manner, even if that goes against their pure profit-maximizing behavior (Hagman et al. 2015). In a way, they can direct consumers to choose environmentally friendly products instead of alternatives that are cheaper but potentially worse for the environment (Sunstein and Reisch 2014).

Green Nudges

The provision of a clean and safe environment has several distinct characteristics. First, greenhouse gas emissions are the biggest market failure the world has seen, as their impact is carried over to the next generations (Stern 2007). Second, there are limitations of the general public's ability to understand the extent of the link between their individual behavior and their contribution to climate change. Because of this gap in understanding, people's perceptions can be influenced by imagery and values (Weber and Stern 2011). Third, environmental issues are also associated with strong moral feelings—either pride when doing something ecologically friendly or shame and guilt when seen not engaging in recycling efforts (Venhoeven et al. 2016). Baddeley (2011) states that energy conservation decisions are often characterized by uncertainty, constraints on learning, social norms, disempowerment, procrastination, and other drivers such as fashion and social pressure, that can influence the decision-making process of individuals. Fourth, environmental decisions are complex in the sense that many mechanisms are interrelated and therefore the change in one activity can have deep and permanent effects on others. Fifth, they have long-term and global effects (Croson and Treich 2014). Finally, there is cognitive dissonance, with a large share of the population denying environmental problems even when experts, like the United States National Research Council, stress that while there is some scientific controversy about the extent of climate change, there is a credible body of evidence documenting that the climate is in fact changing and that such change is largely caused by human activity (Opotow and Weiss 2000).

For Baddeley (2011), these multi-faced, complex, and interconnected characteristics of the environmental problem demand alternative solutions, such as social nudges that encourage behavioral changes within individuals and households. In the words of Elinor Ostrom (2009, 3):

> Waiting for a single worldwide "solution" to emerge from global negotiations is also problematic. . . . To solve climate change in the long run, the day-to-day activities of individuals, families, firms, communities, and governments at multiple levels—particularly those in the more developed world—will need to change substantially.

Altering individual recycling, energy and water use, consumption, commuting patterns, and so on can make a difference. For example, Vandenberg and Steinemann (2007) estimate that using alternative housing insulation and switching to fuel-efficient cars could cumulatively reduce greenhouse gas emission by 30 percent.

There are two instruments that build on behavioral economics and that have been used in environmental policy to target the previous behavioral changes at the individual and household level. The first is green nudging, which as previously mentioned are top-down government responses to individuals' bounded rationality that attempt to incentivize them to change their behavior in the direction of provision or collaboration to a sustainable environment. The second is corporate environmental responsibility, which is a bottom-up approach where firms respond to consumer's preferences toward the environment (Croson and Treich, 2014). This chapter will center on green nudges, which focuses on the concept of biases and bounded rationality rather than corporate environmental responsibility that focuses on changing social preferences.

As stated by Croson and Treich (2014), green nudges should first impact people's decision-making processes without changing their economic incentives, and second, should have low costs and be politically easy to implement—a positive feature compared to the burden associated to increasing taxes. They should be easy to understand, not raise fairness concerns (since they are applied to everyone, even if their impact is more salient for individuals with particular characteristics) and be testable. Green nudges have been shown to achieve major effects on environmental outcomes and are more cost-effective as compared to traditional paternalistic environmental regulations, like mandates and bans, and are potentially more effective than other policy tools, such as simply providing more information, education, moral exhortation, and economic incentives to individuals (Sunstein and Reisch 2014). For example, Benartzi et al. (2017) calculate and compare ratios of impact to cost for different nudge interventions and for traditional policy tools. In the case of energy conservation, they find that a nudge intervention based on sending reports to consumers comparing their energy use to their neighbors saved 27.3 kWh per $1 spent, while consumers receiving discounts if they reduce energy usage (financial incentive) saved 3.41 kWh per $1 spent, and providing financial incentives and education to reduce energy usage saved 14.0 kWh per $1 spent.

Green nudges can be divided into *active nudges*, which make the individual evaluate different alternatives before making a choice, and *passive nudges* that influence automatic behavior and do not require more effort by the individual in the decision-making process (Evans et al. 2017). Table 8.1 describes the different types of both active and passive green nudges.

Momsen and Stoerk (2014) use an online experiment to imitate the situation a consumer faces when deciding between various contract offers from utility companies. They use different nudges—default option, social norms, and mental accounting—to try to see which ones would have an impact on the choice of renewable versus conventional energy. They find that default

Table 8.1   Active and Passive Green Nudges

ACTIVE NUDGES	*PASSIVE NUDGES*
Eco-labeling • Salience: presenting product energy efficiency as a traffic light system • Gain/Losses: presenting energy conservation stickers showing financial gains or losses	Defaults • Opt-in/out: renewable energy as a default in an electricity private contract • Physical: reducing plate sizes to have less food waste that contributes to greenhouse gases
Social Norms • Descriptive: providing households with information about average energy consumption in their neighborhood • Comparative: energy bills showing a household's consumption compared to their neighbors' • Injunctive: energy bills with affective symbols that rate usage • Commitment: goal-setting to decrease private driving behavior	Design • Feature position: putting certain products at eye level in grocery stores • Feature salience: displaying real-time energy usage of different appliances
Active Choice: • Forcing households to choose between renewable and conventional electricity without a default option	Ecological Priming: • Providing environmental information such as paper towel usage in bathroom stalls

Source: Author adapted from Evans et al. (2017, 27).

options and social norms are the most effective at changing behavior toward renewable energy use.

Default Options

Default options change the default setting of certain day-to-day activities that might have an impact on environmental preservation. Examples are changing the default settings of printers to print two-sided, using paperless bills and receipts unless the customer asks for a printed version, or featuring plastic cups that dissuade the usage of straws.

One of the most common default options is the change to double-sided printing. When Rutgers University set printers to print on both sides instead of one by default, 7 million pages (or 620 trees) were saved in one semester. In the first four years, that represented a 44 percent reduction in the use of paper—equivalent to 4,650 trees (Sunstein and Reisch 2014). At a large Swedish university, changing to double-sided printing caused an immediate 15 percent drop in paper consumption, and that such change remained stable over time (Egerbak and Ekstrom 2013).

In some countries, including the United States, consumers are defaulted into a particular source of energy with the option to opt out. The default is usually grey energy, which has more pollutants but is cheaper than other forms of energy. Consumers usually lack the information needed to distinguish between green and grey sources of energy, and therefore may not have the incentive to switch sources unless they are particularly knowledgeable or passionate about the environmental impacts of grey energy. Moreover, even with the information in hand, many times inertia or procrastination can also prevent people from switching to green energy (Sunstein and Reich 2014). Pichert and Katsikopoulos (2008) analyze a natural experiment in southern Germany, where a local energy company decided to establish three separate energy source options—before there was only one. The default was green, and slightly cheaper than the form of energy in place before the change; the second option was a little less green but 8 percent cheaper; and the third option was greener than the default but 23 percent more expensive. A letter was sent offering the different options, and 94 percent kept the default green option, with 4.3 percent changing to the cheaper option and 1.7 percent changing to the most expensive option or switching to a different utility company.

Pichert and Katsikopoulos (2008) also experimented in the lab to present individuals with two options for energy supply: *EcoEnergy*, which highlights its focus on climate protection contribution, and *Acon*, which highlights its economic pricing with no mention of environmental impact. When *EcoEnergy* was the default, 68 percent of participants decided to keep it, but when *Acon* was the default, only 41 percent decided to switch to the greener option. Dinner et al. (2011) also use a lab study to analyze the effects of default options for light bulbs. Subjects were told they were remodeling their house and had to choose between the efficient but costly Compact Fluorescent Light Bulbs (CFLB) or the inefficient but inexpensive Incandescent Light Bulbs (ILB). They were also given information about the cost and benefit of both options, and there was no cost in switching. When ILB was the default, almost 44 percent kept them and 56 percent switched to more environmentally friendly bulbs; however, when CFLB was the default, almost 80 percent kept them (and only 20 percent switched to the cheaper but inefficient option). Additionally, Kallbekken and Saelen (2013) also focus on the use of green defaults to reduce food waste, and, as such, decrease emissions of greenhouse gases by conducting a field experiment on two different nudges at a hotel chain. The first nudge was to reduce the size of the plates used for the buffet services in some hotels. The second one was to display signs in the buffet space of other hotels that read "Welcome back! Again! And Again! Visit our buffet many times. That's better than taking a lot once" (Kallbekken and Saelen 2013, 326) with the idea that it would encourage guests to take less food on their plate on every visit. The authors find that the first nudge decreased food waste by 19.5 percent and that the signs reduced waste by 20.5 percent, with no change in the consumer's satisfaction with the buffet service.

Sunstein and Reisch (2014) point out that the advantage to using green default options is that they can produce the expected changes in behavior at a reduced cost while keeping freedom of choice by allowing consumers to opt out. In fact, not adjusting default settings is also a choice—having the printer set at one-sided printing or keeping larger plates at a buffet impact choice. Therefore, simply changing the default could be an effective way of contributing to public goods without needing to use more expensive and potentially more distortive policy tools. The authors recognize that opting out can be costly for those who have strong preferences against the default option, but that the nudge could still be justified if it produces significant social benefits through emissions reduction. Finally, the authors also state "No one should favor a situation in which choice architects select defaults that cost consumers a great deal and deliver only modest environmental benefits" (Sunstein and Reisch 2014, 157) and therefore, in such cases, an assessment that could even lead to active choosing instead of default options might seem necessary.

Social Norms

Green nudges that build on social norms or social comparisons exploit both the peer effect (providing feedback to individuals comparing their actions to their neighbors) and visibility of actions (making individuals' behavior visible to others) to change behavior regarding environmental issues. The most common form of a green nudge based on social norms are the ones used by utility companies that send out bills showing consumers their performance on energy, water, and/or gas consumption versus their neighbors, while also providing information for ways in which they can reduce that consumption. These practices are commonly known as Home Energy Reports or HERs.

Studies like Allcott and Kessler (2019), Allcott (2011), Ayres et al. (2013), Brandon and Lewis (1999), Costa and Kahn (2010), and Schultz et al. (2007) examine the effectiveness of HERs. The literature overall suggests two observations: first, households that receive HERs tend to actually reduce energy consumption (on average, around 2 percent monthly or 0.52 kWh per day (Allcott 2011)); second, there is heterogeneity in the results based on households' initial level of energy use. Given that the literature overall seems to agree that HERs programs are effective in changing household energy consumption on average in the United States,[2] a set of studies have tried to understand the mechanisms for changing behavior and their impacts on various types of households.

List et al. (2017) ran a field experiment to randomly assign customers of an energy company to three groups: (1) a control group that gets regular utility bills without social comparison; (2) a group that received HERs and is ineligible for the rewards program; and (3) a group that receives HERs and is also encouraged to voluntarily sign up for a rewards program, where they can earn points based on changes in monthly energy use that can be redeemed for purchasing goods online. The idea behind the randomization was to test if there can be complementarities in strategies to reduce energy consumption (nudges plus financial incentives), and if those complementary instruments can affect choices of households that are usually less responsive to social norms. The authors find that receiving HERs reduced energy consumption by 1.3 percent compared to the control group (with those households with higher pretreatment average daily use and variance month-to-month use changing the most). When the effect was analyzed separately for each treatment group, the authors find that the introduction of the rewards program implied a 40 percent reduction in average daily electricity usage than for those who only received the monthly HER. More importantly, when those who actually signed up for the rewards program are compared to those who did not (either because they were ineligible or because they decided not to) the 1.3 percent reduction more than doubled. The authors find that the rewards program incentivized low-level average energy users and those with minimal month-to-month variation, usually the types of users who do not change behavior with just nudges, to reduce their energy consumption. Moreover, the rewards program did not crowd out energy conservation efforts from those who decided not to participate in it. Therefore, even though the combined intervention did not significantly change the behavior of the average household, it created savings for those customers who were selected into the program. As such, List et al.'s (2017, 24) conclusion and policy recommendation is to combine different interventions to design a portfolio of policies that can be "a viable alternative to one-size-fits-all approaches."

Costa and Kahn (2013a) examine the role of ideology in energy conservation nudges through a field experiment. The authors examine the effect of receiving HERs in California while controlling for a set of household characteristics, including their registered political party affiliation, donations to environmental causes, participation in renewable energy programs, and other residential characteristics that may identify environmentalist from non-environmentalist households. They find that the effectiveness in energy conservation nudges depends on the household ideology, contributing to the idea that social comparison nudges are heterogeneously effective. Similarly, Etner et al. (2007) argue that, theoretically, pessimistic individuals contribute more to the public good of "environmental quality" than optimist ones.

While utility companies started using social comparison nudges, this form of green nudge has now been utilized by other companies as well. Goldstein et al. (2008, 474) show that hotels that put up signs regarding the reuse of towels to protect the environment like "[a]lmost 75% of guests who are asked to participate in our new resource savings program do help by using their towels more than once" report that the practice of reusing towels increased by 44 percent and therefore reduced water and electricity consumption.

By using a sample of French farmers who engage in agri-environmental schemes (AESs),[3] Kuhfuss et al. (2016) study the effects of nudging on stated intentions and the impacts of framing and social norms. They find that telling farmers what management practice others are using can influence a farmer's stated decision to keep using the AES technique even after the AES contract and payments end. That means these farmers are conditional cooperators, and thus providing information of what others do can be a powerful policy tool. However, changing the framing of the information about other farmers in either a positive or a negative way does not make the difference. Additionally, Kuhfuss et al.'s (2016) results are aligned with Chen et al. (2009), who find through an experimental survey that farmers' intentions to reenroll in programs that paid them to participate in reforestation in China increased if they had information others would do so too. Czajkowski et al. (2017) found that social comparisons also influenced the level of household home recycling in Poland. Cialdini et al. (1990) found the same for littering, and Schultz et al. (2007) for energy consumption.

The advantage of green nudges in the form of social norms is that their proper application can lead to not just adjusted behavior but the creation of

the norms and institutional change necessary to support sustainable environmental conservation. Social norms or social comparisons rely on the notion
of repeated interactions for conditional cooperation and reciprocity in a localized setting. Just as Ostrom (1990) suggests, those interactions could allow
individuals to systematically engage in collective action to provide local public goods without the need for sanctions. Social comparison provides a space
for cooperation between those who are being nudged, which could contribute
to lasting change.

MECHANISMS OF GREEN NUDGING

Nagatsu (2015) points out two mechanisms through which social nudges
can incentivize people to contribute voluntarily to a broader public good:
the expectations-based mechanism and the frame-based mechanism. The
expectations-based mechanism is the creation of the expectation that others will cooperate in order to induce conditional cooperators to change their
behavior. The frame-based mechanism shifts from an I-frame (asking what *I*
should do) to a we-frame (asking what *we* should do) as a way of maximizing
group benefits by enticing a social mindset. The literature shows that some
conditions need to be satisfied for green nudges to be effective as a policy tool
to increase voluntary contributions to a clean and safe environment.

First, it is necessary that a *substantial portion of subjects are conditional
cooperators* who are willing to cooperate only if other people do so too
(Nagatsu 2015). This is related to Ostrom's (2009, 11) point that "[t]o achieve
its objectives, any policy that tries to improve levels of collective action to
overcome social dilemmas must enhance the level of trust by participants that
others are complying with the policy or else many will seek ways of avoiding
compliance."

Second, given that people might choose different alternatives if they are
presented in different ways, it is necessary for the nudge to be *presented as
meaningful* in order to incentivize people to focus on the social impacts rather
than just their individual impacts (Bacharach 2006). In order to increase the
likelihood of cooperation in situations like the provision of a clean environment, it is not only necessary that there is reliable information about the costs
and benefits of actions but also "the individuals involved see the common
resource as important for their own achievements and have a long-term time
horizon" (Ostrom 2009, 12).

The third condition is that the change in the framing, that is, the alteration
of the relative importance of environmental policy, should be generated from
people who are *credible (*Moseley and Stoker 2013). Citizens often expect
experts or well-known scientists to be the ones explaining why it is important

for them to care about climate change, why the importance of focusing on it now and how their individual actions can have an impact on the issue. Trust and reputation is fundamental when developing nudging strategies (see also chapter 10). The cost of collaboration will be lower if citizens view policy as fair, necessary, and credible.

Fourth, for a nudge to be persuasive and therefore to actually alter the individual behavior, there should be *limited competition* for ideas that challenge the main message. Moseley and Stoker (2013) point out that this is one of the main limitations for the use of green nudges to fight global warming, as there are many different interest groups that give different messages not only about the importance of the subject but also about the types of individual behavior that would need to be changed. Such competition might undermine the power of persuasion of policymakers.

Finally, for the green nudge to have a permanent effect, it needs to create social norms that support the altered behavior. In other words, the nudge needs to create a paradigm shift such that individuals systematically engage in collective action to provide local public goods based on the concepts of conditional cooperation and reciprocity (Moseley and Stoker 2013).

Even though climate change has been framed as a global problem, policies can be implemented at the local level and, collectively, can have a broader impact (Bestill 2001; Ostrom 2009). As Ostrom (2009, 28) states, "Given the severity of the threat, simply waiting for resolution of these issues at a global level, without trying out policies at multiple scales because they lack a global scale, is not a reasonable stance." The main barrier to collective action in this context seems to be the gap between intentions and actions— individuals, for example, usually are in favor of energy from renewable sources even if that entails a higher cost, yet actual use of renewable energy is small.

Green nudges, thus, can work as a compass, directing individuals to what issues they need to pay attention to and become more knowledgeable about, allow them to sort their current biases and begin to adjust their behaviors to align with their environmental goals (Moseley and Stoker 2013). The intention-action gap in environment conservation might differ according to place of residence, exposure to specific threats, or usage of available resources, among others. Therefore, local government—cities, municipalities or metropolitan areas—might be best positioned to understand the reasons behind such gap. For example, as was previously noted, Andor et al. (2020) find that the use of HER interventions was not as efficient to promote reductions in electricity consumption in Germany compared to the United States—mainly because electricity consumption levels and carbon intensities are lower outside the United States. Therefore, the effectiveness of nudges varies according to the specific context in which it is implemented.

Building on the previous point, the literature has also found that green nudges work saliently with people who are overall less individualistic (Croson and Treich 2014); who come from a household with a liberal ideology, understood as affiliating to a liberal political party, donating to environmental causes, and participating in renewable energy programs (Costa and Kahn 2013a), and whose household is situated in an overall liberal community (Costa and Kahn 2013b). Conservative and individualistic citizens tend to have lower risk perceptions of factors like climate change than those with more of a liberal ideology or a communitarian worldview (Kahan 2006; Kahan et al. 2011; Jacquet et al. 2014). Thus, not all green nudges will work the same across all cultural groups. In fact, as Boettke et al. (2008) argue, local norms, customs, and practices in specific locations evolve informally as a product of the individual characteristics of its citizens and the way they interact with each other. Trying to exogenously impose an institutional change that lacks credibility and workability among citizens will be less effective. In other words, trying to implement a one-size-fits-all green nudge approach in different settings will likely not be as effective as one that takes into consideration the characteristics and culture of those being nudged. In this way, nudges should be understood as an agent of transformation of the institutional and cultural status quo (also see chapter 5). Local governments, who are embedded within the local context, may likely have a greater chance of designing green nudge policies targeted at their specific constituency.

Local governments also have the capability of "[d]eveloping the apparatus to build pro-environmental norms" (Moseley and Stoker 2013, 8) by having more opportunities for face-to-face interactions that can help develop trust among citizens and therefore allow them to perform reciprocal acts of governance. As proposed by Ostrom (2009) who encourages efforts to reduce greenhouse emissions at multiple levels of government as a way to commit individuals to change their behavior, "[b]uilding such commitment, and the trust that others are also taking responsibility, can be more effectively undertaken in small-to medium-scale governance units that are linked through information networks and monitoring at all levels" (Ostrom 2009, 39). This polycentric approach, first developed by Ostrom et al. (1961), is based on the principle that many government services are often best provided by multiple, overlapping nodes of authority that interact, compete, and cooperate with one another and higher levels of government. This means that both citizens and officials have more choices in terms of the provision and production of public goods and provide opportunities for feedback and improvement in performance over time. In fact, Ostrom (1990) shows empirically that in small, local communities, rules of use naturally emerge over time between joint users of common resources that are more economically and ecologically efficient.

In addition to the scientific knowledge of experts, the practical and dispersed knowledge among individuals is needed to begin solving the coordination problem that gives rise to the problem of under-provision of a quality environment (Muramatsu and Barbieri 2017). Polycentricism in policy provides an institutional apparatus where those dispersed individuals can bring their knowledge and ideas and find a way to cooperate. In practical terms, it means competition and cooperation at multiple levels. For example, various technological and institutional efforts to reduce greenhouse gas emissions can provide information about which combined sets of actions are the most effective (Ostrom 2009) or the evaluation of different types of nudges—for example, default options implemented at the federal level in countries where the source of energy is national, or local social norms in cities where recycling is done at the city level—can shed a light of which one might be better positioned to change behavior in the expected direction.

In a sense then, green nudges can be multiple-level policy tools intended to act as a catalyst to start the repeated interactions between citizens necessary for engaging in collective action, learning about conditional cooperation and reciprocity, and giving rise to a set of social norms that would eventually allow for an economically and environmentally sustainable use of natural resources. As Moseley and Stoker (2013, 8) state,

> It would seem that the key is for government to cede power to citizens if the forces of norm-creation are to come to fruition. . . . In areas of public policy reliant on citizen cooperation for achieving policy aims . . . such as improving air quality or reducing the use of landfill sites, governments can employ creative methods for harnessing cooperative behavior . . . the State, we argue, needs to work on the development of an institutional apparatus which will permit citizens to cooperate.

In practice, the above can mean supporting the development of community websites or helping organize public events like town hall meetings where environmental issues can be addressed (Moseley and Stoker 2013); in other words, supporting the creation of a space where the different nodes of authority can share experiences and concerns, learn from one another, adapt insights to their specific context, cooperate with each other and coordinate efforts.[4]

LIMITATIONS OF AND CONCERNS
ABOUT GREEN NUDGING

Just as with any other policy tool, there are several limitations to the application of green nudges. The first challenge that the application of green nudges faces is a lack of conditional cooperators—which can happen if people have strong preferences and are not persuaded by the actions of others. Someone who intrinsically does not care about the environment may not be nudged even if there are enough people around her doing so and even if the framing is such so that the importance of saving the planet is clear. It is possible, then, that green nudges which point out at the social aspect of the conservation of the environment will not work in every scenario, but rather will do so in certain societies with citizens that exhibit certain baseline characteristics like non-individualistic behavior or who come from a more liberal ideology.

The second limitation is the possibility of mistakes by the scientists' and experts' conclusions that policymakers follow in order to implement green nudges. The accumulation of mistakes, and, therefore, the application of policy that follow faulty conclusions can undermine the experts' reputation and limit the efficiency of green nudges. For example, Croson and Treich (2014) find that the 75 percent figure of the Goldstein, Cialdini, and Griskevicius (2008) experiment on hotel buffets was exaggerated. This raises concerns about how successful nudges can be and if policymakers will make decisions based on faulty information. Note that the previous is an issue with all public policies. For example, under the Renewable Fuel Standard, refineries in the United States were required to blend ethanol with gasoline as a way to help secure energy independence and the environment (Wardle 2018). At the time of the implementation of the mandate, some scientific studies had concluded that corn ethanol reduced greenhouse gas emissions compared to gasoline (Farrel et al. 2006; Wang 2005). However, after over ten years of implementation, it has been shown that the ethanol mandates actually are contributing to climate change directly by producing air and water pollution as well as indirectly by the expansion of land use for crops and deforestation (Runge 2016). Citizens might be less willing to change their behavior if they distrust the source of the information they receive regarding a specific policy issue like the environment.

Third, in an issue as relevant and global as climate change, with so many different interest groups involved and both political and economic objectives at stake, it is hard to achieve or expect to achieve a limited competition of ideas that challenge the main message. This is already visible in the United States, where "climate change deniers have been remarkably successful in confusing public opinion and delaying decisive action" (Collomb 2014, 1). In fact, even though through their consumption behavior households account for over 70 percent of the global greenhouse gas emissions "there is a gap between how households perceive their responsibility and ability to mitigate climate change and the responsibilities and roles communicated by climate policies" (Dubois et al. 2019, 152). A Gallup survey on climate change in 2018 showed that over 60 percent of Americans believe climate change not only is real but is caused by human activity (Brenan and Saad 2018). However, opinions are politically polarized, with 69 percent of Republicans believing the issue of global warming is greatly exaggerated (versus 34 percent of Independents and 4 percent of Democrats). Similarly, a Pew survey from January 2019 shows that 67 percent of Democrats and Democratic-leaning independents believe global climate change should be a top priority, compared to 21 percent of Republicans (Bowman 2019).

The fourth limitation is the uncertainty of a nudge's effect over time. The long-term effects of nudges depend on their effectiveness in changing citizens' behavioral patterns. For example, Milford et al. (2015) investigate how sending letters that tell households about their recycling patterns and waste habits and their performance as compared to other people in their same municipality, increased the recycled waste by 2 percent in the first 7 months of the study. But, what will happen in 5 years, or even in 10, if these households do not receive additional letters? When implementing a green nudge, the idea is that it will be a catalyst for repeated interactions that will therefore create new social norms and have an effect that goes beyond the initial implementation of the nudge. If the effects of nudges do not persist over time, there is a latent risk that policymakers will transform green nudges into permanent mandates that are hard to reverse. Therefore, more research over time is needed to better understand their long-term effects.

Multiple Voices vs. One Voice and the Role of the Policymaker

[A] polycentric approach to climate governance might provide the best chance we have of accelerating progress toward global climate stabilization by providing more frequent and varied opportunities . . . to engage in face-to-face communications. . . . Those interactions . . . could inculcate the kind of mutual trust that seems necessary for greater cooperation. (Cole 2015, 117)

As previously stated, behind the idea of green nudges lies the notion of repeated interactions as a way to induce conditional cooperation and reciprocity in a localized setting, in a coordinated way. While individuals do not have perfect information, through such a process it is expected that they will be capable of learning and therefore adjusting their behavior. Green nudges would then act as a catalyst within a polycentric approach to start the repeated interactions necessary to engage in collective action and give rise to a set of social norms that will eventually encourage an economically and environmentally sustainable use of natural resources. In a sense then, there is one voice referring to the scientific knowledge of experts that defines the main message: there is a high level of agreement about the existence of climate change, about the human impacts on the global atmosphere (Ostrom 2009), and about the urgency of doing something about it. However, there are multiple voices referring to the knowledge about the actions of individual households and their interactions at multiple levels based on different contexts. Both are needed to solve the coordination problem that gives rise to global warming by providing more opportunities for experimenting and learning.

Even though green nudges can be considered a soft policy tool since they shift behavior rather than mandate action, they still require a policymaker that designs and implements them. While experts and scientists can tell us what to do—for example, highlight that household energy consumption should be reduced by a certain amount—behavioral scientists can tell us how to do so—how to get people to actually decrease their energy usage (Li 2020). However, the decision of putting in place a nudge versus a more traditional policy tool, or even versus doing nothing at all comes from a policymaker. While most of the studies on green nudges are centered around the effects of a nudge on individuals and how they can contribute to the public good, the analysis of how that nudge was designed to begin with and who designed it is not often studied. This deficit is usually the result of the assumption under any green nudge analysis: while individuals are assumed to be self-interested, policy-makers are assumed to maximize social-welfare functions and not their own utility (Berggren 2012). Viscusi and Hamilton (1999) argue that environmental regulators are not rational and benevolent, but rather also have biases, just like the individuals they are attempting to nudge. They suffer, for example, from action bias and, therefore, have a strong political pressure to impulsively nudge people in order to get results. They can also have confirmation bias and, therefore, tend to consider only the information that supports their viewpoint, which goes back to their problem of mixing scientific information with practical knowledge about how people make decisions and interact with each other. Successful interventions require detailed information about dispersed information, and when designing green nudges, policymakers might not listen to all voices, whether because of simply mismanagement or incompetence, or corruption and rent-seeking behavior. In fact, Hayek (1967) argued that policymakers do not have the wisdom and altruistic behavior needed to plan things better than the public itself. Carlsson et al. (2011) also claim that regulators are motivated mainly by their political career and, therefore, hold different beliefs or moral values than the rest of the population.[5]

Moreover, according to Hayek (1967), policymakers can make systematic mistakes and prevent coordination problems from being solved by the market because they focus on technical, scientific, rather than practical, contextual knowledge. While policymakers can have advisors that solve the scientific knowledge problem, it is impossible for them to be familiar with the various dispersed knowledge regarding space and time and the tacit knowledge in the mind of every individual, and to engage the multiple voices needed to solve the coordination problem that is responsible for the under-provision of public goods in the case of the environment. That is why, even if policymakers try to account for every cost and benefit of a nudging intervention there still might be unintended consequences that can "block and distort people's incentives to discover and select some entrepreneurial course of action" (Muramatsu and Barbieri 2017, 3). For example, Hagmann et al. (2019) show that introducing a green energy default nudge with utility companies can crowd out support for policies that seem to have greater impact like carbon taxes. Such green nudges resulted in the unintended consequence of diminished support for other policies, showing that policymakers often do not have full information when designing and implementing nudges. However, this might be the case for most policy applications. For Rizzo and Whitman (2009), policymakers do not have all the relevant information regarding citizen's preferences under each different context. They state, "But lacking such information, we cannot conclude that actual paternalism will make their decision better, under a wide range of circumstances, it will even make it worse" (Rizzo and Whitman 2009, 910). Thus, green nudges—by changing people's behavior in an easy way without changing economic incentives and without being costly to avoid—can be a viable cost-effective alternative to other forms of traditional environmental regulations.

Environmental policy is also an emotional and moral topic, especially with the consequences of climate change being made more visible and more information becoming available. Today, for example, more and more people are deciding to stop using plastic bags or straws because of the perceived effects they might have on the ocean, having heard about and seen pictures of the harm done to marine life. This could be both a pro and a con, as "some policy issues are emotionally charged and can distort policymaker's judgment and decision making" (Muramatsu and Barbieri 2017, 4).

Given that citizens hold different beliefs regarding environmental risks compared to experts, a question that policymakers at the local level might ask themselves when deciding whether to design and implement a green nudge is: "Should the regulator be populist and regulate according to the beliefs of people, or be paternalistic and follow the experts?" (Croson and Treich 2014, 341). Therefore, the analysis of the use of green nudges as a policy tool will not be complete if the actions and constraints related to the role of policymakers are not incorporated. As stated by Buchanan (1949), Buchanan and Tullock (1962), and Brennan and Buchanan (1984, 85), behavioral analysis should be based on a political economy approach that is symmetrical across individuals and policymakers; "whatever model of behavior is used, that model should be applied across all institutions" (Berggren 2012, 201). This type of methodological consistency incorporates the analysis of rationality and cognitive abilities and limitations to both those being nudged and those designing the nudges.

Nudges and Good Governance

The successful implementation of green nudges, like any other policy intervention, is then related to the quality and nature of the political system in which they take place. The extent to which policymakers can act in a manipulative or unethical way when implementing green nudges will depend on whether or not the governance system is participatory, consensus oriented, accountable, transparent, responsive, effective and efficient, equitable and inclusive, and aligned with the rule of law (De la Harpe et al. 2008). In other words, when good governance characterizes the political system, when transparency laws are in place, government green nudges are more likely to be implemented in an accountable and honorable way.

Green nudges can have a manipulative nature (Croson and Treich 2014; Ouvrard and Spaeter 2016). Sunstein (2015) points out that, for example, an information campaign that emphasizes how much individuals might lose by not engaging in an energy conservation program rather than how much they could gain from doing so could be manipulative as "it does not sufficiently appeal to people's deliberative processes but instead tries to trigger the negative feelings that are associated with losses" (Sunstein 2015, 445). Thaler and Sunstein (2009) address this concern by stating that the limit to the manipulative nature of a nudge should be anything that policymakers cannot defend openly to its citizens. However, such a limit is only present in a context of good governance and active citizen engagement. In a political context where, for example, civil participation is limited, like in nondemocratic regimes, policymakers are less accountable and do not have instances or even the need to defend their actions in front of their constituencies.

Hagman et al. (2015) also state that when implementing a social nudge—like green nudges—there can be a clash between liberal ideals, promoting social welfare, and freedom of choice. This means that green nudges may conflict with an individual's autonomy given that they are viewed as instruments aimed at changing individual behavior for social benefit rather than individual benefit (Nagatsu 2015). However, social nudges hinge on conditional cooperation and might promote autonomy if they allow individuals to shift their limited attention to a matter they care about, like the environment (Sunstein and Reisch 2014). Social nudges are defined as "non-coercive behavioral measures that encourage individuals to produce public goods and otherwise overall social welfare, even when doing so is inconsistent with maximizing private welfare" (Hagman et al. 2015, 451). Therefore, as long as the noncoercive aspect of green nudges remains, the potential ethical concerns may be mitigated by the fact that "Our choices are always under the influence of circumstantial factors and unconscious biases that are not under our direct control. . . . Nudging merely alters the set of factors influencing our decision" (Kasperbauer 2017, 52). There are several characteristics of better governance that are necessary to assure that the noncoercive component of green nudges is present. Mainly, it is important that green nudges are implemented following a fair legal framework that will allow citizens to opt out of nudges. Saying it differently, it is important that a system of checks and balances are in place and the enforcement of law is impartial to prevent policymakers from unilaterally transforming green nudges into mandates that will, by their nature, actually restrict choices and therefore autonomy.

Good governance is also necessary to prevent policymakers to act unilaterally and either make systematic mistakes that can obstruct the decentralized learning mechanisms or engage in corrupt or rent-seeking behavior that benefits themselves rather than the common good. As it was previously stated, the nature of political institutions means that policymakers' ability to gather and analyze all the relevant information regarding citizen's preferences under each different context and the biases that might arise needed to design and implement nudges is limited. Under a context of good governance, where the design and implementation of policy is based on reaching consensus among multiple voices and being adaptable when mistakes arise, it is possible to minimize the negative effects of policymakers making systematic errors. It is also important to highlight that having local policymakers who can adapt the implementation of green nudges to the local context can also diminish the possibility of mistakes. Moreover, as it is not only the case for green nudges but for the implementation of any type of policy, making and enforcing decisions in a way that follows existing rules and regulations and having in place mechanisms for holding policymakers accountable might reduce the risk of corruption. As also noted by Nagatsu (2015), social nudges do not seem that different (and therefore no less legitimate) than any other types of policymaking that try to solve social dilemmas. Green nudges can be then an extra tool for policymakers in the quest for solutions to the issue of climate change.

CONCLUSION

Climate change is having real impacts on the world. We can see it not only in the reports that scientists and policymakers distribute but also in our everyday life. More and more, people are starting to be displaced due to the effects of global warming and our routines have to adapt to a new reality (Warner et al. 2009; Carter et al. 2015). According to the 2018 Panel on Climate Change (IPCC), we have limited time to reverse the current trend in climate change before it is too late (IPCC 2018). There is a consensus among scientists that climate change is largely a consequence of disruptive human activity (Anderegg et al. 2010; Jacquet et al. 2014). This raises the question of whether something should and can be done to put a stop to it and to ensure an environment where human life is possible and remains possible for the generations to come.

As global efforts to develop a system that can rapidly deal with climate change in an effective, efficient, and fair way seem not to have worked so far, it seems that there is a need to try out policies at multiple levels of government in smaller scales (Ostrom 2009). In particular, it is relevant to try to design and implement policy solutions that are targeted at individuals and households. As it was exposed in this chapter, even though through their consumption behavior households account for over 70 percent of the global greenhouse gas emissions "there is a gap between how households perceive their responsibility and ability to mitigate climate change and the responsibilities and roles communicated by climate policies" (Dubois et al. 2019, 152). This means that there is a gap between individual intentions and actions that can be a product of lack of information, inertia, or procrastination, among others.

Therefore, under a scenario of multiple and dispersed individuals and actions occurring in different contexts which are interconnected, green nudges as multiple-level policy tools intended to act as a catalyst to start repeated interactions between citizens becomes a plausible and intriguing option. Such repeated interactions are necessary for individuals to engage in collective action, learn about conditional cooperation and reciprocity, and give rise to a set of social norms that would eventually allow for an economically and environmentally sustainable use of natural resources.

This chapter explored the characteristics of different types of green nudges, and provided a review of some—particularly in what refers to default options and social norms—that have been applied so far. Green nudges have been shown to achieve major effects on environmental outcomes and are more cost-effective as compared to traditional paternalistic environmental regulations, like mandates and bans, and are potentially more effective than other policy tools, such as simply providing more information, education, moral exhortation, and economic incentives to individuals (Sunstein and Reisch 2014). However, as Schubert (2017) points out, green nudging by itself will not be enough to solve the problem of climate change but it could be used as a complementary tool in the portfolio of policies that can promote environmental conscious behavior. For example, Kuhfuss et al. (2016) recommend that combining financial incentives with nudges, such as in agri-environmental schemes (AESs), can increase the efficiency of public policies aimed at increasing the provision of environmental quality. In a sense, the policy recommendation of combining different interventions should be seen as "a viable alternative to one-size-fits-all approaches" (List et al. 2017, 24).

Building on the previous, this chapter also discusses how it is important to consider the cultural context in which the green nudge is applied—for which local forms of government might be better positioned to understand the reasons behind the intention-action gap in what refers to individual climate conservation. As such, polycentricism provides an institutional apparatus where different nodes of authority at multiple levels can share experiences and concerns, learn from one another, adapt insights to their specific context, cooperate with each other and coordinate efforts.

The possibility of implementing effective green nudges, as with other public policies, is not unconditional. As it was explored in this chapter, limitations of green nudges, include time-horizon effects; the role of policymakers, their biases, their potential corruption or rent-seeking behavior, and their lack of practical knowledge about the way in which individuals interact with each other. Most of the concerns are related to the quality of the political context in which green nudges exist. Therefore, as analyzed, there are several aspects of good governance that can help mitigate both the practical and ethical considerations of the implementation of green nudges. As Holcombe (2009) states, decision-making is not perfect and takes both time and mistakes to achieve intended goals, both at the individual and also at the social and political levels. As such, feedback and accountability mechanisms should be incorporated when designing green nudges, and policy in general.[6]

The severity of the threat of climate change has proven to be real enough to look for alternative solutions that can be added to the portfolio of policies used to mitigate its consequences. Green nudges, considering both their effectiveness and limitations discussed in this chapter, appear to be a cost-effective tool to add to the policy mix.

NOTES

1. The absence of transaction costs, few private actors affected, and the existence of courts that would allow private actors in the market to negotiate are the initial set of conditions highlighted by Coase (1960) as necessary for private market negotiations to lead to the socially optimal level of pollution regardless of the initial assignment of property rights.

2. Andor et al. (2020) find that in Germany, where electricity consumption levels are lower than in the United States but similar to the OECD average, HERs helped reduced annual electricity consumption only by 0.7 percent or 0.04 kWh per day.

3. AESs are individual contracts signed with farmers who volunteer to implement pro-environmental management practices in return for monetary compensation to offset compliance costs and foregone revenue due to changes in techniques. At the end of the contract, the farmer can decide to stick to the new land management practices or go back to what they did before.

4. Note that cooperation and coordination efforts are important to guarantee that the independent work of each node can contribute to the public good more than one monocentric arrangement (Biddle and Baehler 2019); something that has been evident during the current COVID-19 pandemic (Ross and Perez 2020; Tang and An 2020)

5. For example, in the case of ineffective ethanol mandates, the corn lobby, who has contributed $10.9 million to political campaigns between 2008 and 2014, are major beneficiaries (Koenig 2016).

6. Muramatsu and Barbieri (2017, 5) state that more research is needed to understand the political economy component of behavioral economics; particularly inspect the government failures commonly associated with market regulations; incorporate the analysis of biases and limitations to policymakers; and, incorporate the potential extent of the unintended consequences their implementation might bring as "behaviorally informed policymakers cannot underestimate the fact that it is not that simple to identify what individuals want and what their true preferences are all about."

REFERENCES

Allcott, Hunt. 2011. "Social Norms and Energy Conservation." *Journal of Public Economics* 95 (9–10): 1082–1095.

Allcott, Hunt, and Judd B. Kessler. 2019. "The Welfare Effects of Nudges: A Case Study of Energy Use Social Comparisons." *American Economic Journal: Applied Economics* 11 (1): 236–276.

Anderegg, William R. L., James W. Prall, Jacob Harold and Stephen H. Schneider. 2010. "Expert Cridibility in Climate Change." *Proceedings of the National Academy of Sciences* 107 (27): 12107–12109.

Andor, Mark A., Andreas Gerster, Jorg Peters, and Christoph M. Schmidt. 2020. "Social Norms and Energy Conservation Beyond the US" *Journal of Environmental Economics and Management* 103 (102351): 1–16.

Ayres, Ian, Sophie Raseman, and Alice Shih. 2013. "Evidence From Two Large Field Experiments that Peer Comparison Feedback Can Reduce Residential Energy Usage." *The Journal of Law, Economics, and Organization* 29 (5): 992–1022.

Bacharach, Michael. 2006. *Beyond Individual Choice: Teams and Frames in Game Theory*. Edited by Natalie Gold and Robert Sugden. Princeton, NJ: Princeton University Press.

Baddeley, Michelle. 2011. "Energy, the Environment and Behaviour Change: A Survey of Insights from Behavioural Economics." *CWPE 1162*. doi: 10.17863/CAM.5245.

Benartzi, Shlomo, John Beshears, Katherine L. Milkman, Cass R. Sunstein, Richard H. Thaler, Maya Shankar, Will Tucker-Ray, William J. Congdon, and Steven Galing. 2017. "Should Governments Invest More in Nudging?" *Psychological Science* 28 (8): 1041–1055.

Berggren, Niclas. 2012. "Time for Behavioral Political Economy? An Analysis of Articles in Behavioral Economics." *The Review of Austrian Economics* 25 (3): 199–221.

Betsill, Michele M. 2001. "Mitigating Climate Change in US Cities: Opportunities and Obstacles." *Local Environment* 6 (4):393–406.

Biddle, Jennifer C. and Karen J. Baehler. 2019. "Breaking Bad: When does Polycentricity Lead to Maladaptation Rather than Adaptation?" *Environmental Policy and Governance* 29 (5): 344–359.

Boettke, Peter J., Christopher J. Coyne, and Peter T. Leeson. 2008. "Institutional Stickiness and the New Development Economics." *American Journal of Economics and Sociology* 67 (2): 331–358.

Bowman, Karlyn. 2019. "Democrats and Republicans Divided on Climate Change." *Forbes*, April 19, 2019. https://www.forbes.com/sites/bowmanmarsico/2019/04/19/democrats-and-republicans-divided-on-climate-change/#7e1048bd3198.

Brandon, Gwendolyn, and Alan Lewis. 1999. "Reducing Household Energy Consumption: A Qualitative and Quantitative Field Study." *Journal of Environmental Psychology* 19 (1): 75–85.

Brenan, Megan, and Lydia Saad. 2018. "Global Warming Concern Steady Despite Some Partisan Shifts" *Gallup*, March 28, 2018. https://news.gallup.com/poll/231530/global-warming-concern-steady-despite-partisan-shifts.aspx.

Buchanan, James M. 1949. "The Pure Theory of Government Finance: A Suggested Approach." *Journal of Political Economy* 57 (6): 496–505.

Buchanan, James M., and Gordon Tullock. 1962. *The Calculus of Consent: Logical Foundations of Constitutional Democracy*. Ann Arbor, MI: University of Michigan Press.

Carlsson, Fredrik, Mitesh Kataria, and Elina Lampi. 2011. "Do EPA Administrators Recommend Environmental Policies that Citizens Want?." *Land Economics* 87 (1): 60–74.

Carter, Jeremy G., Gina Cavan, Angela Connelly, Simon Guy, John Handley, and Aleksandra Kazmierczak. 2015. "Climate Change and the City: Building Capacity for Urban Adaptation." *Progress in Planning* 95: 1–66.

Chen, Xiaodong, Frank Lupi, Guangming He. and Jianguo Liu. 2009. "Linking Social Norms to Efficient Conservation Investment in Payments for Ecosystem Services." *Proceedings of the National Academy of Sciences of the United States of America* 106 (28): 11812–11817.

Cialdini, Robert B., Raymond R. Reno, and Carl A. Kallgren. 1990. "A Focus Theory of Normative Conduct: Recycling the Concept of Norms to Reduce Littering in Public Places." *Journal of Personality and Social Psychology* 58 (6): 1015–1026.

Coase, Ronald H. 1960. "The Problem of Social Cost." In Chennat Gopalakrishnan, ed., *Classic Papers in Natural Resource Economics*. London: Palgrave Macmillan, 87–137.

Cole, Daniel H. 2015. "Advantages of a Polycentric Approach to Climate Change Policy." *Nature Climate Change* 5 (2): 114–118.

Collomb, Jean-Daniel. 2014. "The Ideology of Climate Change Denial in the United States." *European Journal of American Studies* 9(1): 1–21.

Costa, Dora L., and Matthew E. Kahn. 2010. "Why has California's Residential Electricity Consumption Been So Flat since the 1980s?: A Microeconometric Approach." *NBER Working Paper* No. 15978. https://www.nber.org/papers/w15978.

Costa, Dora L., and Matthew E. Kahn. 2013a. "Energy Conservation "Nudges" and Environmentalist Ideology: Evidence from a Randomized Residential Electricity Field Experiment." *Journal of the European Economic Association* 11 (3): 680–702.

Costa, Dora L., and Matthew E. Kahn. 2013b. "Do Liberal Home Owners Consume Less Electricity? A Test of the Voluntary Restraint Hypothesis." *Economics Letters* 119 (2): 210–212.

Croson, Rachel, and Nicholas Treich. 2014. "Behavioral Environmental Economics: Promises and Challenges." *Environmental and Resource Economics* 58 (3): 335–351.

Czajkowski, Mikolaj, Nick Hanley, and Karine Nyborg. 2017. "Social Norms, Morals and Self-interest as Determinants of Pro-environment Behaviour: The Case of Recycling." *Environmental and Resource Economics* 66: 647–670.

De la Harpe, Stephen, C.R.J.J. Rijken, and Rolien Roos. 2008. "Good Governance." *PER: Potchefstroomse Elektroniese Regsblad* 11 (2): 2–15.

Dinner, Isaac, Eric J. Johnson, Daniel G. Goldstein, and Kaiya Liu. 2011. "Partitioning Default Effects: Why People Choose Not to Choose." *Journal of Experimental Psychology: Applied* 17 (4): 332–341.

Dubois, Ghislain, Benjamin Sovacool, Carlo Aall, Maria Nilsson, Carine Barbier, Alina Herrmann, Sebastien Bruyere, Camilla Andersson, Bore Skold, Franck Nadaud, Florian Dorner, Karen Richardsen Moberg, Jean Paul Ceron, Helen Fischer, Dorothee Amerlung, Marta Baltruszewicz, Jeremy Fisher, Francois Benevise, Valerie R. Louis, and Rainer Sauerbon. 2019. "It Starts at Home? Climate Policies Targeting Household Consumption and Behavioral Decisions are Key to Low-Carbon Futures." *Energy Research and Social Science* 52: 144–158.

Egebark, Johan, and Mathias Ekstrom. 2013. "Can Indifference Make the World Greener?" *Journal of Environmental Economics and Management* 76: 1–13.

Etner, Johanna., Meglena Jeleva, and Pierre-Andre Jouvet. 2007. "Risk Perceptions, Voluntary Contributions and Environmental Policy." *Research in Economics* 61 (3): 130–139.

Evans, Nicholas, Stephanie Eickers, Leonie Geene, Marijana Todorovic, and Annika Villmow. 2017. "Green Nudging: A Discussion and Preliminary Evaluation of Nudging as an Environmental Policy Instrument." *Environmental Policy Research Center (FFU)* https://refubium.fu-berlin.de/bitstream/handle/fub188/22047/EvansxEickerxGeenexTodorovicxVillmov_FFUxReport_GreenxNudging.pdf?sequence=1.

Farrell, Alexander E., Richard J. Plevin, Brian T. Turner, Andrew D. Jones, Michael O'hare, and Daniel M. Kammen. 2006. "Ethanol Can Contribute to Energy and Environmental Goals." *Science* 311 (5760): 506–508.

Goldstein, Noah, Robert Cialdini, and Viadas Griskevicius. 2008. "A Room with a Viewpoint: Using Norm-Based Appeals to Motivate Conservation Behaviors in a Hotel Setting." *Journal of Consumer Research* 35 (3): 472–482.

Hagmann, David, Emily Ho. and George Loewenstein. 2019. "Nudging Out Support for a Carbon Tax." *Nature Climate Change* 9 (6): 484–489.

Hagman, William, David Andersson, Daniel Västfjäll, and Gustav Tinghög. 2015. "Public views on policies involving nudges." *Review of Philosophy and Psychology* 6 (3): 439–453.

Hayek, Friederich A. 1967. "The Theory of Complex Phenomena." In *Studies in Philosophy, Politics and Economics*. London: Routledge.

Hayek, Friederich A. 1982. *Law, Legislation and Liberty*. Chicago: The Chicago University Press.

Holcombe, Randall G. 2009. "The Behavioral Foundations of Austrian Economics." *The Review of Austrian Economics* 22 (4): 301–313.

IPCC. 2018. "Summary for Policymakers." In: *Global Warming of 1.5°C. An IPCC Special Report on the Impacts of Global Warming of 1.5°C above Pre-industrial Levels and Related Global Greenhouse Gas Emission Pathways, in the Context of Strengthening the Global Response to the Threat of Climate Change, Sustainable Development, and Efforts to Eradicate Poverty*. Edited by Masson-Delmotte, V., P. Zhai, H.-O. Pörtner, D. Roberts, J. Skea, P.R. Shukla, A. Pirani, W. Moufouma-Okia, C. Péan, R. Pidcock, S. Connors, J.B.R. Matthews, Y. Chen, X. Zhou, M.I. Gomis, E. Lonnoy, T. Maycock, M. Tignor, and T. Watereld. Geneva, Switzerland: World Meteorological Organization, 32 pp.

Jacquet, Jennifer, Monica Dietrich, and John T. Jost. 2014. "The Ideological Divide and Climate Change Opinion: "Top-Down" and "Bottom-Up" Approaches." *Frontiers in Psychology* 5 (1458): 1–6.

Kahan, Dan M. 2006. "Cultural Cognition and Public Policy." *Yale Law and Policy Review* 24: 147–170.

Kahan, Dan M., Maggie Wittlin, Ellen Peters, Paul Slovic, Lisa Larrimore Ouellette, Donald Braman, and Gregory N. Mandel. 2011. "The Tragedy of the Risk-Perception Commons: Culture Conflict, Rationality Conflict, and Climate Change." *Temple University Legal Studies Research Paper No. 26, Cultural Cognition Project Working Paper No. 89, Yale Law & Economics Research Paper No. 435, Yale Law School, Public Law Working Paper No. 230*. https://ssrn.com/abstract=1871503

Kallbekken, Steffen., and Hakon Sælen. 2013. "Nudging Hotel Guests to Reduce Food Waste as a Win–Win Environmental Measure." *Economics Letters* 119 (3): 325–327.

Kasperbauer, Tyler J. 2017. "The Permissibility of Nudging for Sustainable Energy Consumption." *Energy Policy* 111: 52–57.

Koenig, Andy. 2016. "Stop Fueling The Corn Lobby's Dirty Ethanol Mandate." *Forbes Media*, January 25, 2016. https://www.forbes.com/sites/realspin/2016/01/25/fuel-the-corn-lobby-ethanol-mandate-rfs/#c7b01182db2e

Kuhfuss, Laure, Raphaele Préget, Sophie Thoyer, Nick Hanley, Philippe Le Coent, and Mathieu Désolé. 2016. "Nudges, Social Norms, and Permanence in Agri-Environmental Schemes." *Land Economics* 92 (4): 641–655.

Li, Rosa. 2020. "The Other Essential Pandemic Office Trump Eliminated." *Slate,* March 18, 2020 https://slate-com.cdn.ampproject.org/c/s/slate.com/technology /2020/03/coronavirus-social-behavior-trump-white-house.amp

List, John A., Robert D. Metcalfe, Michael K. Price, and Florian Rundhammer. 2017. "Harnessing Policy Complementarities to Conserve Energy: Evidence from a Natural Field Experiment." *NBER Working Paper* No. 23355. https://www.nber .org/papers/w23355.

Milford, Anna Birgitte, Arnstein Øvrum, and Hilde Helgesen. 2015. "Nudges to Increase Recycling and Reduce Waste." *Norwegian Agricultural Economics Research Institute Discussion Paper.* https://brage.bibsys.no/xmlui/bitstream/handl e/11250/2437370/NILF-Diskusjonsnotat-2015-01.pdf?sequence=1

Momsen, Katharina, and Thomas Stoerk. 2014. "From Intention to Action: Can Nudges Help Consumers to Choose Renewable Energy?" *Energy Policy* 74: 376–382.

Moseley, Alice, and Gerry Stoker. 2013. "Nudging Citizens? Prospects and Pitfalls Confronting a New Heuristic." *Resources, Conservation and Recycling* 79: 4–10.

Muramatsu, Roberta, and Fablo Barbieri. 2017. "Behavioral Economics and Austrian Economics: Lessons for Policy and the Prospects of Nudges." *Journal of Behavioral Economics for Policy* 1(1): 73–78.

Nagatsu, Michiru. 2015. "Social Nudges: Their Mechanisms and Justification." *Review of Philosophy and Psychology* 6 (3): 481–494.

Nature Climate Change. 2018. "The Price of Fast Fashion." *Nature Climate Change* 8: 1. https://www.nature.com/articles/s41558-017-0058-9

Opotow, Susan, and Leah Weiss. 2000. "New Ways of Thinking about Environmentalism: Denial and the Process of Moral Exclusion in Environmental Conflict." *Journal of Social Issues* 56 (3): 475–490.

Ostrom, Elinor. 1990. *Governing the Commons: The Evolution of Institutions for Collective Action.* Cambridge, UK: Cambridge University Press.

Ostrom, Elinor. 2009. "A Polycentric Approach for Coping with Climate Change." *Policy Research Working Paper* 5095. Washington, DC: The World Bank. https:// elibrary.worldbank.org/doi/abs/10.1596/1813-9450-5095.

Ostrom, Vincent, Charles M. Tiebout, and Robert Warren.1961. "The Organization of Government in Metropolitan Areas: A Theoretical Inquiry." *American Political Science Review* 55 (4): 831–842.

Ouvrard, Benjamin, and Sandrine Spaeter. 2016. "Environmental Incentives: Nudge or Tax?" *Faculté des sciences Èconomiques et de gestion Working Document* N. 23.

Pichert, Daniel, and Konstantinos V. Katsikopoulos. 2008. "Green Defaults: Information Presentation and Pro-Environmental Behaviour." *Journal of Environmental Psychology* 28 (1): 63–73.

Rizzo, Mario J., and Douglas Glen Whitman. 2009. "The Knowledge Problem of New Paternalism." *Brigham Young University Law Review* 1: 905–968.

Ross, Justin and Victoria Perez. 2020. "Federalism and Polycentric Government in a Pandemic." *Mercatus Center Policy Briefs*, April 3, 2020 https://www.mercatus .org/publications/covid-19-policy-brief-series/federalism-and-polycentric-govern ment-pandemic

Runge, C. Ford. 2016. "The Case Against More Ethanol: It's Simply Bad for the Environment." *Yale Environment 360, Yale School of Forestry & Environmental Studies*, May 25, 2016 https://e360.yale.edu/features/the_case_against_ethanol_bad_for_environment

Schubert, Christian. 2017. "Green Nudges: Do They Work? Are They Ethical?" *Ecological Economics* 132: 329–342.

Schultz, Wesley P., Jessica M. Nolan, Robert B. Cialdini, Noah J. Goldstein, and Vladas Griskevicius. 2007. "The Constructive, Destructive, and Reconstructive Power of Social Norms." *Psychological Science* 18 (5): 429–434.

Stern, Nicholas H. 2007. *The Economics of Climate Change: The Stern Review.* Cambridge, UK: Cambridge University Press.

Sunstein, Cass R. 2015. "The Ethics of Nudging." *Yale Journal on Regulation* 32 (2): 413–450.

Sunstein, Cass R. 2017. "Nudges that Fail." *Behavioural Public Policy* 1 (1): 4–25.

Sunstein, Cass R. and Lucia A. Reisch. A. 2014. "Automatically Green: Behavioral Economics and Environmental Protection." *Harvard Environmental Law Review* 38(1): 127–158.

Tang, Shui-Yan, and Brian Y. An. 2020. "Responses to COVID-19 in China and the United States: How Governance Matters." *The National Interest* (forthcoming). https://www.researchgate.net/publication/341535905_Comparing_Emergency_Responses_to_COVID-19_A_Governance_and_Intergovernmental_Perspective

Thaler, Richard. H., and Cass R. Sunstein. 2009. *Nudge: Improving Decisions about Health, Wealth, and Happiness.* Penguin Books.

Vandenberg, Michael P., and Anne C. Steinemann. 2007. "The Carbon-Neutral Individual." *New York University Law Review* 82: 1673–1741.

Venhoeven, Leonie A., Jan Willem Bolderdijk, and Linda Steg. 2016. "Why Acting Environmentally-Friendly Feels Good: Exploring the Role of Self-Image." *Frontiers in Psychology* 7 (1846): 1–8.

Viscusi, W. Kip, and James T. Hamilton. 1999. "Are Risk Regulators Rational? Evidence from Hazardous Waste Cleanup Decisions." *American Economic Review* 89 (4): 1010–1027.

Wang, Michael. 2005. "Updated Energy and Greenhouse Gas Emission Results of Fuel Ethanol." In *The 15th International Symposium on Alcohol Fuels, San Diego*: 26–28.

Wardle, Arthur R. 2018. "The Ethanol Mandate has Failed in its Original Purpose." *Washington Examiner*, October 09, 2018. https://www.washingtonexaminer.com/opinion/op-eds/the-ethanol-mandate-has-failed-in-its-original-purpose

Warner, Koko, Charles Ehrhart, A. de Sherbinin, Susana Adamo, and Tricia Chai-Onn. "In Search of Shelter: Mapping the Effects of Climate Change on Human Migration and Displacement." *Climate Change CARE International.* https://www.cabdirect.org/cabdirect/abstract/20103085728

Weber, Elke U., and Paul C. Stern. 2011. "Public Understanding of Climate Change in the United States." *American Psychologist* 66 (4): 315–328.

Chapter 9

The Paradoxes of the Privacy Paradox

Will Rinehart

Among the most impactful parts of the European Union's General Data Protection Regulation (GDPR) is the requirement that users have to say yes to every instance of data collection. California Representative Ro Khanna pushed the idea as a central feature of his Internet Bill of Rights (Swisher 2018). Yet, he pointed out that, "if you have to click on something 50 times, it kind of defeats the purpose" (Swisher 2018, n.p.). Access Now, an Internet rights group, pushed the idea as a key component of their guidelines for lawmakers in adopting a new U.S.-wide privacy law (Access Now 2018). And Eric Null, senior policy counsel at the Open Technology Institute who has long been involved in privacy discussions, made the case for an opt-in regime. He explained, "The benefit of opt-in is making sure consumer data isn't used in ways they didn't know about, understand, or agree to. Opt-out assumes they know, when in reality we all know they don't. How do you solve that without opt-in?" (Null 2018, n.p.).

Arguments about opt-in mandates are connected by a common thread: user choice, in whatever they may decide, must be supported by knowledge about the costs and benefits of the service. Since consumers do not have that knowledge, their decisions do not reflect their actual preferences. So, until consumers know what they are agreeing to, the default must be set to no collection.

Decision-making biases are said to necessitate behavioral nudges like opt-in defaults. But the reality is far less dire than imagined. Importantly, users are cognizant of the relevant trade-offs that come with data collection (Fuller 2019). As research has shown, users know about advertising and data collection, they are aware of their privacy settings, and they consider online networks generally a good deal even after considering privacy issues. A unique kind of exchange occurs between users and platforms like Google, Facebook, and Twitter. Importantly, consumers experience a zero price. The only cost to social media platforms comes in signing up and maintaining a presence. As such, zero-priced services display special characteristics (Gans 2020). Finally, the transition to opt-in mandates pushes significant costs onto everyone in the online ecosystem, an outcome explicitly decried by the original purveyors of nudge theory.

Changing the default of information sharing is but one example of the centrality that knowledge plays within the construction of privacy laws and regulations. Indeed, as a group of privacy scholars noted, various elements of privacy laws and privacy interventions were connected "in informing and guiding users' decisions toward safer, better choices, without imposing a particular decision" (Acquisti et al. 2017, 11). Nudge theory serves as a foundation for privacy legislation, a middle way between self-regulatory mechanisms, which have seemingly failed in privacy, and hard paternalistic regulation, which imposes significant costs. As Acquisti et al. (2017, 11) frame it, "Regulation might fail (or cause unintended consequences), and self-regulatory approaches may not adequately address problems—such as smoking among minors or privacy protection."

This chapter examines the knowledge problem that opt-in mandates are purportedly meant to solve. As should be apparent by the end, opt-in mandates do little to correct this problem, if it is indeed a problem that should be corrected. Just because privacy is an important value does not mean privacy regulations should not be subject to a thorough detailing and assessment of their costs and benefits. Policymakers, students, and scholars should be keenly aware of the pitfalls of privacy regulations, especially their inefficacy, and should be far more skeptical in calling for increased regulations.

THE RHETORIC OF PRIVACY AND
PRIVACY REGULATION

Privacy scholarships are plagued by a lack of clarity in terms. Like other contested ideas, *the concept* of privacy needs to be distinguished from *the conceptions* of privacy. Following the categories laid down by legal philosopher Ronald Dworkin (1994), privacy is associated with an abstraction notion or concept, as well as all those particular instantiations of the idea, or their conceptions.

Both the concept of a privacy right and its first conception can be traced to a now-famous law article on the topic by Samuel Warren and future justice of the Supreme Court of the United States Louis Brandeis. In the aptly named, "The Right to Privacy," Warren and Brandeis (1890) describe privacy as the right to be left alone. In 1928, Brandeis wrote this argument into a dissent in *Olmstead v. United States*, creating the now dominant argument within government surveillance law. Brandeis might have created a lasting legacy in surveillance law, but the rise of computers and large databases in the 1960s caused Alan Westin to rethink the concept of privacy, expand it, and then pen "Privacy and Freedom" (1967). This book laid down the foundation for modern privacy law and the sectoral approach by defining privacy as the control over and safeguard of personal information. Other, more recent interpretations of privacy see it as an aspect of dignity, autonomy, and human freedom (Schoeman 1992). Helen Nissenbaum (2004) explained that privacy should be understood as an abrogation of contextual norms. The variety of understandings of privacy, explained Law Professor Daniel Solove (2006, 485), suggests the idea "is too complicated a concept to be boiled down to a single essence." Instead, we should understand privacy as "an umbrella term, referring to a wide and disparate group of related things" (Solove 2006, 485).

Privacy laws often include two broad classes of legal mandates meant to redress different kinds of privacy conceptions. Protecting digital data from the unwanted actions of unauthorized users, which includes cyberattacks, data breaches, or fraud, is an issue of *data security*. In contrast, *data privacy* denotes a class of laws and regulations that limit legitimate actors from using, disclosing, or collecting information. Data security experts are thus worried about the integrity of a database, whereas data privacy experts are concerned about the appropriate collection and use of that data in relation to the users. In practice, the distinction often becomes muddied, because the terms security and privacy are so closely associated.

Properly designed surveys help to show that these associated concepts are in fact distinct. Together, the National Telecommunications and Information Administration and the Census have surveyed Internet users on their concerns about Internet use by offering a range of different categories. Identity theft and credit card or banking fraud top the list. Most recently, those concerns troubled 57 percent and 45 percent of users, respectively (Goldberg 2018). But data collection and loss of control over personal information, respectively, rank far lower. At 22 percent and 21 percent, collection or loss of control over data seems to concern nearly half of the population concerned with fraud. When privacy is broken into its conceptions of data security and data privacy, fraudulent activity is leaps and bounds more of a concern than ere control of data, by nearly three times (DiVall 2018).

The difference comes from the expected cost of fraud, which simply is not present in the loss of control of data. Identity theft and fraud are costly, require attention and time to rectify, and necessitate future monitoring. Individuals affected by the Equifax breach, for example, were entitled to compensation up to 20 hours at $25 per hour for the time they spent dealing with the identity theft (Belmonte 2019). They were also eligible for up to $20,000 for out-of-pocket losses and free credit monitoring services.

Importantly for this chapter, privacy will reference data privacy and not data security, unless otherwise noted.

PRIVACY LAWS IN THE UNITED STATES AND NUDGE THEORY

Federal privacy law in the United States has traditionally been governed by the sectoral approach. Sensitive data, like health or financial data, are protected by narrow laws, which limit disclosure or grant specific rights to classes of individuals, while other types of data are restricted less.

Among other mandates, sectoral privacy laws often dictate defaults choices. The Children's Online Privacy Protection Act (COPPA) requires that the parent or guardian of a child under the age of 13 must affirmatively opt-in before companies can collect or use their personal information, for example (FTC 2002). Other federal laws have chosen instead to give consumers an opt-out choice, such as with the Gramm-Leach-Bliley Act (GLBA), which includes financial privacy protections (McQuinn and Castro 2019). Both instances are limited in scope and apply to data that is considered sensitive.

Nudges in the form of opt-in and opt-outs have been used as regulatory correctives in privacy law, but it was not until the work of Richard Thaler and Cass Sunstein (2009) that they were classified as such. In *Nudge*, Thaler and Sunstein (2009, 14) first categorized and named this type of policy, noting that,

> A nudge, as we will use the term, is any aspect of the choice architecture that alters people's behavior in a predictable way without forbidding any options or significantly changing their economic incentives. To count as a mere nudge, the intervention must be easy and cheap to avoid. Nudges are not mandates. Putting fruit at eye level counts as a nudge. Banning junk food does not.

For Thaler and Sunstein, nudges are tools that help to achieve better outcomes or reduce costs that come from ill-considered actions. Thaler and Sunstein (2009) open their book by laying out how better displaying food could help kids live a healthier life, and indeed, nudges are rife within healthcare and food services. In countries other than the United States, cigarette boxes are plastered with images of dying children or blackened lungs. Under the Affordable Care Act, chain restaurants are required to have menus with calorie counts, in the hope that people will choose healthier options (Filloon 2018). Speaking on these changes, the authors argue that "setting default options, and other similar seemingly trivial menu-changing strategies, can have huge effect on outcomes" (Thaler and Sunstein 2009, 8).

Printing new menus or changing around the packaging is relatively low-cost affairs, as is changing where healthy food is placed on buffets or in grocery stores. But for choices made online, changing defaults shifts economic incentives because buyers and suppliers of data must comply with all of the other requirements within the law. In some cases, opt-out requirements mean that companies can no longer sell their core services or products.

The recently passed California Consumer Privacy Act (CCPA), which just applies to the state of California, established the right to opt-out of allowing a business to sell personal information to third parties. The seemingly innocuous creation of a default was passed alongside the right to have personal data deleted as well as the mandate to receive equal service and pricing. Thaler and Sunstein limited the scope of nudges by insisting they had to be easy and cheap to avoid. In practice, nudges are bundled with other requirements and enforced with fines (GDPR EU 2020).

Nudge theory holds a prominent place within privacy because opt-out and opt-in requirements are key provisions within the laws. Nudge theory also straddles two spaces within the scholarship where there is constant debate: privacy preferences and the value of privacy. Both need interrogation. First, what are privacy preferences and how are they formed? It is often, unfortunately, assumed blithely that new choice regimes will be better for consumers and reduce costs from ill-considered actions. But the demand for privacy, as was alluded to earlier, is highly contingent on context. Second, how do the costs imposed by changing the defaults of privacy change the total options offered to consumers? The goal of nudge is to influence people to make better decisions, but what happens when those legal requirements subtly shift the underlying landscape?

PRIVACY PREFERENCES

People do not know and cannot know their preferences until they discover them through the experience of real choice (Plott 1996; Buchanan 1982). Not surprisingly, preferences are highly contingent on how survey questions and experimental designs are framed, as Baruch Fischhoff (1991) and Paul Slovic (1995) extensively detail. Online experiences are especially influenced by differences in framing, which in turn make it difficult to accurately elicit the value of privacy. Indeed, a central conflict within privacy is known as the privacy paradox, a purported inconsistency between privacy attitudes and revealed choices. As one review of the literature described it, "while many users show theoretical interest in their privacy and maintain a positive attitude towards privacy-protection behavior, this rarely translates into actual protective behavior" (Barth and de Jong 2017, 1039).

A cottage industry has popped up detailing instances when consumers say one thing but act dissonantly. One experiment showed that customers clearly preferred buying DVDs from a more privacy-invasive firm because they were offering a slightly lower price (Preibusch et al. 2013). As the researchers discovered, when this game was played over a number of interactions, the more privacy-invasive company tended toward a larger market share and higher revenue than their competitors. Researchers working in another context were able to persuade a third of their test group to give up personal passwords for a bar of chocolate (Happ et al. 2016). But the bar of chocolate might not be a price floor since one paper famously found that "most subjects happily accepted to sell their personal information even for just 25 cents" (Grossklags and Acquisti 2007, 16).

The value of privacy clearly hinges on the elicitation method, as illustrated by the work of Cass Sunstein (2018, n.p.). To drill down on this problem, Sunstein asked two groups of people similar questions about the value of Facebook. The first group was asked, "Suppose that you had to pay for the use of Facebook. How much would you be willing to pay, at most, per month?" The second group, on the other hand, was asked: "Suppose that you are being offered money to stop using Facebook. How much would you have to be paid per month, at a minimum, to make it worth your while to stop using Facebook?" For those asked the first question, known as a willingness-to-pay (WTP) value, the average answer was about $1 per month. Those asked the second question, known as a willingness-to-accept (WTA) value, averaged $59 per month. Depending on the framing, the value of Facebook varied widely, a tendency known as the endowment effect.

Angela Winegar and Cass Sunstein (2019, 3) interpret this large gap in privacy preferences as evidence against valuing privacy altogether, saying that "both WTP and WTA answers are largely expressive, and hence do not give a helpful account of the welfare effects of maintaining or relinquishing data privacy." Because of the informational problems, they conclude that "consumer preferences might be endogenous to the method of elicitation, raising serious questions about whether they are stable and also about their normative standing" (Winegar and Sunstein 2019, 13). The same kind of criticism can just as easily be applied to privacy laws.

Privacy scholarship has a deep roster of research detailing how decisions about sharing or keeping information private online are afflicted by cognitive biases and instability of preferences (Acquisti et al. 2016). Benefit immediacy, one such inconsistency, results from the intertemporal nature of choice (Wilson and Valacich 2012). The benefit of information collection is immediate in that users get access to a service or a platform, but the potential costs of disclosing that information are deferred until some other point in time, creating a conflict.

The need for consumer choices to be consistent across time in economics initially arose from model tractability requirements. Paul Samuelson, for example, did not endorse his intertemporal model as a normative model of choice, noting that "any connection between utility as discussed here and any welfare concept is disavowed" (quoted in Frederick et al. 2002, 355). In other contexts, inconsistent choices indicate dynamism, not irrationality. Consumer churn between businesses, for example, suggests that consumers have inconsistent preferences, but they are especially rational when the quality of a business's product drops. Over time, people's circumstances change and they gather new information, naturally leading to shifts in tastes.

Online users might realize that they no longer benefit from the costs of sharing, cancel their account, and delete their data. A concrete example of this phenomenon occurred in 2018 when some 15 million people left Facebook, largely as a result of the news surrounding Cambridge Analytica (Statt 2019). Were these individuals irrational when they signed up, but then rational when they left? A much simpler explanation is that both choices were optimal for the individuals, but the context had changed when new information had been revealed.

People know that disclosing information can be beneficial. Indeed, even in a situation where disclosure can be harmful to one person in a transaction, it can be worthwhile to another in that same transaction, as Geoffrey Manne et al. (2018, 11) explain:

> To take one example from a recent [Federal Trade Commission] FTC workshop on the issue, consumers may (understandably) strongly prefer to keep hidden from their social network connections ads that could appear indicating that the user purchased a home HIV test kit, if such data is used by the network to target ads to the users' connections. It may be that the revelation that the user bought an HIV test imposes a high cost on the user. But it may also be that the revelation would alert the user's sexual partners to their risk of infection and cause them to take their own precautions. Under these circumstances, the net benefit from the sharing of the information may be quite positive, even though the user may not take account of those external benefits.

Information thus serves dual roles. Individuals can benefit if information is not shared (kept private) but can also benefit if information is shared (Acquisti et al. 2016). It is here that theories of nudge become important for public policy.

Policymakers and scholars often reference the privacy paradox literature when arguing for the imposition of an opt-in requirement for all forms of data collection (Grassley 2019). What unites the above examples, and others like them, is again the conflict created when people said that they cared about privacy and then acted in contrast with their stated values. So, perhaps if they were reminded of their values and told about the long-term risks in sharing information, then they would adjust their behavior accordingly. In testing this hypothesis, Omri Ben-Shahar and Adam Chilton (2016) found that many people did not respond to more information. In a study that simplified privacy policies and laid out the costs, they found that people did not change their behavior all that much. Even with a better comprehension of what the disclosure entailed, participants were neither just as willing to share personal information, nor did they adjust in their expectations about the long-term consequences (Ben-Shahar and Chilton 2016).

Ben-Shahar and Chilton's (2016) result is not a one-off finding. As another study found, "the ability of even improved transparency solutions or additional control tools to better align consumer attitudes towards privacy with actual behavior and reduce regret from oversharing is ultimately questionable" (Adjerid et al. 2013, 1). Interestingly enough, when users have an increased feeling of control over the publication of their data, they often engage in riskier disclosures measures (Brandimarte et al. 2013). So, even when people are faced with the potential consequences of their disclosure, benefit immediacy is not reduced. Informational nudges have limited effectiveness.

Moreover, many people knowingly do not read the terms of service contracts and yet still agree to them anyway (Vedantam 2016). One study suggested that only about one in a thousand people click on a site's terms of service (Bakos et al. 2014). So, there is a tenuous connection *at best* between affirmative consent in agreeing to online services and absolute knowledge of what that consent fully entails. At the heart of the opt-in regime is a nudge that does not represent knowledge on the part of participants.

In some contexts, the distance between privacy actions and privacy intentions is perceived as a market failure (Acquisti et al. 2016). The experimental evidence undercuts the claim of market failure, however. Even when consumers are given information about the impact of their choices, there seem to be limited effects on user understanding and choices. As Mario Rizzo and Glen Whitman (2009, 924) note, "identifying an inconsistency in someone's behavioral preferences (meaning those that actually determine choice) is not the same as identifying someone's true preferences." User preferences do not seem to reflect the true costs and benefits of the available options because the risks are not fully understood. But a more fundamental question remains: what are the real risks of information disclosure? There are good reasons to think that risks cannot be appropriately estimated and thus people (including users and policymakers) find it difficult to accurately incorporate these downsides.

ZERO-PRICED AND PRICED EXCHANGES

There is another way to understand the inconsistencies that seem to plague privacy preferences. Rather than seeing revealed preferences as conflicting with stated preferences, stated preferences should be compared against human action. Human action, not merely preferences, helps to form the order of exchange within a market. Borrowing from James Buchanan (1982), the order of the market should be understood as emerging from the interactions of individuals as they make genuine choices. Indeed, Buchanan seemed to have tackled the clash between revealed and stated preferences when he commented,

> [I]ndividuals are presumed to carry around with them fully determined utility functions, and, in the market, they act always to maximize utilities subject to the constraints they confront. As I have noted elsewhere, however, in this presumed setting, there is no genuine choice behavior on the part of anyone. In this model of market process, the relative efficiency of institutional arrangements allowing for spontaneous adjustment stems solely from the *informational* aspects.
>
> This emphasis is misleading. Individuals do not act so as to maximize utilities described in *independently existing functions*. They confront genuine choices, and the sequence of decisions taken may be conceptualized, *ex post* (after the choices), in terms of "as if" functions that are maximized. But these "as if" functions are, themselves, generated in the choosing process, not separately from such process. (Buchanan 1982, 5; italics in the original)

In other words, the terminology of revealed and stated preferences obfuscates the reality that these ideas hope to capture. Stated preferences are truly preferences. They speak to the utility of a good and how individuals might rank or choose among alternatives, say between cash and privacy, in an ideal setting. Revealed preferences are something else entirely. They are the product of preferences that have been transformed by the constraints of the world. In the language of calculus that permeates economics, utility functions (preferences) are subject to constraints (allocation). Economics uses calculus and optimization because it can crudely capture both elements. Preferences are always over real-world allocations.

To see this in action, notice how the commentary around a digital dividend deals with the unique choices offered by the price of zero. Tim Wu (2015, n.p.), for example, advocated for a data payment system in *The New Yorker*, stating that: "Most people don't feel like they are actually paying when the payment is personal data and when there is no specific sensation of having handed anything over." Still, Wu presses onward asking, "So what does it really mean, then, to pay with data?" (Wu 2015, n.p.). Wu is right that there is not a payment, but he missteps by conflating different spheres of exchange when he continues with his analysis. The price system is one kind of order, but prices are not the only method of exchange. Just as there are different orders for services and goods, there is a unique order for zero-priced services online that involves exchange without payment.

Wu's solution to this perceived conflict in exchange would legally require platforms to give users an explicit payout, a digital dividend. The imagined world of the digital dividend includes two allocations, one where the price of the digital service is zero, and another where the price is negative because of the payout. But little attention has been focused on explaining why negative prices do not emerge on social media platforms in the first place. Why aren't users confronted with this kind of allocation in the real world? Negative prices have emerged on other platforms, most notably, credit card payment systems. In formal modeling of this problem, economist Joshua Gans (2020) found that a zero price has the effect of either attracting or repelling mass consumption. Moving beyond that point to negative prices, however, does not improve total welfare for the entire platform. Gans' (2020) work suggests that the decision to offer a free service is actually an optimal allocation.

In real-world experiments, zero clearly carries a special meaning in exchange. Kristina Shampanier et al. (2007) found that people much prefer a free product than an inexpensive product that offers much greater value. In their test, people were given the choice between receiving a Hershey's kiss for one cent and a Ferrero Rocher chocolate for 26 cents, as well as the option to not buy anything. In this first test, around 40 percent of participants choose either of the two chocolates. When researchers offered this same group a Hershey's kiss for a zero price and a Ferrero Rocher chocolate for 25 cents, nine out of ten participants chose the Hershey's kiss. Palmeira (2011) argues that the zero effectively removes a reference point that can offer guidance in comparing between products. As one review of the literature explained it, "the comparison with zero is meaningless because any number is infinitely larger than zero" (Zhang and Slovic 2018, 1).

Making a good explicitly priced changes how it is perceived. Bruno Frey and Felix Oberholzer-Gee (1997) catalogued a unique incidence of this phenomenon just as Switzerland was preparing to take a national vote on where to site nuclear waste dumps. In a door-to-door survey, around 50 percent of respondents supported putting a potentially dangerous nuclear waste dump in their backyard. Yet, when asked whether they would be willing to have the dumps in their communities for about 10 percent of median income, willingness-to-accept dropped and only 25 percent supported the plan. The addition of a price cut acceptance in half.

Alvin Roth (2007) calls this trade a repugnant market. Why is it, he asks, that you cannot eat horse or dog meat in a restaurant in California, which has people from all over the world, including places that serve those kinds of meals? As he explains, "The answer is that many Californians not only don't wish to eat horses or dogs themselves, but find it repugnant that anyone else should do so, and they enacted this repugnance into California law by referendum in 1998" (Roth 2007, 37). Charging interest was considered distasteful at one point in history, just as selling blood is still considered taboo in some countries. Similarly, selling kidneys is portrayed as being inappropriate in the United States, but is commonplace in Iran (Bengali and Mostaghim 2017). Dowries, which were once common in the West, are the provenance of a world epochs different than ours. Life insurance is another example, as Virginia Postrel (2007, n.p.) pointed out,

> When you think about it, life insurance is a really ghoulish thing. I mean you have insurance that's going to pay your relatives if you die. That's kind of disgusting. And it was considered disgusting until fairly late in history, until the early 20th century. There was a big shift where life insurance went from being considered immoral, ghoulish, to being considered something that a responsible person should buy.

Repugnance is also encountered when pulling apart that often-repeated comment about platforms: "If you are not paying for the product, you are the product." It might be a pithy phrase, but it is a wholly incorrect one. The product is actually an ad, positioned on the site and tailored for you. Countless weeklies across the United States run under a free model and have done so for decades. And yet, this exchange is not questioned like ads on Facebook and Google are. The difference lies in a perceived repugnance in the exchange of data. The phrase conjures a sense of being objectified and the unease it entails.

Instead of calling online services repugnant, commenters tend to call them creepy (Tene and Polonestky 2013). Indeed, the term has become so commonplace that scholars Omer Tene and Jules Polonetsky developed a theory of creepiness in privacy to help practitioners navigate potential blowback. As they explain, "The word 'creepy' has become something of a term of art in privacy policy" but the term is typically employed for "new technologies and services that grate against social norms, often resulting in negative public response" (Tene and Polonestky 2013, 60). Other research confirms that unpredictability undergirds creepiness (McAndrew and Koehnke 2016).

Repugnance and creepiness are natural reactions to a dynamic online environment. New services bring with them opportunity but also uncertain consequences. Consumers must navigate areas no one has traversed before, and with that comes unease. The unease does not represent a failing that needs correction via regulation but rather signals the indefinite nature of online experiences. As the next section helps to lay out, most privacy harms are precarious.

THE RISKS OF DISCLOSURE AND ITS IMPACT ON THE PRIVACY PARADOX

To better understand the harms related to control of data, it is helpful to contrast it with the explicit costs involved with a data breach, a kind of data security issue as outlined earlier. The 2013 Target data breach exemplifies the classic data breach in that credit card information was collected and adversely distributed over the dark web for money. All told, the breach cost the retailer $252 million in various lawsuits. As for the company's financials, in the weeks following the initial reports, sales slipped 5.3 percent and profits dropped 46 percent. Consumers wary of Target's reputation stayed away from the retailer, leading to a 7–8 percent decline in traffic (Phillips 2014).

Improper informational disclosure does not normally translate into explicit costs because the data shared on Facebook, Google, and Twitter cannot easily be used for fraud or other kinds of harmful activity. Violating norms on a platform are far more complicated since they cannot be easily price-denominated. While users might not want their data shared, sharing does not normally lead to harmful acts. Smoking increases cancer and the potential for heart attack, both clear harms that might be mitigated by label warnings detailing those risks (Hammond 2006). Calorie counts on menus seem to reduce total caloric intake in some environments and thus help mitigate heart problems and other weight-related diseases (Block and Roberto 2014). Yet, the risk of informational disclosure is not like cancer or heart disease. Oftentimes, these risks simply do not materialize in any tangible way.

Informational harms, a broader term for privacy harms, are notoriously difficult to pin down. In 2017, leadership at the FTC conducted a workshop to explore the limits of a legal injury in information. The official report offered few substantive examples:

[E]xposure of personal information that a consumer wishes to keep private, such as sensitive medical information, sexual orientation, or gender identity, may cause both market and non-market harm to the consumer. For example, one participant noted that exposure of such information may affect a consumer's ability to obtain or keep employment. Another stated that it may negatively affect the consumer's relationships with family, friends, and coworkers. (FTC 2018, 2)

As the FTC pointed out, there is little agreement on what should be included and even less agreement on how to resolve harms where explicit costs are not involved, especially since changes might limit consumer benefits.

While credit card and banking fraud might be rampant, instances of real harm from information sharing are uncommon. Indeed, one story is often used as the case study to explain the harm from improper information disclosure. Around 2012, Target started sending direct mail to addresses where recent purchases suggested a woman in the household was pregnant (Duhigg 2012). Not long after the program began, a man walked into a Target outside Minneapolis and demanded to see the manager because the company was sending his daughter these coupons and he insisted there must be some mistake. As was later revealed in a *New York Times* article, his teenage daughter was in fact pregnant. This singular instance is said to necessitate a rule (Balkin 2016). On the flip side, if Target were to send coupons to a home where a child was not expected, most people would probably just throw the flier away. Since the context is different, the informational harm no longer exists. Because the risk of disclosure is exceptionally rare, some scholars resist laws built on these kinds of harms (Khan and Pozen 2019).

It is common for privacy harms to be artfully constructed. Daniel Solove (2004) frames it as a digital dossier. Seven days a week, twenty-four hours a day, electronic databases are compiling information about you, he warns, creating a profile of activities, interests, and preferences used to investigate backgrounds, check credit, market products, and make a wide variety of decisions affecting our lives. Even though no such thing exists, Solove (2004) explains why such a ledger poses a grave threat to our privacy. Frank Pasquale (2016) calls it the "black box." Ryan Calo (2014, 999) calls it "digital market manipulation," the belief that, "[f]irms will increasingly be able to trigger irrationality or vulnerability in consumers—leading to actual and perceived harms that challenge the limits of consumer protection law, but which regulators can scarcely ignore."

CONSUMERS KNOW THE ONLINE ENVIRONMENT

Nudges might be helpful if consumers are making choices but do not clearly understand the trade-offs. Yet, Internet users have been found to understand that they are engaged in a trade-off (Rader 2014). Caleb Fuller (2019) found that nine out of ten people who use Google are aware that it collects information to serve ads. Moreover, as users search more often, or consume more, they are more aware of the information collection. For those that use Google about once a day, a lower bound, 78 percent are aware of information collection. But for those that search dozens of times a day or more, their understanding jumps to 93 percent. Fuller also found that "86% of respondents express no willingness to pay for additional privacy when interacting with Google" (Fuller 2019, 1). It should come as no surprise that people want it all, limiting both disclosure and their financial outlays.

Pew found, for example, that "there are a variety of circumstances under which many Americans would share personal information or permit surveillance in return for getting something of perceived value" (Rainie and Duggan 2016, n.p.). As those researchers found, users are fine with sharing shopping histories for a discount card but are not fine with car insurance companies offering cheaper rates if a tracking device is installed. The trade association NetChoice worked with Zogby Analytics to find that only 16 percent of people are willing to pay for online platform services (Winterton 2018). Lior Jacob Strahilevitz and Matthew Kugler (2016) found that 65 percent of email users, even though they knew their email service scans emails to serve ads, would not pay for an alternative service. Countless other studies underpinning this thesis beget a more refined version of the informational critique of privacy: consumers do indeed understand that trade-offs are occurring but think the terms of the deal are unfair. But then again, consumers think this about all products, every purchase is too costly (Bolton et al. 2003).

There is a paradox in the privacy paradox. Why is it that users would take steps to manage their online privacy experiences? Indeed, if people had an incorrect perception of the risk, as has been claimed, it would make little sense why so many have adopted technologies and techniques to limit disclosure. A comScore found that about 3 in every 10 Internet users delete their cookies every month, a technique to limit disclosure (Lipsman 2007). Similarly, one of every four Internet users in the United States uses ad-blocking technologies, like uBlock Origin or AdBlock Plus (eMarketer 2017). Moreover, those aged 18–45 are far more active in deploying techniques to limit information sharing. Teens also use coded language to maintain a linguistic distance from their parents who also might be on a platform. The practice of hiding messages and meanings within otherwise non-secret media goes by the name of steganography (Newman 2017). Survey results from Reuters also suggest that 3 out of 4 Facebook users are aware of their privacy settings, while nearly 8 in 10 know how to change their privacy settings (Reuters 2018). Users are far more educated about their choices and disclosure of information than is typically suggested.

OPT-IN MANDATES AND THE COST
OF REGIME CHANGE

Overall, users largely seem to care about limiting disclosure and are aware of the tools that platforms provide to change their privacy settings. Still, opt-in regulations are argued as a corrective to informational gaps (Spiezio 2019). The debate over opt-in or opt-out might be framed as being a knowledge-centric policy change, but users are hardly more informed in a pure opt-in system.

Opt-in mandates present users with three big hurdles as decisionmakers. First, consumers have substantially less information about the decisions they make. Before any additional service can be provided, a user must imagine all of the potential benefits, which will be especially difficult for untested ideas and startups. Second, consumers will think that the defaults are suggestions by the company or experts. In other words, they will assume that it is a recommended action, and may be more likely to adhere to it than change their settings. Lastly, these defaults will become the status quo. Any further change from this baseline will require significant effort by a company and will be understood by the decisionmaker as a trade-off. A seminal paper by William Samuelson and Richard Zeckhauser (1988) documents countless cases where one option was presented as the status quo, inflating its attractiveness, even when that option was randomly assigned.

Opt-in regimes are also meant to tackle time inconsistencies. But consider a contract where you have only one option, you can either opt-in or not to data collection before you consume the good or service. If you say yes, then the negotiations have effectively ended. No further choices can be expressed unless you exit from the service completely. The contract is explicit and agreed to upfront. If, however, you are given the choice to opt out, then users always retain certain kinds of information processing rights in the future. The relationship between you and the provider becomes one of an extended negotiation, a repeated game where a contract is implicitly agreed to but can be modified at some future point. In short, opt-out regimes open the range of contractual relationships (Klein 1996). The ability to exit from this negotiation becomes a powerful tactic.

Nicklas Lundblad and Betsy Masiello (2010, 160) explain the importance,

> This ought to evolve into an ongoing negotiation and game of repeated trust between the service provider and the user. But what we observe in account-based opt-in decisions is a one-time ex-ante limited choice which applies over the lifetime of a service contract. This actually risks the user's privacy over the long term because the deal requires no further negotiation on the part of the service provider.

Moving data industries to opt-in regimes modifies the user's relationship with the processor in a way that changes the relative positions within the negotiation process. Currently, privacy is, as Kevin Haggerty and Richard Ericson (2000, 616) explain, "less a line in the sand beyond which transgression is not permitted, as a shifting space of negotiation where privacy is traded for products, better services or special deals."

The impact of moving toward an opt-in system is hardly innocuous. Opt-in defaults often show markedly lower participation rates to opt-out defaults even though the good or service is exactly the same (Johnson et al. 2002). The classic example is organ donation. Although there is widespread support for organ donation, only about 28 percent actually volunteer to be donors, despite the fact that around 85 percent claim to want to be donors (Johnson et al. 2002). Some countries automatically enroll everyone for organ donation and then allow for opting out, which results in participation rates of 85 percent and higher. Examples of countries moving from one system to another are few, but the Welsh government reformed their system in 2013 by passing legislation that assumed consent for organ donation. The result was hardly stellar: "Covering the period from January 2010 or January 2011 to September 2017, all donation data show no change [in the number of people donating] since the legislation's introduction" (Parsons 2018, 943).

Opt-in privacy regimes have been tried before in the United States in the context of communication networks and were found to be costly endeavors. In a court case in 2000, US West, a telephone company that is now part of CenturyLink, revealed that getting permission to sell their services cost the company between $21 and $34 per consumer (Tuan 2000). The company was challenging a law passed in the wake of the 1996 Telecommunication Act that was clearly aimed at limiting expansion by the Baby Bells. By their own internal calculations, US West had to make 4.8 calls to each customer household before they reached an adult who could grant consent to share information. In one-third of households called, US West never reached the customer. Altogether, customers received more calls from the opt-in regime than in an opt-out system even though many were not able to enjoy the benefits of new services. The consent regime was burdensome to the company and the users.

Opt-in regimes have been imposed in other policy domains, and studies have also found higher costs and slowed innovation in those industries. A 2000 Ernst and Young study of financial institutions found that opt-in mandates cost the entire financial industry $56 billion (Nott 2004). An estimate of a new law for charities suggested that the cost of compliance with an opt-in privacy law would have been nearly 21 percent of their total revenue (Cate 2003). Industry estimates from the American Banker suggest that around 5 percent of people choose to opt out of sharing financial information under GLBA requirements, a significantly smaller impact (Lee 2001).

While still early, research from the AdChoices program illuminates how users approach opt-in regimes. In AdChoices, which covers the bulk of advertising online, consumers are given the ability to opt out of online behavioral advertising via a dedicated website. The real-world uptake of AdChoices is minimal, only 0.23 percent of American ad impressions arise from users who opted out of online behavioral advertising (Johnson et al. 2017).

SHIFTING THE CONSENT ENVIRONMENT

While sometimes framed as costless, creating opt-ins or opt-outs does indeed impose costs. Changing defaults requires that every person affirmatively consents to a data collection service. Companies involved in data collection and processing must comply with the rules. Opt-in choices reduce the total number of people choosing yes, driving down the effectiveness of data processing. For those companies that rely on the processing of data, which is increasingly every company, they will actually be collecting data more intensely from fewer people, which could diminish their ability to service new consumers and limit their effectiveness. This in turn will affect the overall choice set available to consumers.

Opt-in mandates are a feature within the General Data Protection Regulation (GDPR), which came into effect in Europe in 2018 (Radley-Gardner et al. 2016). Early research on the regulatory impact of the GDPR finds that the biggest players have been able to weather the storm while smaller firms have been wiped out (Bergemann 2018). The proclivity of information disclosure laws to narrow the range of options has also been found. Smaller advertising firms have lost between 28 and 32 percent of their placements on websites, while Google was able to increase their web presence by 1 percent (Grelf 2018).

Economists focused on privacy predicted exactly this result years earlier (Campbell et al. 2015). The biggest players had to tighten the reins on the entire ad network, and effectively crowded out websites that could not guarantee consent from users (Markman 2018). In a feature on the subject, reporting from the *Wall Street Journal* confirms the extent to which GDPR is drawing advertising money toward Google's online-ad services and away from competitors (Kostov and Schechner 2018). Paris-based Smart, a player in the ad space, says it has seen a roughly 50 percent drop in overall traffic (Kostov and Schechner 2018). Because Google has to ensure consent, the company has bought more ad inventory from its own exchange, where it is sure to have user consent for targeted advertising.

Early work from Jian Jia et al. (2020) points to large impacts from GDPR on nascent industries. By using a difference-in-difference analysis with the

United States as the control, the researchers were able to pinpoint the effect of GDPR on European venture capital deals. By comparing data on venture deals in the EU and United States between July 2017 and October 2018 from Crunchbase, it was calculated that the EU saw double digit declines in venture-funding. As the authors explain, this reduction takes place in both the intensive margin in that the average dollar amount raised per round of funding decreased by 39 percent and the extensive margin in that the number of deals incurred a 17 percent drop (Jia et al. 2020).

This comes with little surprise. Earlier privacy regulation in Europe found the impact on small sites could be massive. The implementation of restricted information sharing rules under e-Privacy decreased the efficacy of advertising by 65 percent relative to the rest of the world, cutting off the lifeblood of Internet startups (Goldfarb and Tucker 2011). Those hardest hit were general content sites like news outlets.

The GDPR, like every other privacy law, imposes three kinds of costs on firms. First, the regulation forces firms to retool data processes to realign with the new demands. Refactoring, as it is called, is a costly process that can sink a company because the costs are overwhelming (Leitch and Stroulia 2003). For privacy regimes, this is generally a one-time fixed fee that raises the cost of all information-using entities. Second, the regime adds risk compliance costs, causing companies to staff up to ensure compliance. Finally, GDPR has changed the investment dynamics for all those affected industries.

Currently, the retooling costs and the risk compliance costs are going hand-in-hand, so it is difficult to determine the costs of each. Still, they are substantial. A McDermott-Ponemon survey on GDPR preparedness found that almost two-thirds of all companies say the regulation will "significantly change" their informational workflows (Winton et al. 2018). For just over 50 percent of companies expecting to be ready for the changes, the average budget for getting to compliance tops $13 million, by this estimate. Among all the new requirements, this survey found that companies were particularly struggling with the data-breach notification requirement. The inability to comply with the notification requirement was cited by 68 percent of companies as posing the greatest risk because of the size of levied fines.

The International Association of Privacy Professionals (IAPP) estimated the regulation will cost Fortune 500 companies around $7.8 billion to get up to speed with the law (IAPP 2017). And these will not be one-time costs, since "Global 500 companies will be hiring on average five full-time privacy employees and filling five other roles with staff members handling compliance rules" (IAPP 2017, n.p.). A PwC survey on the rule change found that 88 percent of companies surveyed spent more than $1 million on GDPR preparations, and 40 percent more than $10 million (Cline 2018).

It might take some time to truly understand the impact of GDPR, but the law will surely change the dynamics of countless industries. For example, when the EU adopted the e-Privacy Directive in 2002, Avi Goldfarb and Catherine Tucker (2011) found that advertising became far less effective. The impact seems to have reverberated throughout the online ecosystem as venture capital investment in online news, online advertising, and cloud computing dropped by between 58 and 75 percent (McQuinn and Castro 2018). Information restrictions shift consumer choices. In Chile, for example, credit bureaus were forced to stop reporting defaults in 2012, which was found to reduce the costs for most of the poorer defaulters but raised the costs for non-defaulters (Liberman et al. 2018). Overall, the law led to a 3.5 percent decrease in lending and reduced aggregate welfare.

PUTTING THE THREADS TOGETHER

Thaler and Sunstein's (2009, 5) unifying aim with nudge theory is to merely persuade choices "without forbidding any options or significantly changing their economic incentives." Within privacy scholarship, setting defaults are seen as costless nudges. Since they are coupled with other rules and fines, these changes slip out of the realm of mere suggestions and quickly become mandates. As work on the GDPR has found, a mandated choice system changes the incentives for all the companies involved. In practice, privacy nudges translate into costly compliance regimes, resulting in skewed economic choices in the long run.

Privacy laws tend to hit the smallest players the hardest, and if those entrepreneurs have new ideas or ways of doing business, mandates will make it harder for new ideas to take hold. In the hectic but dynamic process that is the market, privacy laws make the discovery of new innovations less likely.

Opt-in mandates are also meant to ensure consumers express their true preferences, but preferences are highly contextual and personal, as are privacy harms. As such, consumer preferences must be discovered through interactions with allocations as they exist in the real world. Importantly then, consumers cannot express anything akin to a choice if they are not faced with trade-offs. In other words, the lack of knowledge that opt-in mandates foist upon users severely undercuts their expression of preferences. Experimental economics has only supported this insight first elaborated by Buchanan: efficient exchange occurs even when many of the classical assumptions of perfect market don't hold, like the need for complete information.

In total, opt-in mandates will not yield a better world with more informed choices. Rather, they will yield a different world with different choices. In many contexts, it should be expected that these different choices may be worse. Consumers benefit when their data is combined with others to offer new services, and they also benefit when they are made aware of new opportunities through advertisement. Shutting down these paths to discovery upends the very root purpose of opt-ins and other nudges.

The idea pushed by Thaler and Sunstein (2009) finds its limits in privacy policy. Mandating choices translates into real costs on the economy, on innovation, and on real lives. Those who are engaged in the policy discussion and who believe in strong privacy regulations should not be dismissing the fact that regulations are costly. Rather, they should be upfront with what they are willing to sacrifice for more data control. A mature approach to public policy and privacy would celebrate trade-offs instead of wishing them away.

REFERENCES

Access Now. 2018. "Creating a Data Protection Framework: A Do's and Don'ts Guide for Lawmakers—Lessons from the EU General Data Protection Regulation to Contribute to the Global Discourse on Data Protection." November. https://www.accessnow.org/cms/assets/uploads/2018/01/Data-Protection-Guilde-for-Lawmakers-Access-Now.pdf.

Acquisti, Alessandro, Idris Adjerid, Rebecca Balebako, Laura Brandimarte, Lorrie Faith Cranor, Saranga Komanduri, Pedro Giovanni Leon, Norman Sadeh, Florian Schaub, Manya Sleeper, Yang Wang, and Shomir Wilson. 2017. "Nudges for Privacy and Security: Understanding and Assisting Users' Choices Online." *ACM Computer Surveys* 50 (3): 11–41.

Acquisti, Alessandro, Curtis Taylor, and Liad Wagman. 2016. "The Economics of Privacy." *Journal of Economic Literature* 54 (2): 442–92.

Adjerid, Idris, Alessandro Acquisti, Laura Brandimarte, and George Loewenstein. 2013. "Sleights of Privacy: Framing, Disclosures, and the Limits of Transparency." *Proceedings of the Ninth Symposium on Usable Privacy and Security* 9: 1–11.

Bakos, Yannis, Florencia Marotta-Wurgler, and David R. Trossen. 2014. "Does Anyone Read the Fine Print?: Consumer Attention to Standard-Form Contracts." *The Journal of Legal Studies* 43 (1): 1–25.

Balkin, Jack M. 2016. "Information Fiduciaries and the First Amendment." *University of California Davis Law Review* 49: 1183–234.

Barth, Susanne and Menno D. T. de Jong. 2017. "The Privacy Paradox – Investigating Discrepancies between Expressed Privacy Concerns and Actual Online Behavior – A Systematic Literature Review." *Telematics and Informatics* 34 (7): 1038–58.

Belmonte, Adriana. 2019. "Here's How Much You Could Get from The Equifax Data Breach Settlement." *HuffPost*, July 25. https://www.huffpost.com/entry/how-to-get-equifax-money-data-breach-lawsuit_l_5d38bd4be4b004b6adba579a.

Bengali, Shashank and Ramin Mostaghim. 2017. "'Kidney for Sale': Iran Has a Legal Market for the Organs, but the System Doesn't Always Work." *Los Angeles Times*, October 15. https://www.latimes.com/world/middleeast/la-fg-iran-kidney-201710 15-story.html.

Ben-Shahar, Omri and Adam Chilton. 2016. "Simplification of Privacy Disclosures: An Experimental Test." *The Journal of Legal Studies* 45 (S2): S41–S68.

Bergemann, Benjamin. 2018. "The Consent Paradox: Accounting for the Prominent Role of Consent in Data Protection." In *Privacy and Identity Management. The Smart Revolution*, edited by Marit Hansen, Eleni Kosta, Igor Nai-Fovino, and Simone Fischer-Hübner, 111–31. Cham, CH: Springer International Publishing.

Block, Jason P. and Christina A. Roberto. 2014. "Potential Benefits of Calorie Labeling in Restaurants." *Jama* 312 (9): 887–88.

Bolton, Lisa E., Luk Warlop, and Joseph W. Alba. 2003. "Consumer Perceptions of Price (Un)Fairness." *Journal of Consumer Research* 29 (4): 474–91.

Brandimarte, Laura, Alessandro Acquisti, and George Lo. 2013. "Misplaced Confidences: Privacy and the Control Paradox." *Social Psychological and Personality Science* 4 (3): 340–47.

Buchanan, James M. 1982. "Order Defined in the Process of Its Emergence." *Literature of Liberty* 5 (4): 5.

Calo, Ryan. 2014. "Digital Market Manipulation." *George Washington Law Review* 82 (4): 995–1051.

Campbell, James, Avi Goldfarb, and Catherine Tucker. 2015. "Privacy Regulation and Market Structure." *Journal of Economics and Management Strategy* 24 (1): 47–73.

Cate, Fred H. 2003. "The Privacy Problem: A Broader View of Information Privacy and the Costs and Consequences of Protecting It." *First Amendment Center*, March. Accessed August 1, 2019. https://www.freedomforuminstitute.org/wp-cont ent/uploads/2016/10/FirstReport.privacyproblem.pdf.

Cline, Jay. 2018. "Pulse Survey: GDPR Budgets Top $10 Million for 40% of Surveyed Companies." PricewaterhouseCoopers.

DiVall, Linda. 2018. "American Action Forum Title II Survey Findings." *American Action Forum*, June 29. Accessed August 1, 2019. https://www.americanactionforu m.org/wp-content/uploads/2018/07/AVP-Memo-7-2018.pdf.

Duhigg, Charles. 2012. "How Companies Learn Your Secrets." *The New York Times Magazine*, February 16. https://www.nytimes.com/2012/02/19/magazine/shopping -habits.html?pagewanted=1&_r=1&hp.

Dworkin, Ronald. 1994. *Life's Dominion: An Argument about Abortion, Euthanasia, and Individual Freedom.* New York: Vintage.

eMarketer. 2017. "eMarketer Scales Back Estimates of Ad Blocking in the US." February 15. https://www.emarketer.com/Article/eMarketer-Scales-Back-Esti mates-of-Ad-Blocking-US/1015243?ecid=NL1001.

Federal Trade Commission (FTC). 2002. *Protecting Children's Privacy under COPPA: A Survey on Compliance.* April. https://www.ftc.gov/sites/default/files/ documents/rules/children's-online-privacy-protection-rule-coppa/coppasurvey.pdf.

———. 2018. *FTC Informational Injury Workshop.* October. https://www.ftc.gov/ system/files/documents/reports/ftc-informational-injury-workshop-be-bcp-staff-pe rspective/informational_injury_workshop_staff_report_-_oct_2018_0.pdf.

Filloon, Whitney. 2018. "Chain Restaurants Are Now Legally Required to Display Calorie Counts." *Eater*, May 7. https://www.eater.com/2018/5/7/17326574/calorie -count-menu-nutrition-fda-law.

Fischhoff, Baruch. 1991. "Value Elicitation: Is There Anything in There?" *American Psychologist* 46: 835–47.

Frederick, Shane, George Loewenstein, and Ted O'Donoghue. 2002. "Time Discounting and Time Preference: A Critical Review." *Journal of Economic Literature* 40 (2): 351–401.

Frey, Bruno S. and Felix Oberholzer-Gee. 1997. "The Cost of Price Incentives: An Empirical Analysis of Motivation Crowding-Out." *American Economic Association* 87 (4): 746–55.

Fuller, Caleb. 2019. "Is the Market for Digital Privacy a Failure?" *Public Choice* 180 (3–4): 353–81.

Gans, Joshua S. "The Specialness of Zero." Working Paper, National Bureau of Economic Research No. w26485.

GDPR EU. 2020. "GDPR Fines & Data Breach Penalties." December 14. https://ww w.gdpreu.org/compliance/fines-and-penalties/.

Goldberg, Rafi. 2018. "Most Americans Continue to Have Privacy and Security Concerns, NTIA Survey Finds." *National Telecommunications and Information Administration Blog*, August 20. https://www.ntia.doc.gov/blog/2018/most-ameri cans-continue-have-privacy-and-security-concerns-ntia-survey-finds.

Goldfarb, Avi and Catherine E. Tucker. 2011. "Privacy Regulation and Online Advertising." *Management Science* 57 (1): 57–71.

Grassley, Chuck. 2019. *GDPR & CCPA: Opt-ins, Consumer Control, and the Impact on Competition and Innovation: Hearing before the Committee on the Judiciary,* 116th Cong. (statement of Senator Chuck Grassley, Ranking Member).

Grelf, Bjorn. 2018. "Study: Google Is the Biggest Beneficiary of the GDPR." *Cliqz*, October 10. https://cliqz.com/en/magazine/study-google-is-the-biggest-beneficia ry-of-the-gdpr.

Grossklags, Jens and Alessandro Acquisti. 2007. "When 25 Cents Is Too Much: An Experiment on Willingness-To-Sell and Willingness-To-Protect Personal Information." *Proceedings of the Sixth Workshop on the Economics of Information Security.* https://econinfosec.org/archive/weis2007/papers/66.pdf.

Haggerty, Kevin D. and Richard V. Ericson. 2000. "The Surveillant Assemblage." *The British Journal of Sociology* 51 (4): 605–22.

Hammond, David. 2006. "Effectiveness of Cigarette Warning Labels in Informing Smokers about the Risks of Smoking: Findings from the International Tobacco Control (ITC) Four Country Survey." *Tobacco Control* 15 (Suppl_3): iii19–iii25.

Happ, Christian, André Melzer, and Georges Steffgen. 2016. "Trick with Treat – Reciprocity Increases the Willingness to Communicate Personal Data." *Computers in Human Behavior* 61: 372–77.

International Association of Privacy Professionals (IAPP). 2017. "Global 500 Companies to Spend $7.8B on GDPR Compliance." November 20. https://iapp.org /news/a/survey-fortune-500-companies-to-spend-7-8b-on-gdpr-compliance/.

Jia, Jian, Ginger Zhe Jin, and Liad Wagman. 2020. "GDPR and the Localness of Venture Investment." SSRN Working Paper, No. 3436535.

Johnson, Eric J., Steven Bellman, and Gerald L. Lohse. 2002. "Defaults, Framing and Privacy: Why Opting In-Opting Out." *Marketing Letters* 13 (1): 5–15.

Johnson, Garrett, Scott Shriver, and Shaoyin Du. 2017. "Consumer Privacy Choice in Online Advertising: Who Opts Out and at What Cost to Industry?" Working Paper, Simon Business School.

Khan, Lina and David E. Pozen. 2019. "A Skeptical View of Information Fiduciaries." *Harvard Law Review* 133: 497–541.

Klein, Benjamin. 1996. "Why Hold-ups Occur: The Self-Enforcing Range of Contractual Relationship." *Economic Inquiry* 34 (3): 444–63.

Kostov, Nick and Sam Schechner. 2018. "Google Emerges as Early Winner From Europe's New Data Privacy Law." *The Wall Street Journal*, May 31. https:// www.wsj.com/articles/eus-strict-new-privacy-law-is-sending-more-ad-money-to-g oogle-1527759001.

Lee, W. A. 2001. "Opt-Out Notices Give No One a Thrill." *American Banker*, July 10. https://www.americanbanker.com/news/opt-out-notices-give-no-one-a-thrill.

Leitch, Rob and Eleni Stroulia. 2003. "Understanding the Economics of Refactoring." *Proceedings of the Fifth ICSE Workshop on Economics-Driven Software Engineering Research*. Accessed August 1, 2019. http://www.soberit.hut.fi/edser -5/Papers/E05_LeitchStroulia.pdf.

Liberman, Andres, Christopher Neilson, Luis Opazo, and Seth D. Zimmerman. 2018. "The Equilibrium Effects of Information Deletion: Evidence from Consumer Credit Markets." National Bureau of Economic Research Working Paper No. w25097.

Lipsman, Andrew. 2007. "Cookie Deletion Rates and the Impact on Unique Visitor Counts." *Comscore, Inc.*, April 16. https://www.comscore.com/chi/Insights/Bl og/Cookie-Deletion-Rates-and-the-Impact-on-Unique-Visitor-Counts?cs_edgesca pe_cc=US.

Lundblad, Nicklas and Betsy Masiello. 2010. "Opt-In Dystopias." *Scripted* 7 (1): 155–65.

Manne, Geoffrey, Kristian Stout, and Dirk Auer. 2018. "Comments on Developing the Administration's Approach to Consumer Privacy." *International Center for Law and Economics*. November 9. Accessed July 31, 2019. https://laweconcente r.org/wp-content/uploads/2018/11/ICLE-Comments-NTIA-Developing-Adminis trations-Approach-to-Privacy.pdf.

Markman, Jon. 2018. "GDPR Is Great News for Google and Facebook, Really." *Forbes*, May 23. https://www.forbes.com/sites/jonmarkman/2018/05/22/gdpr-is-g reat-news-for-google-and-facebook-really/#3b2b5be748f6.

McAndrew, Francis T. and Sara S. Koehnke. 2016. "On the Nature of Creepiness." *New Ideas in Psychology* 43: 10–15.

McQuinn, Alan and Daniel Castro. 2018. "Why Stronger Privacy Regulations Do Not Spur Increased Internet Use." *Information Technology & Innovation Foundation.* July. http://www2.itif.org/2018-trust-privacy.pdf.

———. 2019. "A Grand Bargain on Data Privacy Legislation for America." *Information Technology & Innovation Foundation.* January. http://www2.itif.org /2019-grand-bargain-privacy.pdf?_ga=2.111927044.1237727920.1564666708- 2071049777.1564666708.

Newman, Lily Hay. 2017. "What Is Steganography?" *Wired*, June 26. https://www .wired.com/story/steganography-hacker-lexicon/.

Nissenbaum, Helen. 2004. "Privacy as Contextual Integrity." *Washington Law Review* 79 (1): 119–57.

Nott, Loretta. 2004 "Financial Privacy: The Economics of Opt-In vs Opt-Out." *Congressional Research Service (CRS)*, February 12.

Null, Eric (@EricNull). 2018. "I agree on right to be forgotten. The benefit of opt-in is making sure consumer data isn't used in ways they didn't know about/understand/ agree to. Opt-out assumes they know, when in reality we all know they don't. How do you solve that without opt-in?" Twitter, May 23. https://twitter.com/ericnull/s tatus/999360346396741632.

Palmeira, Mauricio. 2011. "The Zero-Comparison Effect." *Journal of Consumer Research* 38 (1): 16–26.

Parsons, Jordan Alexander. 2018. "Welsh 2013 Deemed Consent Legislation Falls Short of Expectations." *Health Policy* 122 (9): 941–44.

Pasquale, Frank. 2016. *The Black Box Society: The Secret Algorithms That Control Money and Information.* Cambridge, MA: Harvard University Press.

Phillips, Matt. 2014. "Shoppers Decided to Avoid Target after Its Giant Data Breach." *Quartz*, February 26. https://qz.com/181703/shoppers-decided-to-avoid-target- after-its-giant-data-breach/#/h/50164,2/.

Plott, Charles R. 1996. "Rational Individual Behavior in Markets and Social Choice Processes." In *The Rational Foundations of Economic Behavior,* edited by Kenneth Arrow, Enrico Colombatto, Mark Perlman, and Christian Schmidt. New York: Palgrave Macmillan, 225–50.

Postrel, Virginia. 2007. "Radio 4 Current Affairs." *BBC Radio*, December 7. http://news.bbc.co.uk/nol/shared/spl/hi/programmes/analysis/transcripts/12_07 _07.txt.

Preibusch, Sören, Dorothea Kübler, and Alastair R. Beresford. 2013. "Price ver- sus Privacy: An Experiment into the Competitive Advantage of Collecting Less Personal Information." *Electronic Commerce Research* 13 (4): 423–55.

Rader, Emilee. 2014. "Awareness of Behavioral Tracking and Information Privacy Concern in Facebook and Google." *Proceedings of the Tenth USENIX Conference on Usable Privacy and Security* 10: 51–67.

Radley-Gardner, Oliver, Hugh Beale, and Reinhard Zimmermann, eds. 2016. *Fundamental Texts on European Private Law.* Oxford: Hart Publishing.

Rainie, Lee and Maeve Duggan. 2016. "Privacy and Information Sharing." *Pew Research Center*, January 14. https://www.pewinternet.org/2016/01/14/privacy -and-information-sharing/.

Reuters. 2018. "Reuters Poll Data: Social Media Usage Poll." May 3. Accessed August 1, 2019. https://web.archive.org/web/20200916080543/http://fingfx.thomsonreuters .com/gfx/rngs/FACEBOOK-PRIVACY-POLL/010062SJ4QF/2018%20Reuters%2 0Tracking%20-%20Social%20Media%20Usage%205%203%202018.pdf.

Rizzo, Mario J. and Douglas Glen Whitman. 2009. "The Knowledge Problem of New Paternalism." *Brigham Young University Law Review* 4: 905–68.

Roth, Alvin. 2007. "Repugnance as a Constraint on Markets." *Journal of Economic Perspectives* 21 (3): 37–58.

Samuelson, William and Richard Zeckhauser. 1988. "Status Quo Bias in Decision Making." *Journal of Risk and Uncertainty* 1 (1): 7–59.

Schoeman, Ferdinand David. 1992. *Privacy and Social Freedom*. Cambridge, UK: Cambridge University Press.

Shampanier, Kristina, Nina Mazar, and Dan Ariely. 2007. "Zero as a Special Price: The True Value of Free Products." *Marketing Science* 26 (6): 731–902.

Slovic, Paul. 1995. "The Construction of Preference." *American Psychologist* 50 (5): 364–371.

Solove, Daniel J. 2004. *The Digital Person Technology and Privacy in the Information Age*. New York: New York University Press.

———. 2006. "A Taxonomy of Privacy." *University of Pennsylvania Law Review* 154 (3): 477–564.

Spiezio, Caroline. 2019. "Privacy Notices, Opt-In Clauses Debated as US Regulators Shape Federal Privacy Law." *Corporate Counsel*, March 12. https://www.law .com/corpcounsel/2019/03/12/privacy-notices-opt-in-clauses-debated-as-us-re gulators-shape-federal-privacy-law/?slreturn=20190701155942.

Statt, Nick. 2019. "Facebook's US User Base Declined by 15 Million since 2017, According to Survey." *The Verge*, March 6. https://www.theverge.com/2019/3 /6/18253274/facebook-users-decline-15-million-people-united-states-privacy-scan dals.

Strahilevitz, Lior Jacob and Matthew B. Kugler. 2016. "Is Privacy Policy Language Irrelevant to Consumers?" *The Journal of Legal Studies* 45 (S2): S69–S95.

Sunstein, Cass. 2018. "How Much Is It Worth to Use Facebook? It Depends." *Bloomberg*, May 3. https://www.bloomberg.com/opinion/articles/2018-05-03/f acebook-users-want-to-be-paid-a-lot-to-quit.

Swisher, Kara. 2018. "Introducing the Internet Bill of Rights." *The New York Times*, October 4. https://www.nytimes.com/2018/10/04/opinion/ro-khanna-internet-bill -of-rights.html.

Tene, Omer and Jules Polonetsky. 2013. "A Theory of Creepy: Technology, Privacy and Shifting Social Norms." *Yale Journal of Law and Technology* 16: 59–133.

Thaler, Richard H. and Cass R. Sunstein. 2009. *Nudge: Improving Decisions about Health, Wealth, and Happiness*. New York: Penguin Books.

Tuan, Julie. 2000. "U.S. West, Inc. v. FCC." *Berkeley Technology Law Journal* 15 (1): 353–72.

Vedantam, Shankar. "Do You Read Terms of Service Contracts? Not Many Do, Research Shows." *NPR*, August 23. https://www.npr.org/2016/08/23/491024846/ do-you-read-terms-of-service-contracts-not-many-do-research-shows.

Warren, Samuel and Louis Brandeis. 1890. "The Right to Privacy." *Harvard Law Review* 4 (5): 193–220.

Westin, Alan F. 1967. *Privacy and Freedom.* New York: Anthenum.

Wilson, David W. and Joseph S. Valacich. 2012. "Unpacking the Privacy Paradox: Irrational Decision-Making within the Privacy Calculus." *International Conference on Information Systems* 5: 4152–62.

Winegar, Angela G. and Cass R. Sunstein. 2019. "How Much Is Data Privacy Worth? A Preliminary Investigation." *Journal of Consumer Policy* 42: 425–440

Winterton, Robert. 2018. "American Consumers Reject Backlash Against Tech." *NetChoice*, September 12. https://netchoice.org/techlashpoll/#release.

Winton, Ashely, Larry Ponemon, and Mark E. Schreiber. 2018. "New Study Highlights Lack of GDPR Preparedness." *IAPP*, April 25. https://iapp.org/news/a/new-study-highlights-lack-of-gdpr-preparedness/.

Wu, Tim. 2015. "Facebook Should Pay All of Us." *The New Yorker*, August 14. https://www.newyorker.com/business/currency/facebook-should-pay-all-of-us.

Zhang, Yufeng and Paul Slovic. 2019. "Much Ado about Nothing: The Zero Effect in Life-Saving Decisions." *Journal of Behavioral Decision Making* 32 (1): 30–37.

Chapter 10

Nudging, Trust, and the "Sharing Economy" in Latin America

Luis H. Lozano-Paredes

In this chapter, I explore the intersection of the sharing economy and behavioral "nudging" (see Thaler and Sunstein 2009) in Latin America. This is done with a transdisciplinary perspective extracting from urban studies, as the city is the place where the sharing economy has had its greatest expansion (Davidson and Infranca 2016; Salice and Pais 2017), together with organizational science which helps to frame the agency of actors within the sharing economy. This exploration focuses its analysis on the period between 2015 and 2019 when there was a proliferation of nudging policies related to the sharing economy in Latin American cities. Moreover, and due to, the abrupt changes emerging from the 2020 COVID-19 crisis, I accompany this analysis with a critical evaluation, observing how the year 2020 proved to be a good testing ground to conclude that "nudging" simply does not work.

I use the term *sharing economy* here to describe any marketplace that uses platforms to connect distributed networks of individuals for sharing or exchanging otherwise underutilized assets (Koopman et al. 2015). I also use the concept of *trust* to understand the sharing economy in Latin America and how it intersects with a reality of emergent orders (Hayek [1969] 1996; DiZerega and Montuori 2000; Tao 2016), where trust cannot be nudged via public policy.

As it will be discussed in the following sections, the nudging public-policy strategies developed from 2015 to 2019 propose to introduce trust mechanisms for the sharing economy platforms' participating peers (producers and users). These policy strategies have the express intention of avoiding externalities regarding job insecurity and backlash from other actors in the urban ecosystem, while improving people's relationship and trust with this disruptive economic phenomenon.

Up to 2019, policymakers, academics, and other stakeholders in Latin America, such as the Inter-American Development Bank (IADB 2017), explored policy strategies and responses related to the emergence of the sharing economy. Committees and nongovernmental organizations in Latin American countries began advocating for regulation of the sharing economy in their policy planning documents and recommendations for policymakers.

There is already some regulation on specific cases, such as in São Paulo, Brazil, which regulated sharing economy platforms according to its official gazette on July 07, 2017, (Prefecture of São Paulo 2019), together with the federal district in Mexico which regulated Uber and other transportation platforms according to a resolution on July 15, 2015 (Government of Mexico City 2015). However, even if there are many regulatory projects linked to platforms development in the region (Reilly 2020), as of early 2021, the sharing economy platforms remain largely unregulated in Latin American cities and countries.

The issue of trust-nudging has been present in these preliminary policy recommendations and initial regulations (IADB 2017); specifically, that sharing economy platforms should establish "trust-enhancing mechanisms" for users, mostly for security concerns as recommended by the National Commission of Productivity in Chile in an article on April 14, 2018 (National Commission of Productivity, Chile 2018). Equally, the concept of maintaining control over the development of these platforms by "trusted" entrepreneurs is also present, for example, it is established by the Ministry of Information and Communications Technology in Colombia in its decree on April 20, 2018 (Ministry of Information and Communications Technology, Colombia 2018).

It should be noted here that in Latin American countries, the institutional nature of the regulatory system is slow, tied to political change, manipulation, and rent-seeking, and lacks strong contract enforcement that fosters trust with, and in, the government. Therefore, the reason many urban services in which sharing economy platforms have flourished is their response to otherwise the failed provision of these services by government monopolies (Pirez 2016). Furthermore, the sharing economy also creates an environment where individuals harness alternative strategies to facilitate and improve personal growth outside of the institutional ecosystem.

Therefore, I argue that the phenomenon of the sharing economy and its platforms in Latin America is built on a base of self-organized institutions already present in society. These institutions cannot be "nudged" as the tacit knowledge (Polanyi [1966] 1983) that structures them, and the spontaneous orders for trust between peers are preexisting to any intervention. In this chapter, I will advocate for discouraging interventions on the social fabric behind the sharing economy that attempt to impose nudges that will simply not work. Equally, I will suggest that related regulation should seek to achieve minimum standards rather than directly intervene in the sharing economy. This will be, to my best knowledge, the first approach to the issues of the sharing economy in Latin America that analyzes nudging and trust, while promoting public policies that recognize the preexistent characteristics and social institutions of this setting.

The chapter is divided into six sections. First, I elaborate on the relation of sharing economy platforms within the complex Latin American setting. Second, I discuss the concept of trust and the idea of nudging trust-enhancing mechanisms into the sharing economy platforms in Latin America. Third, I analyze the nudging strategies developed between 2015 and 2019 in the case studies of Argentina, Brazil, Chile, Colombia, and Mexico. Fourth, I engage with nudging and the nature of emergent institutions in Latin America that will lead to an analysis on the evolving situation of the 2020 COVID-19 crisis and its visible consequences as the fifth section. Finally, in the sixth section, I propose some policy implications and conclusions.

THE SHARING ECONOMY, POLICYMAKING, AND THE COMPLEXITY OF LATIN AMERICA

In urban studies, the concept of "planning for complexity" (AESOP 2015; Roo and Porter [2007] 2016), has been developed to acknowledge that urban spaces (and the communities and individuals within them) are self-organizing and complex systems. Moreover, that the constant desire of authorities to regulate and centralize urban areas leads to unintended consequences as it fails to recognize their inherent complexities. Cities are hubs of market and social participation, and in them people seek lodging, transportation, social services, and public spaces. Cities are also nodes for innovation and entrepreneurship, both built from relationships between denizens that cannot be "managed" nor "nudged" into preestablished or planned outcomes.

Historically, and particularly in Latin America, this has led to the emergence of peer-to-peer informal networks for the provision of urban services, enabled by twenty-first-century platform technology, which are framing relationships under what is now called the sharing economy. From this perspective, it is not hard to imagine that regulation and other government interventions are currently (and probably permanently) unable to cope with the processes defining urban complexity or the sharing economy in developing countries.

This new approach to urban studies, as with any dramatic change in methods and preconceived models, is a not so silent revolution where international publications and research journals specializing in urban issues are treating the issue as a transformation from the inside. The crisis in the top-down perspective of urban planning and the problems of the city is linked to a predictable change in the role of the state (Roo and Porter [2007] 2016), which demands a need to rethink the nature of urban policy processes. Older models are being replaced by diffuse models of governance, where the roles and responsibilities expected of planning authorities are no longer as direct. Instead, governance is viewed as an array of activities by a wide range of actors in and beyond government agencies. This approach acknowledges the new and innovative elements of participation in the urban space.

On the other hand, the characteristics of cities in developing countries have also seen a recent development of literature around the concept of "fragile governance" (Montero and Chapple 2018). Understood here as the governance framework in which people in cities innovate and implement nonorthodox, informal, and self-regulated solutions to achieve a territorial, localized, and advanced vision of development and welfare, transforming and fostering new kinds of local associations, mutual learning, innovation in leadership and conflict management. Equally, the concept of "conflicting rationalities" (Watson 2003; Satgé and Watson 2018) engages with the characteristics of southern settings and illustrates the gap between the notions of the "what ought to be" and "proper living" to the "nature of the rationality guiding the actions of the other parties involved" (Watson 2003, 395).

The "formal" institutional failure, and unrecognition of social informal institutions, is also present explicitly in cronyism and political maneuvering. Specifically, prolific in contexts such as Latin America, where, using Frye and Shleifer's (1997) terminology of a "grabbing-hand," the state and government act as excluding, and unhelpful actors. Thus, leading to a large part of the population toward a context in which the legal framework of integration and inclusion into the economic system has failed, causing the emergence of informality as the only possibility for millions to be included in economic progress and welfare.

It is interesting to note that the preexisting informal processes in the cities of the developing world (Ghersi 1997) were already based on processes of mutual approval, feedback, and social interaction long before the advent of the sharing economy (Vergara 2017). Thus, as I will continue to argue in this chapter, in the Latin American setting, the sharing economy aligns with informal practices already in place.

The intersection of emergent orders and the need for renewed models of urban governance have an alternative in the theoretical framework of urban polycentrism (see Ostrom et al. 1961; Ostrom 2010; Boettke et al. 2013), which highlights how cities could be studied, governed, and transformed worldwide and aims for a recognition of the importance of emergent models and bottom-up approaches. Informality in the management, access, and procurement of common resources in the urban space, such as the sharing economy platforms, is also addressed in the literature (Postrel [1998] 2011) and can be classified as a process of self-regulation in emergent economic interaction agreements.

These processes of self-regulation and control are exactly the ones building the framework of trust, where "good faith" is built on the familiarity brought by the localized and decentralized nature of actions, interactions, and outcomes. This dynamic exposes a duality of stasis and dynamism as defined by the work of Postrel ([1998] 2011) in terms of a relation toward innovation and the unexpected outcomes of disruption. The attitude of openness, embracement, and evolution by variation to reach a favorable outcome is called "dynamism," whereas the position of envisioning stability while fearing and fighting disruptive phenomena is defined as "stasis."

What has been achieved by the recent disruption of the sharing economy in Latin America, however, is still up for debate. Current literature examines various forms of governance in the Latin American context, to analyze and propose if better policies can be attained by the recognition of the reality that has shaped the growth of Latin American cities through history, including informality (Pirez 2016; Soto [1986] 2002).

There is, however, a research gap regarding the impact of the sharing economy in Latin America, especially concerning its relationship with emergent networks of urban services. This gap has oriented Latin American governments to outright ignore the emergent phenomenon or to engage in policy practices that do not deal with the issue of sharing economy platforms. Thus, proposing alternatives, which are, at best, designed to constrain the sharing economy to outdated regulatory frameworks. Indeed, the needed exploration of innovative ways of urban governance in terms of action, development, and implementation of policies is currently at odds with the perspective developed by policy units in Latin American countries. Policy proposals and recommendations so far have failed to grasp the nature of the disruption by the sharing economy and the intrinsic nature of informality, and they lack the capacity necessary to respond creatively to these systems without thwarting them.

TRUST-ENHANCING MECHANISMS, NUDGES, AND SHARING ECONOMY PLATFORMS IN LATIN AMERICA

In a context where institutions do not perform as expected, the forced implementation of planned policies can breed unintended results (Mayorga and Córdova 2007). Particularly when these policies are related to the digital platforms of the sharing economy, where their societal impacts are still insufficiently studied (Reilly 2020). Such unintended consequences are, among others, a diminished trust in government functions and its institutions (OECD et al. 2019), and because of this, I argue, an expansion of trust building and organization between citizens (Vergara 2017). Trust between peers in Latin America is built by citizens in a process of collective action that demonstrates the organizational capacity of individuals with a common goal. Which in most cases is public, spontaneous, and nonrecurrent (Vergara 2017), leading to different ways of trust creation and association construction unique to the Latin American context, manifesting in a particularized and generalized manner:

> The first is between people who know each other and the second between strangers . . . in a certain association, between each activity carried out in it, members create trusting relationships among themselves, so that when a problem arises there will be sufficient confidence to resort to one of their association partners since there is less uncertainty about the return of the favor. . . . In the second, social or generalized trust, the explanatory mechanism is different. The people who are part of the association are considered by the individual as a representative part of society, in such a way that expectations are created about the behavior of new people based on the experiences emergent within the group, that is, if positive events have occurred in this interaction there will be a better willingness to trust people outside the group. (Vergara 2017, 6)

This perspective on how trust is built among citizens in associative processes, such as the ones necessary for the development of the sharing economy as exposed by Coolican and Coffman (2016).

However, one perspective from behavioral economics theory is that trust and trustworthiness related to the sharing economy are starting to fall apart due to specific failures originating from the actors involved in the platforms (Coolican and Coffman 2016). This includes poor behavior from service providers and unethical transactions in monetary digital platforms. Trust works as a constant feedback mechanism, where if one of the parties involved in the transaction shows trust, the other actor will act accordingly. For instance,

> The stranger that is welcomed into someone's Airbnb might be a little more conscientious of a guest knowing that the owner has trusted them to act appropriately. After all, trust does beget trustworthiness. This positive—and counter-intuitive—outcome helps show that people are more trusting than skeptics usually assume, especially when someone else goes out on that limb first. (Coolican and Coffman 2016, n.p.)

It is also argued that trust and reciprocity in the sharing economy is not permanent and requires constant maintenance. Since interactions in the sharing economy are limited in time and scope, it could result in a lack of "social prox-imity" which endangers social ties and decreases the degree of cooperation in a context where trust is essential. Thus, the sharing economy could risk damag-ing the working, yet intangible, mechanisms of faith and trust necessary for its success (Coolican and Coffman 2016). Consequently, "re-gaining the public's trust after it has been lost can be an extraordinarily difficult task" (Coolican and Coffman 2016, n.p.). For every startup or platform that fails to understand the trust and social relations risks damage to the entire industry of the sharing economy. In other words, trust is a prerequisite for a thriving sharing economy.

Other sources in the behavioral economics literature also focus on trust as a principle of interaction and feedback between actors in any given eco-nomic transaction or social development. Especially in how these interactions require the element of trust between peers or trust in the government, policy unit, or institution if an intervention in the form of a "nudge" is going to be developed. The concept of trust is, thus, important and ubiquitous for nudg-ing policy implementation and the effectiveness of the nudge depends on the level of trustworthiness the governmental authority or policymaker has among the population (Sunstein et al. 2019).

Trust is also viewed as a commitment toward an institution, with nudging policies being more persuasive when coming from governments or private organizations that have a form of brand loyalty (Nudel and Wiik 2017). The behavioral economics perspective also focuses on the predisposed biological and psychological systems of reaction present in humans, in both interactions between peers and between institutions and citizens (Thaler and Sunstein 2009).

Here, a connection toward the evolution of the sharing economy is clear where the comportment and agency of people is studied in view of their participation and relationship with topics of privacy, power, and interactions. But mainly with relation to trust, toward both the governmental level regulat-ing the sharing economy and the platforms providing the service (Newlands et al. 2020). Thus, it has been concluded by policy units that the issue of "ensuring" trust should be at the cornerstone of every policy related to the sharing economy in the years to come.

This type of analysis and conclusions, however, has primarily been devel-oped in the United States and in European countries but not in developing countries. The following section of this chapter aims to solve that gap by examining examples of the sharing economy and corresponding nudge policies currently being developed in Latin American countries and how the literature on nudges is influencing such policies. Even if it is not addressed in an explicit way, the policy recommendations being developed by national governments in Latin America show an approach that resembles the efforts of other nudge policy units, especially from European countries.

This is not to say that Latin American governmental units in charge of dealing with the sharing economy disruptions are not bringing original solutions to local problems, but it is evident that some factors of behavioral economics have influenced their approaches. There has been a knowledge spillover from the literature of developed countries that is being currently applied and transmitted by international organizations, such as the Inter-American Development Bank (Scartascini 2018), and this knowledge, I argue, wrongly influenced the mindset of policymakers in Latin America.

NUDGING STRATEGIES IN LATIN AMERICAN COUNTRIES

This section discusses how five countries, with different institutional arrangements and contextual settings, developed policies and policy recommendations between 2015 and 2019 for dealing with the disruption caused by the sharing economy platforms: Brazil, Chile, Colombia, Mexico, and Argentina. In all these case studies, the further approval, introduction, and implementation of the proposed policies were radically thwarted by the 2020 COVID-19 pandemic, which redirected state capacity toward the public-health and economic crises and delayed further discussions related to other issues. Specifically, congressional sessions were often suspended, and the executive branch governed mostly by emergency decree.

Brazil

One of the settings where the sharing economy has had its greatest expansion in Latin America is the massive market of Brazil, one of the first countries where regulation was implemented to deal with the sharing economy. Specifically, a law was passed to regulate ride-sharing platforms in the city of Sao Paulo. This law was then scaled up by the Public Prosecutor's Office of Brazil in 2016, proposing a federal regulation of ride-sharing platforms and the creation of a free market for taxicabs at the national level (Public Prosecutor's Office of Brazil 2016) and countersigned by a new state-level decree in 2019 (Prefecture of Sao Paulo 2019).

This first approach has stimulated local regulators and policymakers to elaborate nonbinding recommendations from the legislative body, which has now created a commission for the regulation of the sharing economy in Brazil. The most prolific recommendation from the commission and elaborated by the Ministry of Economics was to include a specific section aimed at a federal control of the platforms in order to avoid potential manipulation (i.e., false advertisement, price gouging, etc.) of the behavior of users by the platform companies (Secretariat of Economic Partnership, Brazil 2018).

These recommendations vaguely asked for a policy that would mandate Uber and similar apps to stop including incentives for competition among platform workers (i.e., drivers), to inform users about the "social cost" of market variables manipulation (like demand-induced "surge pricing"), and to provide disclaimers about undesired practices (such as user exclusion from platforms for no reason, a common practice by platform companies like Uber). The latter is not explicitly prohibited by Brazilian law but is deemed by policymakers as "contentious" and "problematic" (Secretariat of Economic Partnership, Brazil 2018, 2–3).

The text of the regulation does not provide specific warning language or requirements for providers of rides, but it does refer to a supposed inclination of the population to distrust entities with practices such as those previously described (Secretariat of Economic Partnership, Brazil 2018). It also argues for mechanisms to use that mistrust for "convincing" the population to take into account the problems generated by the disruption of platforms and produce a more "conscious" use of the sharing economy.

Among the Brazilian population, however, there seems to be resistance toward these suggestions by the government as evidenced by previous popular incorporation of trust toward the sharing economy (O GLOBO 2015). Furthermore, by considering that in the year 2018, the then Brazilian federal government of the Socialist Worker's Party and the Social Democrat MDB party were enduring heavy corruption scandals linked to misusage of public resources and very low popularity, which eventually led to the election of the candidate from the Social Liberal Party (Jair Messias Bolsonaro), the government seems to face more distrust from citizens than the sharing economy. Bolsonaro, a populist but pro-market newcomer against developing more regulations on any type of markets (Carvalho 2019), promoted an agenda of radical economic liberalization and likely stalled further regulation debates on the sharing economy.

Chile

Chile is the most comprehensive, at least in terms of theoretical construction and the evolution of institutional structures, case of sharing economy regulation. A specific unit was created to examine productivity, disruption, and the impacts on civil society from technology and the sharing economy (National Commission of Productivity, Chile 2018).

The commission is a consultancy institution, with an independent and autonomous character, and with a goal of advising the Chilean central government on subjects oriented toward increasing productivity and well-being.

Inside this commission, the study and policy recommendations regarding disruptive technologies and the regulation of digital platforms of the sharing economy, including policy papers on the economy and digital platforms, transportation platforms, lodging platforms, financial services/fintech, and telemedicine. All these recommendations to the national government highlight the issue of nudging trust by citizens and local (Municipal and Regional) governments to better "harness" the benefits of the sharing economy. Particularly in the realm of lodging, where it is stated that the national government shall promote that all lodging businesses adopt the system of mutual evaluation by hosts and guests used by sharing economy platforms, as to improve the institutional feedback mechanisms and relations with users (National Commission of Productivity, Chile 2018). The provision, however, is not to be considered mandatory for all businesses in the eventual case of a comprehensive national regulation of sharing economy lodging platforms, but rather a recommendation at the institutional level for the businesses operating in the traditional lodging sector.

Equally, recommendations regarding trust and normalization between the traditional and sharing economy sectors are also present in the study of telemedicine (National Commission of Productivity, Chile 2018, Telemedicine). In this policy paper, it is suggested that for the future implementation of nationwide medical attention by digital platforms all patients and health personnel, even those outside the new telemedicine framework, start working with the policies of trust and incentives used by sharing economy platforms. The latter recommending the need for nationwide implementation of education and training in this regard. Again, these suggestions and "active promotions" are not considered mandatory or binding for all businesses in the future; however, they are powerful suggestions at the institutional level with a possible goal of national normalization of medicine services.

Regarding the sharing economy in general, the central government has failed to produce actual binding regulation to date, which could solve the legal limbo in which the different platforms are working. Only for the case of transportation platforms, on July 9, 2019, the Chilean Senate gave green light to a so-called "Uber Law," which is, however, as of February 2021, still under discussion in the finance committee to later go to debate in the upper house. Yet again, Chileans have been using the different platforms since their disruption in the market, without governmental intervention. Thus, I argue that the creation of a specific unit from the government to deal with the issue (together with the provided recommendations for "harnessing" the benefits of the sharing economy) may be a misallocation of valuable public resources.

Colombia

The Colombian case is paradigmatic because there has been a wave of regulatory intentions regarding the evolution of the sharing economy platforms in the country, especially in the realms of lodging, tourism, and transportation. However, these regulatory frameworks were modeled after the traditional lodging and transportation sectors (Ministry of Transportation of Colombia 2015) and made assumptions that were inappropriate for this emergent, technology-based market.

The failure of these intentions, however, appears to have been recognized by the Colombian government, as the National Ministry of Information and Communications Technology has created a special commission, together with the Ministry of Education and the National Planning Department among other administrative units, to address these issues (Ministry of Information and Communications Technology, Colombia 2018). This commission is designed to produce recommendations to be considered by the Presidency of the Republic and the legislative bodies when drafting a possible future law for the sharing economy in the country.

Within the official decree creating the new commission, a subtle and vague introduction of a nudge related to trust in the sharing and digital economy can also be found (Ministry of Information and Communications Technology, Colombia 2018). It is established by the decree that the national government, by means of the Ministry of Education, will foment the "appropriation" of the sharing economy by the general population. With an indication of the benefits and prejudices that the new schemes bring to society, to "allow that the public policies adopted by the state in relation to the digital economy are maintained in the long run" (Ministry of Information and Communications Technology, Colombia 2018, 3). The application and regulation of this decree is currently stalled, but from its language, it can be inferred that an educational campaign will be established to nudge people toward the "preferred" usage of sharing economy platforms, whatever that might be. This process has already begun in the Ministry of Education under the premise of the promotion of appropriation of the sharing economy (Ministry of Information and Communications Technology, Colombia 2018).

More recently, a new "Law Project" has been introduced in the Colombian congress as an accumulation of different projects presented by representatives and senators of parties in all the spectrum of ideological allegiance (House of Representatives, Colombia 2020). This project incorporates an element of trust and, particularly, the idea of regulating the sharing economy platforms to allow that the market and security rules to be imposed by the Colombian state generate trust among their users for the continued growth of the platforms.

This law project should be debated by mid-2021 if the circumstances of the pandemic allow it. Finally, and we can see a pattern here, the Colombian population is using the different sharing economy platforms despite their illegality and outright persecution by the authorities. Moreover, this has been the case since the first platforms began operating in Colombia (around 2014 and 2015), and therefore, a process of nudging toward the proper usage and appropriation of the platforms is, at best, irrelevant.

Mexico and Argentina: An Interesting Paradox

Mexico and Argentina show a very interesting development in regulating the sharing economy. In the Mexican case, policies and regulations were established in the states and the federal district, leading to the normalization of the sharing economy platforms. On the other hand, in the Argentinean case, only one province (Mendoza) has legalized and regulated these platforms as of 2019, and only one city court (Buenos Aires) has deemed them legal, while punitive measures have been developed for persecuting sharing economy activities elsewhere in the country.

In this context, the absence of policy or congressional units dedicated to the analysis and the promotion of recommendations toward the sharing economy is telling. Some academic institutions in both countries have developed recommendations and studies, but there are, to the knowledge of the author, no policy-oriented institutions, administrative departments, ministries, or legislative commissions that are tackling the present nature of the sharing economy in these two countries. This can be explained by observing different strategies which were used by local governments in both countries: the institutional promotion for the interaction with would-be users of the sharing economy platforms, focusing on the public procurement of alternatives that fulfill the same role and compete with the disruptive platforms and startups from the private sector.

In transportation, for instance, the case is evident for the city of Buenos Aires, where the city's Ministry of Transportation created applications for hailing taxis, owned and promoted publicly by the government, and in direct competition with platforms, such as Uber as well as platforms like EasyTaxi, a regular taxi ride-hailing, privately procured app that is considered illegal in the jurisdiction (City Government of Buenos Aires 2018). In the same city, the government created a lodging app intended to compete with Airbnb, and in the meantime, it charges taxes to platforms that are not recognized as "legal." As of 2021, both these government-provided platforms failed to gain critical mass of popularity and were discontinued.

Nudging in these failed platforms manifested in "choice architecture" mechanisms (Thaler and Sunstein 2009) to the promotion of the government-owned app in the public transit system, by means of publicity, merchandizing, and even fare-reduction mechanisms. Which attempted to induce people to use the government-owned app, instead of simply grabbing a taxicab on the street or renting by traditional forms. This situation generated an odd reality, where the government was not only competing with the digital provision of services, but also traditional provisions. These efforts shared the urban space with tacitly recognized sharing economy platforms that, even if deemed illegal or unregulated, were still growing in everyday use (Infobae 2018). Moreover, since the government platforms were operating in a nonmarket environment, prices were distorted and provided economic actors with incorrect information about the relative costs and benefits of their choices.

Similarly, in Mexico, different states were promoting their own apps to directly compete with transportation and lodging platforms. But again, these apps also ended up competing with the traditional industry providers, nudging people to use the services provided by the government. The implementation of these government-produced alternatives both in Argentina and Mexico has failed. By looking at the latest data published by Uber in 2018 (Uber is not prone to publish or updating its data openly) for Buenos Aires, which showed a growth of 55,000 new drivers, a million users and a daily incorporation of 400 drivers and 7,000 users, this should hardly be a surprise (Infobae 2018).

The analysis of the cases in this section highlights the governmental intentions toward the sharing economy in Latin America, and how the use of nudging is present in different ways but always linked to sustaining future regulation regarding the development of platforms. In table 10.1, a comparison between the analyzed cases is drafted to clarify the nature of the policy recommendations, the implementation of policies for competing with the sharing economy by choice architecture processes, and the reception by the population. This comparison sheds light on the effectiveness of nudging policies (hidden or not) and its application in the Latin American region. There are even more cases to be mentioned in the Latin American context, but the diversification of policy intentions, and the proposed nudges for different kinds of sectors in these five countries give a good example of what is going on inside the public institutions of the region. As currently drafted, these policy recommendations are sometimes a straightforward but subtle way to introduce policy planning regarding the behavior of people and institutions in the sharing economy. As well as the type of nudges deemed appropriate for the "proper" functioning of the sharing economy and the reduction of its social costs or externalities.

However, I argue that it is probable that the future reception of the population will continue to be null or low at best, deeming the nudges and the policy units and governmental products themselves unnecessary. To strengthen this last argument, I must attest that there is a tendency from Latin Americans,

Table 10.1 Case Studies Policy Comparison

Country	Argentina	Brazil	Chile	Colombia	Mexico
Nudge Language Used	Choice architecture and economic incentives (no policy unit involved)	Suggested as a process of "convincing" the population (vague)	Policy recommendations and provision suggested for older schemes (suggestive—active promotion)	Focus on regulations of platforms and sharing economy to create trust (educative, suggestive, active promotion)	Choice architecture and economic incentives (no policy unit involved, no draft)
Reception by Population	Usage of (private) sharing economy platforms not reduced	Null or low (no trust in the state)	Null or low (previous usage of platforms while informal)	Null of low (previous usage of platforms while informal)	Usage of (private) sharing economy platforms not reduced
Working Policy	Implemented and working in some jurisdictions	Partially implemented	Partially implemented	Not implemented (still in discussion)	Implemented and working in some jurisdictions

Source: Author created.

particularly policymakers, to expect that great social transformations will come mainly from the political arena, while underestimating the role of private initiative. We as Latin Americans often believe too much in the so-called "written law." However, ironically, when laws are put in writing, our natural response is to consider it "respected but not fulfilled," and whatever policy proposition, recommendation or regulation many times ends up being mere ink over paper that no one follows.

In the next section of this chapter, I will argue that bottom-up institutions generated by civil society, which are established and stable, can be more effective for achieving both trust and the efficient usage of the benefits of the sharing economy. Thus, generating the need to revise all policy intentions currently developing (and failing) in the region.

DISCUSSION ON NUDGING AND EMERGENT INSTITUTIONS IN LATIN AMERICA

It would be tempting to suggest that the previously mentioned nudging policy recommendations in Latin American countries are simple statements coming from well-intended policy planners with a positivist perspective. That they simply have not been able to fully grasp the phenomenon of the sharing economy and are proposing preliminary, vague, yet failing, perspectives of how to harness the benefits and tackle the challenges of this new economy. However, local contexts need to be considered, and in Latin America, the history of governance and policy planning is prolific with interventionist and paternalist visions, which end up transforming preliminary public-policy intentions into extensive overregulation.

Here, nudging proposals, such as the ones in Brazil, Chile, and Colombia, have in their conception a problem of paternalism. The issue of paternalism, behavioral economics, and nudges transformed into active public policy is correctly identified as a knowledge problem by this literature and others dealing with the impossibility of centralized policy planning (Lavoie [1985] 2016; Rizzo and Whitman 2009). This perspective applies to emergent orders in Latin American cities and countries, where policymakers are incapable of properly identifying all the possible cognitive reactions and interactions of the actors involved in the processes linked to the sharing economy. Moreover, they are incapable of having the complete knowledge to properly identify all individual preferences toward the economic interactions of users and providers, as well as any social mechanisms already in place in the context where the intervention is proposed (Rizzo and Whitman 2009).

I argue here that pursuing an idealized vision in which the government tries to enhance the usage of disruptive market forces, such as the Colombian case, or even the Chilean experiment of trying to transfer the mechanisms of the sharing economy to the traditional schemes of exchange of services, is deemed to fail. Where no attention is paid to preexistent local, and usually informal, institutions, policy will be ineffective. Such as the case of the property rights and land-titling in Perú (Kerekes and Williamson 2010), where not recognizing preexistent institutions, together with lack of trust in institutions imposed from the top-down (even if they favored property rights enforcement and worked in favor of market processes), made these policies fail to realize its purposes and be durable in time. A classical case of lack of institutional "stickiness" in which institutions, as good as they may be in theory, fail when imposed and do not consider preexistent structures and traditions (Boettke et al. 2008).

The sharing economy platforms are used by people in the region to reduce transaction costs and make more efficient exchanges between provider and consumer. Sharing economy platforms are, I argue, being used to socially institutionalize (generally informal) economic relations already happening at the level of civil society. However, these preexisting relations, depending equally in cognitive systems such as mutually acquired trust, simply cannot be "nudged" by policy units' suggestions or recommendations formed by regulators trying to apply outdated concepts to a disruptive phenomenon (Koopman et al. 2015).

Multiple examples of the institutionalization and digitalization of informal economic relations into the sharing economy framework exist in Latin America, such as the case of Colombia, where in many intermediate cities, the sharing economy platforms have disrupted and reorganized the informal schemes of transportation, and even promoted more self-organized networks of for-profit urban services provision (CIPPEC 2018). Or the case of peer-to-peer rents for lodging or tourism, deemed informal by the Mexican government (López-Bosch Martineau 2017), which was a phenomenon long present in the Mexican housing and lodging market but was expanded greatly by the arrival of Airbnb (González Sánchez 2006). This latter practice is embraced by people looking to avoid the excessive tax load from the federal and state governments, and the extensive requirements toward lodging provision, which effectively expulse small economic actors from this lucrative procurement.

Other, much less studied cases (due to their nature of informality, and the general refusal from academia and governmental units to analyze them) can be found by scanning secondary sources that show hints of the reproduction of informality using sharing economy platforms. For example, informal peer-to-peer lodging in Uruguay (iProfesional 2007) or the appearance of fintech bottom-up alternatives, which use messaging platforms such as WhatsApp (El Universal 2019) are good examples that are already frightening authorities in the region. What is known about these emergent groups of economic interrelation using digital platforms is that enterprising individuals, and their peers, create these institutions, establish rules, self-regulate their economic relations, and generate greater welfare for themselves.

For example, some ride-hailing drivers in Colombia pay a fee to join emergent platform-based communities, which neither demand verification of data nor compliance with technical or mechanical norms but offer the possibility of more earnings (Reilly and Lozano-Paredes 2019). For female drivers, these communities offer the possibility to enjoy the security of knowing that passengers have been vetted by trusted community members, such as security guards posted at known buildings. Local collaborations (built on trust) also help drivers (male and female) within these communities to connect via WhatsApp with potential users when there is high demand, and other "traditional" platforms such as Uber are saturated. In addition, these local systems allow drivers to enhance their service offering through the delivery of packages, or carpooling.

Much of these economic relations and emergent phenomena have yet to be fully studied, but I can state with confidence that they are a common ground for understanding the nature of the impacts of the sharing economy in the region, and most of the developing world. Moreover, the study of these economic relations is useful to factually scrutinize and criticize the proposed nudging strategies by policymakers in these countries, which can be confronted with emergent processes of self-regulation and de-biasing from the bottom-up (Rizzo and Whitman 2009). Processes that are building and making these networks successful and resilient and that show an adequate harnessing of the benefits of the sharing economy.

Pretending to nudge and advocate the artificial creation of mechanisms for "protecting" people and "promoting trust" in relation to sharing economy platforms seems, at best, misguided. Trust is already there and cannot be nudged; doing this can pose a risk of losing the existing social capital used by people in their individual and communal progress (Kerekes and Williamson 2010).

In terms of practical application and implementation of policies, all the contextualization of trust and self-regulation shows a dynamic in which policymakers are advancing erroneous propositions. For the case of Latin America, a position of reactionary stasis (Chassin and Msaid 2016) takes place in the policymakers' intentions and recommendations toward the sharing economy, together with the pretension of knowledge of all outcomes. In promoting to nudge the personal preferences and natural interactions of familiarity and trust in the sharing economy, what policymakers are really doing is reacting with static, old, and unadaptable regulations and concepts on disruptive innovation. Regulation proposals that are contradictory, and regrettably, do not recognize the evolution of peer-to-peer and other informal economic interactions.

In the next section, I will continue the discussion by updating the analysis considering the impacts of the 2020 COVID-19 pandemic, and what I define as the conflict between classic paternalism versus organized anarchies. A conflict that has proven that a middle ground of "libertarian paternalism" (Thaler and Sunstein 2003) of behavioral economics is simply not applicable for Latin American countries, especially when those countries are now confronted by severe public-health and economic crises.

COVID-19 AND THE DUEL OF PATERNALISM VERSUS ORGANIZED ANARCHIES

The 2020 COVID-19 pandemic has caused a direct impact on how sharing economy platforms are developing in Latin America. It is important to attest that even if there are policies of social distancing affecting public transportation and lodging, for example, there is evidence that the sharing economy platforms are still present and growing. This will surely create a new institutional environment and breed tensions with the traditional industries that are affected by both platforms and the pandemic-related city lockdowns.

The lockdown measures decreed by almost all Latin American governments in 2020 included some flexibility for essential workers and other professions. This flexibility has been harnessed by ride-hailing platforms such as Uber, Cabify, and DiDi, which introduced different services for social distancing and exclusively for people working in the quarantine-excluded jobs. At the same time, dissident networks in emergent platform-based communities have organized themselves in their social media outlets (mainly Facebook) to keep providing their services to people included in the exceptions, but also to others and, thus, breaking the lockdown rules (Driver's Club Bogotá 2020). There is evidence that this breaking of lockdown rules is a process affecting the whole institutional ecosystem, as the exceptions were varied and somewhat vague and people were increasingly moving through Latin American cities by different means, such as carpooling, ride-hailing platforms and more artisanal forms such as emergent platform-based communities. Regarding the governmental response to date, the enforcement of restrictions related to the irregularity of sharing economy platforms is almost nonexistent as the efforts are still allocated for the response to the COVID-19 pandemic.

It is difficult to know what exactly is going to be the outcome and the effects of the COVID-19 pandemic on the sharing economy in Latin America.

However, it is necessary to take this into account for revising the validity and applicability of the previously presented nudging policy recommendations.

During 2020, we were confronted by a paradigm of a growing "classic" state paternalism, visible in the enforcement of lockdowns and quarantine, on one hand. And on the other hand, a response to this paternalism by locally bred alternatives (Driver's Club Bogotá 2020; Golden Drivers 2020) that can be classified under what has been defined in organization science as "organized anarchies." Organized anarchies are understood here in their conceptualization related to alternative organizations (Schwartzman 1989). Organized anarchy, first outlined by Cohen et al. 1972) and focusing on the forms of organization emerging from higher education institutions, is nonetheless a constantly updated (Lomi and Harrisson 2012) and useful perspective (Carrington et al. 2005) to consider when dealing with different societal organizations and decision-making processes (Manning [2013] 2018).

When observing the impacts of sharing economy platforms in Latin America, I can see that organized anarchies, as organizations of great choice opportunities, high level of uncertainty, low information, and fluid participation are a better-suited framework to understand the behavior of actors and the development of the sharing economy. In a still-unregulated sharing economy, a model of organization and decision-making where participants, problems, solutions, and choice opportunities are put together (and beneficial decisions emerge) is more succinct than nudging behavioral outcomes.

The opposite of organized anarchies are the traditional forms of decision and organization theory: either normative decision theory, dealing with "ideal" optimization of decision-making, or descriptive decision theory focused on the assumption of behaviorism under consistent rules or procedures. However, if something has emerged from the 2020 pandemic and the enforcement of lockdowns and quarantines in Latin America, it is that people are not bound by these parameters of decision-making and organization even in critical circumstances. Instead, they utilize any organizations and mechanisms they can to obtain income and survive.

The need for survival is aggravated by the incapacity of government services, such as urban sanitary services, and the need to access the job market, particularly in a context where most of the population works in informality (Baker and Velasco-Guachalla 2018; Altamirano 2019). Indeed, collective life in Latin America (and other developing countries) is different than in developed countries, where these types of requirements of sanitation and digitalization of work are possible. In most developing countries, these are luxuries (Bhan et al. 2020).

Even before the pandemic, emergent needs lead the population to find income solutions in the sharing economy and other digital platforms. This has only expanded since the pandemic. Virtuality will not only prevail as a

work tool, but as a way of life, the same person in the same day will be able
to edit a video, receive a traveler at home, take a passenger in his car, take out
walk the neighbor's dog, and prepare a programming project for a company
located anywhere in the world. In the end, the measure of the success of the
contracted work will be to meet efficient results, in fragmented schedules and
partial times. Hourly and on-demand work will be seen more frequently, as
it is consistent with the sustainability of the companies and the survival of
the worker.

On the other hand, however, and as we saw in the policy recommendations dealing with the sharing economy before the pandemic, the proposed
regulations and institutions were designed for radically different models.
Moreover, they do not respond to a situation in which the crisis linked to the
pandemic is still looming, and its results are difficult to predict or even to
critically report.

There is no "libertarian paternalism" or "nudging" in a context where
lockdowns and quarantines (however necessary) are imposed without sufficient preparation and attention to the consequences. "Flattening the curve"
as a goal to enhance the medical systems and capacities of a country, and that
were intended to be periods of 15 days to 40 days, were extended to months in
Latin America and were quickly reintroduced during the second wave of the
disease in early 2021. Such efforts are not based on "middle-ground" ideas
of nudging (Rizzo and Whitman 2009). Rather the state is increasingly aban-
doning the vision of "nudging" as a possible way to develop public policy.

Given this, I argue that the COVID-19 pandemic revealed that the two
actors currently at odds as models of organization of society and decision-
making are the purely "traditional" paternalistic state and the response in the
form of organized anarchies. Based on the presented research on the policy
intentions in selected countries, it can be argued that whatever "soft" or
"middle-ground" intention on regulating the sharing economy and framing
the decisions of its actors, confronts the challenge of reality.

In addition, that the case for intervention in familiar economic interactions
between people using nudges, being vague or direct, must be challenged
as its outcomes may destroy the social fabric that sustains and enrich the
advancement of the sharing economy in Latin America, particularly at a time
of crisis. The generation of trust in the state will tend to weaken, so nudging
this trust into the development of the sharing economy clearly looks at this
time, pointless. While we live in a time where uncertainty rules, there is no
way to predict or claim to attest what are going to be the consequences of
increased paternalism for our democracies, and what will be the development
of organized anarchies in the core of Latin American societies. The best we
can do, as social scientists, is to critically report the current situation, observe

the practices (in this case the growth of the sharing economy even in times of pandemic), and focus our attention on a radical alternative which leaves the market as a way to engage with the possible paths to the future (see Lavoie [1985] 2016).

CONCLUSION AND POLICY RECOMMENDATIONS

Behavioral interventions that attempt to increase trust between peers, or from individuals to institutions, may produce unintended consequences, such as reducing familiarity between actors and thwarting the naturalness of the emergent orders built in localized informal economic interrelations, decision-making processes, and ultimately collective action. This problem is aggravated by the incapacity of policymakers creating the nudge interventions to be aware of all possible cognitive reactions, mechanisms, biases, actions, decisions, and outcomes of the actors in the sharing economy. These issues have been exacerbated by the COVID-19 pandemic and corresponding policies.

Latin American governments aiming to regulate the sharing economy should instead focus on addressing basic security, both physical and juridical, of people using and working with these platforms. Further, they should allow the organized anarchy mechanisms to frame decision-making collective action by participating actors, while providing outcomes that people in Latin America need. Even more now when the economic consequences of the pandemic and lockdowns are suggesting a bleak future.

Any future policies to be developed in the region must be evaluated in the context of emergent business and decision-making models that have significant implications for society. Policymakers need to consider the importance and relevance of community innovations, and policy proposals need to take into consideration the impossibility of centralized governance and planning.

But most of all, it is necessary to recognize the entrepreneurial spirit behind the sharing economy actors, the nature of peer-to-peer relationships and governance and stop importing conceptual models for policymaking and the study of people's behavior in Latin America. These conflicting rationalities (Watson 2003) of "ought to be" behaviors and actions versus "what really happens" have framed the development of public policy in Latin America for many years, being necessary to start observing practices in the "real world," which complement and build a bridge with the theory. In emerging and developing countries, attention should be fixed on ways that encourage people to empower themselves to be entrepreneurs and innovators, especially during times of crisis, instead of interfering in how they trust and relate to each other.

REFERENCES

AESOP. 2015. "AESOP Prague Annual Congress 2015." https://www.aesop-plannin
g.eu/events/en_GB/2015/01/16/readabout/aesop-congress-2015-in-prague.

Altamirano, Melina. 2019. "Economic Vulnerability and Partisanship in Latin
America." *Latin American Politics and Society* 61 (3): 80–103.

Baker, Andy and Vania Ximena Velasco-Guachalla. 2018. "Is the Informal Sector
Politically Different? (Null) Answers from Latin America." *World Development*
102: 170–82.

Bazan, Víctor. 2013. "El Federalismo Argentino: Situación Actual, Cuestiones
Conflictivas y Perspectivas." *Estudios Constitucionales* 11 (1): 37–88.

Bhan, Gautam, Teresa Caldeira, Kelly Gillespie, and AbdouMaliq Simone. 2020.
"The Pandemic, Southern Urbanisms and Collective Life." *Society and Space
Magazine*, August 3. https://www.societyandspace.org/articles/the-pandemic-s
outhern-urbanisms-and-collective-life.

Boettke, Peter J., Christopher J. Coyne, and Peter T. Leeson. 2008. "Institutional
Stickiness and the New Development Economics." *American Journal of Economics
and Sociology* 67 (2): 331–58.

Boettke, Peter J., Liya Palagashvili, and Jayme Lemke. 2013. "Riding in Cars with
Boys: Elinor Ostrom's Adventures with the Police." *Journal of Institutional
Economics* 9 (4): 407–25.

Buenadicha Sánchez, César, Albert Cañigueral Bagó, and Ignacio L. De León.
2017. "Retos y Posibilidades de la Economía Colaborativa en América Latina y
el Caribe." *Inter-American Development Bank (IADB)*, June. https://publications
.iadb.org/es/retos-y-posibilidades-de-la-economia-colaborativa-en-america-latina
-y-el-caribe.

Carrington, Peter J., John Scott, and Stanley Wasserman, eds. 2005. *Models and
Methods in Social Network Analysis*. Cambridge, UK: Cambridge University
Press.

Carvalho, Laura. 2019. "How Did the Brazilian Economy Help to Elect Bolsonaro?"
The London School of Economics and Political Science Blogs, October 2. https://bl
ogs.lse.ac.uk/latamcaribbean/2019/10/02/how-did-the-brazilian-economy-help-to
-elect-bolsonaro/.

Chassin, Youri and Youcef Msaid. 2016. "Viewpoint—Uber and Taxis: Australia
Opens the Door to Reforms." *Montreal Economic Institute*, February 8. Accessed
June 5, 2019. https://www.iedm.org/58042-viewpoint-uber-and-taxis-australia-ope
ns-the-door-to-reforms.

City Government of Buenos Aires. 2018. "BA Taxi: Innovación en Tus Viajes."
Accessed March 5, 2019. https://www.buenosaires.gob.ar/taxis/ba-taxi-innovacion
-para-mejorar-tus-viajes.

Cohen, Michael D., James G. March, and Johan P. Olsen. 1972. "A Garbage Can
Model of Organizational Choice." *Administrative Science Quarterly* 17 (1): 1–25.

Coolican, D'Arcy and Lucas Coffman. 2016. "Trust, the Sharing Economy and
Behavioral Economics." *BehavioralEconomics.com*, July 14. https://www.beh
avioraleconomics.com/trust-the-sharing-economy-and-behavioral-economics/.

Davidson, Nestor M. and John J. Infranca. 2016. "The Sharing Economy as an Urban Phenomenon." *Yale Law and Policy Review* 34 (2): 215–79.

DiZerega, Gus and Alfonso Montuori. 2000. *Persuasion, Power and Polity: A Theory of Democratic Self-Organization.* New York: Hampton Press.

Driver's Club Bogotá. 2020. "Driver's Club Bogotá." *Facebook.* https://www.facebook.com/Driversbogota/.

El Universal. 2019. "Superfinanciera Alertó sobre Pirámides en Grupos de Plataformas de Chat." *El Universal*, February 12. https://www.eluniversal.com.co/colombia/super financiera-alerto-sobre-piramides-en-grupos- de-plataformas-de-chat-LJ748841.

Frye, Timothy and Andrei Shleifer. 1997. "The Invisible Hand and the Grabbing Hand." *The American Economic Review* 87 (2): 354–58.

Gabardo, Emerson. 2015. "La Inexistencia de un Criterio Constitucional de Subsidiariedad en la Definición de Potestades Federativas en Brasil." *Estudios Constitucionales* 13 (1): 91–122.

Ghersi, Enrique. 1997. "The Informal Economy in Latin America." *Cato Journal* 17 (1): 99–108.

Golden Drivers Bogotá. 2020. "Golden Drivers." *Facebook.* https://www.facebook .com/goldendrivers1/.

González Sánchez, Jorge. 2006. "Dinámica Reciente en la Vivienda en Renta en la Ciudad de México." *Scripta Nova: Revista Electrónica de Geografía y Ciencias Sociales* 10 (218): 49.

Government of Mexico City. 2015. "Administración Pública del Distrito Federal." July 15. https://data.consejeria.cdmx.gob.mx/portal_old/uploads/gacetas/c9b9972 feb6fa4501f6facffc2b9a9bf.pdf.

Hayek, Friedrich A. [1969] 1996. *Studies in Philosophy, Politics and Economics.* New York: Touchstone.

House of Representatives of Colombia. 2020. "Informe de Ponencia Primer Debate Proyecto de Ley No. 003 de 2020." December 16.

Infobae. 2018. "Argentina Registró el Mayor Crecimiento de Uber en Todo el Mundo." *Infobae*, September 25. https://www.infobae.com/economia/2018/09/25/ argentina-registro-el-mayor-crecimiento-de-uber-en-todo-el-mundo/.

iProfesional. 2007. "Alto Nivel de Informalidad en Alquileres en Punta del Este." *iProfessional*, November 26. https://www.iprofesional.com/impuestos/57563-Alto-nivel-de-informalidad-de-alquileres-en-Punta-del-Este.

Isabel Vergara, Rosario Martiza. 2017. "La Relación de la Confianza Social y el Asociacionismo Formal e Informal en el Capital Social: México en el Contexto Latinoamericano." *Proceedings of the XIII Congress of Asociación Española de Ciencia Política y de la Administración*, September. https://aecpa.es/es-es/la-relacion-de-la-confianza-social-y-el-asociacionismo-formal-e-inform/congress-papers/2030/.

Kerekes, Carrie B. and Claudia R. Williamson. 2010. "Propertyless in Peru, Even with a Government Land Title." *American Journal of Economics and Sociology* 69 (3): 1011–33.

Koopman, Christopher, Matthew Mitchell, and Adam Thierer. 2015. "The Sharing Economy and Consumer Protection Regulation: The Case for Policy Change." *The Journal of Business, Entrepreneurship and the Law* 8 (2): 529–45.

Lafloufa, Jacqueline. 2015. "Pode Confiar: A Economia Compartilhada Ganha Força no Brasil." *Galileu*, February 26. https://revistagalileu.globo.com/Revista/noticia/2015/02/pode-confiar.html.

Lavoie, Don. [1985] 2016. *National Economic Planning: What Is Left?* Arlington, VA: Mercatus Center at George Mason University.

Lomi, Alessandro, and J. Richard Harrison. 2012. "The Garbage Can Model of Organizational Choice: Looking Forward at Forty." In *The Garbage Can Model of Organizational Choice: Looking Forward at Forty*, edited by Lomi Alessandro and J. Richard Harrison, 3–19. Bingley, UK: Emerald Publishing.

López-Bosch Martineau, Cedrian. 2017. "Regulación de la Renta de Alojamientos entre Pares para el Desarrollo Turístico en México." Master diss., Center of Economic Research and Teaching, Mexico City.

Lozano-Paredes, Luis H. and Katherine Reilly. 2018. "Decent Work for Ride Hailing Workers in the Platform Economy in Cali, Colombia." In *Urban Transport in the Sharing Economy Era Collaborative Cities*, 92–127. Buenos Aires, Argentina: CIPPEC.

Manning, Kathleen. [2013] 2018. *Organizational Theory in Higher Education*. New York: Routledge.

Mayorga, Fernando and Eduardo Córdova. 2007. "Gobernabilidad y Gobernanza en América Latina." Working Paper, NCCR North-South.

Ministry of Information and Communications Technology of Colombia. 2018. "Decreto 0704 de 20 de Abril del 2018." April 20. Accessed March 5, 2019. https://www.mintic.gov.co/portal/604/w3-article-72799.html.

Ministry of Transportation of Colombia. 2015. "Decreto 1079 de 2015." May 26. https://www.mintransporte.gov.co/descargar.php?idFile=12801.

Montero, Sergio and Karen Chapple. 2018. *Fragile Governance and Local Economic Development: Theory and Evidence from Peripheral Regions in Latin America*. London: Routledge.

National Productivity Commission of Chile. 2018. "Tecnologías Disruptivas: Regulación de Plataformas Digitales." January 9. http://www.comisiondeproductividad.cl/2018/04/tecnologias-disruptivas-regulacion-de-plataformas-digitales/.

Newlands, Gemma, Christoph Lutz, and Christian Fieseler. 2020. "European Perspectives on Power in the Sharing Economy." *Report from the EU H2020 Research Project Ps2Share: Participation, Privacy, and Power in the Sharing Economy*.

Nudel, Leon and Emilia Wiik. 2017. "Nudge Is All around—but What Is around the Nudge?" Master's diss., Stockholm School of Economics.

OECD, Economic Commission for Latin America and the Caribbean, CAF Development Bank of Latin American, and European Union. 2019. *Latin American Economic Outlook. 2019: Development in Transition*. Paris: OECD Publishing.

Ostrom, Elinor. 2010. "Beyond Markets and States: Polycentric Governance of Complex Economic Systems." *The American Economic Review* 100 (3): 641–72.

Ostrom, Vincent, Charles M. Tiebout, and Robert Warren. 1961. "The Organization of Government in Metropolitan Areas: A Theoretical Inquiry." *The American Political Science Review* 55 (4): 831–42.

Pirez, Pedro. 2016. "Las Heterogeneidades en la Producción de Urbanización y los Servicios Urbanos en América Latina." *Territorios* 34: 87–112.

Polanyi, Michael. [1966] 1983. *The Tacit Dimension.* Gloucester, MA: Peter Smith.

Postrel, Virginia. [1998] 2011. *The Future and Its Enemies: The Growing Conflict Over Creativity, Enterprise, and Progress.* New York: Free Press.

Prefecture of São Paulo 2019. "Comitê Municipal de Uso do Viário: Resolução Nº 21, de 28 de Março de 2019." March 28. https://www.prefeitura.sp.gov.br/ci dade/secretarias/upload/Resolu%C3%A7%C3%A3o%20CMUV%20n%C2%BA %2021%20-%202019.pdf.

Public Prosecutor's Office of Brazil. 2016. "Nota Pública sobre o 'Uber.'" Ministério Público Federal. Accessed March 5, 2019. http://www.mpf.mp.br/pgr/documentos /nota-publica-uber.

Reilly, Katherine. 2020. "Platform Developmentalism: Leveraging Platform Innovation for National Development in Latin America." *Internet Policy Review* 9(4): 1–29.

Reilly, Katherine and Luis H. Lozano-Paredes. 2019. "Ride Hailing Regulations in Cali, Colombia: Towards Autonomous and Decent Work." In *Information and Communication Technologies for Development: Strengthening Southern-Driven Cooperation as a Catalyst for ICT4D*, edited by Petter Nielsen and Honest Christopher Kimaro, 425–35. Cham, CH: Springer.

Rizzo, Mario and Glen Whitman. 2009. "The Knowledge Problem of New Paternalism." *BYU Law Review* 4 (4): 905–68.

Roo, Gert de and Geoff Porter. [2007] 2016. *Fuzzy Planning: The Role of Actors in a Fuzzy Governance Environment.* Farnham, UK: Ashgate Publishing.

Salice, Silvia and Ivana Pais. 2017. "Sharing Economy as an Urban Phenomenon: Examining Policies for Sharing Cities." In *Policy Implications of Virtual Work*, edited by Pamela Meil and Vassil Kirov, 199–228. Cham, CH: Palgrave Macmillan.

Satgé, Richard de and Vanessa Watson. 2018. "Conflicting Rationalities and Southern Planning Theory." In *Urban Planning in the Global South: Conflicting Rationalities in Contested Urban Space*, 11–34. Cham, CH: Palgrave Macmillan.

Scartascini, Carlos. 2018. "Nudging Latin Americans to Healthier, More Prosperous Lives." *Inter-American Development Bank Blogs*, January 18. https://blogs.iadb .org/ideas-matter/en/nudging-latin-americans-to-healthier-more-prosperous-lives/.

Schwartzman, Helen B. 1989. "An Organized Anarchy." In *The Meeting: Gatherings in Organizations and Communities*, 89–114. Boston, MA: Springer US.

Secretariat of Economic Partnership. 2018. "Economia Colaborativa ou Economia do Compartilhamento: Reporte da Secretaria de Acompanhamento Econômico." Accessed March 5, 2019. https://www2.camara.leg.br/atividade-legislativa/comiss oes/comissoes-temporarias/especiais/55a-legislatura/cesp-marco-regulatorio-da-ec onomiacolaborativa/documentos/audienciaspublicas/ANGELOApresentaoCDAbr il2018.pdf

Soto, Hernando de. [1986] 2002. *El Otro Sendero: La Revolución Informal.* Lima, PE: Editorial El Barranco.

Sunstein, Cass R., Lucia A. Reisch, and Micha Kaiser. 2019. "Trusting Nudges? Lessons from an International Survey." *Journal of European Public Policy* 26 (10): 1417–43.

Tao, Yong. 2016. "Spontaneous Economic Order." *Journal of Evolutionary Economics* 26 (3): 467–500.

Thaler, Richard H., and Cass R. Sunstein. 2003. "Libertarian Paternalism." *The American Economic Review* 93 (2): 175–79.

———. 2009. *Nudge: Improving Decisions about Health, Wealth, and Happiness.* New York: Penguin Books.

Watson, Vanessa. 2003. "Conflicting Rationalities: Implications for Planning Theory and Ethics." *Planning Theory and Practice* 4 (4): 395–407.

Index

Page numbers in italics indicate tables and figures.

on sanctions versus nudges, 26, 28, 78; on testing and evidence, 63; on vigilance against nudging, 84
Swedberg, R., 96
Switzerland, 212
syphilis, 77

Target, 214, 215
taxes, 37, 38
Teacher Loan Forgiveness, 163
telemedicine, 238
Tene, Omer, 213
terms of service contracts, 210
testing hypotheses, 63
test scores, 157–58
Texas education policy, 156–57
text message alerts, 158
Thaler, Richard: on biases, 126, 162; on checks on choice architects, 72; on choice architecture's inevitability, 51; on default rules, 127; on educational choice, 147, 151, 152, 154, 156, 158; on information costs, 164; on libertarian paternalism's aims, 2, 71, 100, 221; on libertarian paternalism's beneficiaries, 92–93; on nudge's definition, 23, 25, 50, 71, 78, 101, 126, 176, 206; on nudges' efficacy, 206; on paternalism and coercion, 52; on restaurant hygiene grading, 78; on sanctions versus nudges, 26, 28, 78; on vigilance against nudging, 84
third party damages, 72–73, 79, 81–83, 85
Thomas, Herschel F., III, 124, 126
Tiebout, Charles M., 62
Tiebout competition, 62
tobacco companies, 102
Tocqueville, Alexis de, 74, 75, 85
tort law, 43
totalitarianism, 44n4
tourism, 77–78
towel reuse, 183

traditions, 97
transparency: benefits of, 119–20, 123; history of, 121–22; of nudges, 53, 86; nudging to promote, 126–29, 136–38; regulation versus, 119, 124–26
transportation technology, 75
Treich, Nicholas, 178, 188
trust, 230, 233–35, 238–39, 244–45
tuberculosis, 77
Tucker, Catherine, 221
Tullock, Gordon, 58–60, 62, 191
Turner, Sarah, 157–58
Tversky, Amos, 18
"Two is Enough" campaign, 109–11

unemployment, 73, 75, 78
uniform policies, 57–58
unintended consequences, 32, 191, 196n6
United States vs. Harriss, 139n2
University of Chicago, 127
urban planning, 36–37, 231–32
urban poor, 73, 75–76, 78–80, 84, 87n3
Uruguay, 244
U.S. government, 81–82. *See also specific agencies*
U.S. military, 154–55
U.S. News and World Report, 161–62
U.S. South, 137
U.S. Supreme Court, 139n2, 204–205
US West (company), 87n7, 218
U.S. West (region), 81–83
utility functions, 13, 17, 209, 211

Vandenberg, Michael P., 178
venture capital, 220–21
Verba, Sidney, 122
Vietnam War, 154
Viscusi, W. Kip, 52, 59, 190
voter preferences, 58–60
voting with feet, 62

Wales, 218

About the Contributors

Cynthia Boruchowicz is a PhD candidate in policy studies at the University of Maryland.

Jeffrey Bristol is an independent scholar.

Erin Dunne is a public affairs professional.

Rosemarie Fike is an instructor of economics at Texas Christian University.

Stefanie Haeffele is a senior fellow in the F. A. Hayek Program for Advanced Study in Philosophy, Politics, and Economics at the Mercatus Center, George Mason University.

Katarina Hall is profesora de economía aplicada at Universidad Francisco Marroquín, Guatemala.

Arielle John is a senior fellow in the F. A. Hayek Program for Advanced Study in Philosophy, Politics, and Economics at the Mercatus Center, George Mason University.

Shannon Lee is a research associate in the Office of Planning, Assessment, and Institutional Research at Pennsylvania State University.

Luis H. Lozano-Paredes is a PhD candidate in built environment-urban governance at the University of Technology Sydney.

Oliver McPherson-Smith is a DPhil student in politics at Oxford University.

Will Rinehart is a senior research fellow at the Center for Growth and Opportunity at Utah State University.

Mario J. Rizzo is associate professor of economics and director of the Foundations of the Market Economy Program at New York University.

James M. Strickland is assistant professor in the School of Politics and Global Studies at Arizona State University.

www.ingramcontent.com/pod-product-compliance
Lightning Source LLC
Chambersburg PA
CBHW021811270326
41932CB00007B/144